Architecting the Industrial Internet

The architect's guide to designing Industrial Internet solutions

Shyam Nath
Robert Stackowiak
Carla Romano

BIRMINGHAM - MUMBAI

Architecting the Industrial Internet

First published: September 2017

Production reference: 1200917

Published by Packt Publishing Ltd.
Livery Place
35 Livery Street
Birmingham
B3 2PB, UK.

ISBN 978-1-78728-275-9

www.packtpub.com

Credits

Authors
Shyam Nath
Robert Stackowiak
Carla Romano

Reviewers
William Bathurst
Doug Ortiz

Commissioning Editor
Aaron Lazar

Acquisition Editor
Alok Dhuri

Content Development Editor
Rohit Kumar Singh

Technical Editor
Pavan Ramchandani

Copy Editor
Safis Editing

Project Coordinator
Vaidehi Sawant

Proofreader
Safis Editing

Indexer
Francy Puthiry

Graphics
Abhinash Sahu

Production Coordinator
Nilesh Mohite

About the Authors

Shyam Nath is the director of technology integrations for Industrial IoT at GE Digital. His area of focus is building-go-to market solutions. His technical expertise lies in big data and analytics architecture and solutions with focus on IoT. He joined GE in Sep 2013. He has worked in IBM, Deloitte, Oracle, and Halliburton, prior to that. He is the Founder/President of the BIWA Group, a global community of professional in Big Data, analytics and IoT. He is author of the IoT Architecture chapter in *Internet of Things and Data Analytics Handbook*, published by *Wiley*. He has often been listed as one of the top social media influencers for Industrial IoT. He is very active on Twitter (@ShyamVaran).

I would like to thank my professional colleagues at GE, for enriching my experience in the field of Industrial Internet. I would also thank the Industrial Internet Consortium (IIC), who facilitated the testbeds and provided the key insights for this book. Finally, I will thank my family and friends who were part of my journey while I was writing this book.

Robert Stackowiak is a technology business strategist at the Microsoft Technology Center in Chicago where he gathers business and technical requirements during client briefings and defines Internet of Things and analytics architecture solutions, including those that reside in the Microsoft Azure cloud. He joined Microsoft in 2016 after a 20-year stint at Oracle where he was Executive Director of Big Data in North America. Bob (his nickname) has spoken at industry conferences around the world and co-authored many books on analytics and data management including *Big Data and the Internet of Things: Enterprise Architecture for A New Age,* published by *Apress,* five editions of *Oracle Essentials, published by O'Reilly Media, Oracle Big Data Handbook,* published by *Oracle Press, Achieving Extreme Performance with Oracle Exadata,* published by *Oracle Press*, and *Oracle Data Warehousing and Business Intelligence Solutions,* published by *Wiley.* You can follow him on Twitter at @rstackow.

I would like to thank my teammates for their input and guidance in the Chicago Microsoft Technology Center as this book was being written. I thank Paul Edlund, Bob Gabriel, Matthew Housholder, Ross LoForte, and Mark Skoog for providing important insight. I have received great support and encouragement from Microsoft management, especially Beth Malloy, the Director of the Chicago Microsoft Technology Center and a trusted and favorite collaborator there. Other co-workers at Microsoft provided extensive IoT and analytics related documentation that was frequently referenced during the creation of several sections in this book. Their experience helped us explain where and how to apply technology components across the entire architecture. I would also thank the many customers I met with while at Microsoft and Oracle over the years. They provided real examples of Industrial Internet use cases and projects, often years ahead of where others were. Finally, I would thank Jodie Stackowiak, my wife, partner, and the love of my life who remains supportive during weekends of book writing and in my pursuit of a career that always seems to align with technologies in the early days of their widespread adoption.

Carla Romano is director of development for big data and data warehousing at Oracle, focusing on industry solutions, including the Industry Data Model suite of products for airlines and transportation, telecommunications, retail, and utilities industries. She has an extensive background in Business Intelligence and data management, and is a frequent presenter at Oracle Openworld and the BIWA-SIG conferences. She is also a member of the IIC testbeds committee. She is currently developing utilities for Oracle Big Data Cloud Service. She previously worked at Lockheed Engineering Sciences and Unisys under contracts from NASA.

I would like to thank Shyam and Sudip Majumder for introducing me to the world of IIoT, and my many colleagues at Oracle for creating an interesting and challenging environment. Many thanks to Shyam and Bob for their support during a grim time. I would also like to thank my husband and my friends for their encouragement and tolerance.

About the Reviewers

William Bathurst is a development manager at M2Mi with over 25 years of industry experience. He is currently working with the Industrial Internet Consortium to work out advanced tracking solutions for the Airline Industries.

Doug Ortiz is a senior big data architect at ByteCubed who has been architecting, developing, and integrating enterprise solutions throughout his career. Organizations that leverage his skillset have been able to rediscover and reuse their underutilized data via existing and emerging technologies such as Amazon Web Services, Microsoft Azure, Google Cloud, Microsoft BI Stack, Hadoop, Spark, NoSQL Databases, and SharePoint, along with related toolsets and technologies. He is also the founder of Illustris and LLC, and you can reach him at dougortiz@illustris.org.

Doug has experience in integrating multiple platforms and products and holds certifications in big data, data sciences, R, and Python. He helps organizations gain a deeper understanding and value of their current investments in data and existing resources, turning them into useful sources of information, and he has improved, salvaged, and architected projects by utilizing unique and innovative techniques.

Doug regularly reviews books on topics such as Amazon Web Services, data science, machine learning, R, and cloud technologies. His hobbies include yoga and scuba diving.

I would like to thank my wonderful wife, Mila, for all her help and support, as well as our wonderful children, Maria and Nikolay.

www.PacktPub.com

For support files and downloads related to your book, please visit www.PacktPub.com.

Did you know that Packt offers eBook versions of every book published, with PDF and ePub files available? You can upgrade to the eBook version at www.PacktPub.com and as a print book customer, you are entitled to a discount on the eBook copy. Get in touch with us at service@packtpub.com for more details.

At www.PacktPub.com, you can also read a collection of free technical articles, sign up for a range of free newsletters and receive exclusive discounts and offers on Packt books and eBooks.

https://www.packtpub.com/mapt

Get the most in-demand software skills with Mapt. Mapt gives you full access to all Packt books and video courses, as well as industry-leading tools to help you plan your personal development and advance your career.

Why subscribe?

- Fully searchable across every book published by Packt
- Copy and paste, print, and bookmark content
- On demand and accessible via a web browser

Customer Feedback

Thanks for purchasing this Packt book. At Packt, quality is at the heart of our editorial process. To help us improve, please leave us an honest review on this book's Amazon page at https://www.amazon.com/dp/1787282759.

If you'd like to join our team of regular reviewers, you can e-mail us at customerreviews@packtpub.com. We award our regular reviewers with free eBooks and videos in exchange for their valuable feedback. Help us be relentless in improving our products!

Table of Contents

Preface   1

Chapter 1: The Industrial Internet Revolution   7

    How today's Industrial Internet came about   9
        Earlier generations of the Industrial Revolution   10
        Why is it time for the Industrial Internet?   15
        Challenges to IIoT   18
    The architect's roles and skills   19
    Architectural approaches for success   22
        Reference architectures for the Industrial Internet   22
        The multi-tier IIoT architecture   24
        A security framework for the Industrial Internet   25
        A connectivity framework for the Industrial Internet   26
        The industrial data analytics framework   27
        Cloud and user experience considerations   29
            Business strategy framework for the Industrial Internet   30
    Summary   31

Chapter 2: Architectural Approaches for Success   33

    Architectural framework   34
    Architectural viewpoints   35
        Business viewpoint   36
            Security considerations for the business viewpoint   37
        Usage viewpoint   38
            Security considerations for the usage viewpoint   40
        Functional viewpoint   40
            Control domain   41
            Operations domain   42
            Information domain   44
            Application domain   45
            Business domain   45
                Cross-cutting functions and system characteristics   46
                Computational deployment patterns   47
            Security considerations for the functional viewpoint   48
        Implementation viewpoint   48
            Security considerations for the implementation viewpoint   54
    Data and analytics   55
        Data management   57

Analytics and advanced data processing   58
Integrability, interoperability, and composability   58
Connectivity   59
Intelligent and resilient control   59
Dynamic composition and automated interoperability   60
Using PoCs to evaluate design   61
Scope definition   61
Business case considerations   62
Solution definition   62
Building the PoC   65
Prototype scale   67
Evaluate/modify   68
Production scale   68
Architecture   69
Components   69
Continuing engineering   69
Summary   69

Chapter 3: Gathering Business Requirements   71

Initial business discovery   74
Getting ready for business discovery   75
Gathering CSFs   76
Gathering KPIs   78
From data sources to KPI delivery   80
Prioritizing the building of solutions   82
Building the business case   84
Components of backend infrastructure cost models   85
Smart device and networking costs   89
Estimating implementation costs   90
Documenting future benefits   90
Financial justification of our supply chain project   91
Selling the project   97
Summary   99

Chapter 4: Mapping Requirements to a Functional Viewpoint   101

The control domain   103
Basic edge device capabilities   104
Smarter edge device configurations   106
Selecting sensors and edge devices   106
The supply chain optimization control domain   107
The operations domain   108

The information domain   110
   Solving information domain functional requirements   111
   A supply chain optimization information domain   112
The application domain   113
   Assessing business analysts and user skills   113
   The supply chain optimization application domain   115
The business domain   116
DevOps and the agile movement   118
   Agile approaches   119
   Using microservices and containers to speed DevOps   120
Summary   121

Chapter 5: Assessing Industrial Internet Applications   123
   Architecture patterns for the Industrial Internet   124
   Build versus buy decisions   125
   Asset Performance Management (APM)   127
   Assessing the analytics applications   132
      Descriptive analytics   133
      Diagnostic analytics   133
      Predictive analytics   134
      Prescriptive analytics   136
      Fit gap analysis   137
      Brilliant Manufacturing   141
      Field Service Management (FSM) application   142
   Summary   144

Chapter 6: Defining the Data and Analytics Architecture   145
   Data and analytics requirements and capabilities   146
      Data reduction and analytics   148
      Publish and subscribe   148
      Query   148
      Storage persistence and retrieval   149
      Integration   149
      Description and presence   150
      Data framework   151
      Rights management   151
      Creating business value   152
      Analytics functionality   152
      Mapping analytics architecture to reference architecture   154
      Advanced analytics   155

The Lambda architecture and IIoT   156
Analytics, machine learning, and analyst tools   158
  A process for advanced analytics creation   159
  Machine learning tools   160
  Other analyst tools   161
Early Industrial Internet applications and historians   163
The speed layer and field gateways   164
The batch layer   167
  Data lakes and Hadoop   167
    Graph database   169
  Data warehouses, data marts, and relational databases   169
  Supply chain optimization in the batch layer   171
Summary   171

Chapter 7: Defining a Deployment Architecture   173
  Current state of deployment architectures for IT systems   174
  Hosted systems and the cloud   176
    Hosted services   176
      Single-tenant hosting   178
      Multi-tenancy   179
    Cloud computing   180
      Public cloud   181
      Private cloud   181
      Hybrid cloud   181
      Billing   182
  Enterprise Resource Planning (ERP)   183
    Considerations for SaaS cloud versus on-premises   183
    Customer Relationship Management (CRM)   185
    Human Resource Management Systems   186
  Data warehousing and big data   187
    Data warehouse and decision support   188
      Management considerations for data warehouse   189
      Big data   190
      Hadoop file systems   190
      Data lakes   192
      Management considerations for data lakes   192
      Big data analytics and data science   193
  Converged infrastructure and engineered systems   194
    Deployment considerations   195
  IIoT constraints   195
    Incremental upgrades   195
    On-premises versus cloud   196
      Consumption models   197
    Analytics capacity considerations   198

Analytics considerations   199
    Key constraints in analytics architecture design   199
Design for the edge tier   203
Networking considerations   204
    Connectivity transport layer   206
        Network layer consideration   206
        Topology   207
    Edge connectivity   208
Management and support infrastructure   210
Summary   210

Chapter 8: Securing the Industrial Internet   211

Examples of cybersecurity attacks   213
IIoT security core building blocks   217
NIST cybersecurity frameworks   220
IIoT security guidelines   221
Securing devices and the edge to the cloud gateway   223
    Device considerations   224
    Device to gateway connections   227
Securing the backend   229
    Data lake security   231
    Securing other NoSQL databases   232
    Data warehouse security   233
Risk assessments and best security practices   234
Planning for security in the supply chain example   236
Summary   238

Chapter 9: Governance and Assuring Compliance   239

Assessing governance, risk, and compliance   240
    Data governance   241
    Assessing risk and trustworthiness   242
International compliance certifications   245
International consortia and emerging standards   248
Government and public institution compliance   250
    Non-U.S. government standards and certifications   251
    U.S. government standards   253
Industry compliance certifications   255
    Which guidelines apply   257
GRC in the supply chain optimization example   259
Summary   262

Chapter 10: Industrial Internet Use Cases in Various Industries   265

Use cases versus case studies   266
Use cases within industry vertical   267
  Use cases in agribusiness   268
    Use cases in alternative energy and environmental control   268
    Use cases in construction   269
    Use cases in logistics and transportation   270
    Use cases in manufacturing and CPGs   271
    Use cases in oil and gas   271
    Use cases in pharmaceuticals, medical equipment, and healthcare   272
    Use cases in utility companies   273
Manufacturing IIoT architectures and examples   274
  A manufacturing test bed   274
    Factory operation visibility and intelligence   276
    Omnichannel initiatives   278
Predictive maintenance   279
  Airline industry background   280
    Airline proactive and preventive maintenance   282
    Preventive maintenance as a business   289
Asset tracking and handling   289
  Baggage and cargo handling   290
    Expanded baggage-handling services   295
    Tracking tools in manufacturing and construction   296
    Chemical industry automated tracking and replenishment   297
Environmental impact and abatement   300
Summary   302

Chapter 11: A Vision of the Future   305

Maturing IIoT frameworks and applications   307
Evolving edge devices   310
The evolution of networking   311
Cognitive and mixed reality HMIs and deep learning   315
The impact on robotics and mobile devices   318
Improved security through blockchain technology   319
Quantum computing   320
The Industrial Internet's impact on society   322
Summary   324

Appendix: Sources   327

Index   333

Preface

It seems that every day, one can pick up a technology journal or view an online technology article about the Industrial Internet of Things (IIoT). The articles usually provide insights into specific solutions to business problems or how a specific technology component is evolving to provide a function necessary in deploying an Industrial Internet solution.

If you are undertaking one of your first IIoT projects, this book will provide you with the background needed. The authors have attempted to provide both timely and timeless guidance. The IIoT ecosystem is rapidly evolving, and we'll describe some of those changes in various locations in this book. Yet, we also see that justifications for these projects and use cases are falling into repeatable patterns. The overall architecture is generally well-understood and is also largely repeated, even while individual technology components are growing more capable and sophisticated.

The Industrial Internet Consortium (IIC) provides useful documentation in defining key aspects of the IIoT architecture that the architect must consider. We'll reference the IIC documentation frequently in this book. However, we also felt a desire to provide guidance as to how the architecture is applied in projects as these solutions are defined.

An area of intense interest, as this book was published, is securing the IIoT and the governance of Industrial Internet solutions. In a portion of the book that covers these topics, we'll provide what we believe is practical guidance and point to the many worldwide, regional, and industry standards that can impact your designs.

Solutions, component capabilities, and certifications around standards are very fluid and will probably have changed between the time we wrote this book and the time you read this. In areas where rapid change is occurring, the content should provide you with a launching point for you to do your own further discovery. We have a lengthy list of sources in an appendix in this book.

The authors of this book work at some of the leading providers of IIoT frameworks and solutions; we have called upon that experience in writing this book, but have sought to do so in a manner that should be largely vendor agnostic.

Our goal is to help you fully realize the complexity and promises of these projects, but also help you gain the experience needed to architect successful solutions. You are probably at an early stage in your journey that will consist of many stages. We hope that you will find the book a useful place to start or add knowledge where you currently have gaps.

What this book covers

Chapter 1, *The Industrial Internet Revolution*, describes how we reached today's IIoT solutions and the role of the architect.

Chapter 2, *Architectural Approaches for Success*, talks about architecture viewpoints, the implementation viewpoint, data and analytics, and using proof of concepts to evaluate design.

Chapter 3, *Gathering Business Requirements*, covers topics such as preparing for business discovery, gathering critical success factors, business benefits and key performance indicators, gaining an understanding of skills, evaluating data sources, value from early mockups and proof of concepts, prioritizing stages, building the business case, and selling the project.

Chapter 4, *Mapping Requirements to a Functional Viewpoint*, describes the control, operations, information, application, and business domains, and DevOps and the agile development movement.

Chapter 5, *Assessing Industrial Internet Applications*, covers architecture patterns, build versus buy considerations, asset performance management, analytics, the Brilliant Factory, and a field services application.

Chapter 6, *Defining the Data and Analytics Architecture*, describes typical requirements and capabilities, the Lambda architecture, analytics, machine learning and analyst tools, early Industrial Internet applications and historians, and the speed and batch layers in the architecture.

Chapter 7, *Defining a Deployment Architecture*, covers past and current architecture, on-premises and cloud deployment, designing for the edge, networking considerations, device management, management and support infrastructure, and consumption models.

Chapter 8, *Securing the Industrial Internet*, describes examples of cybersecurity attacks, core building blocks, NIST cybersecurity frameworks, security guidelines, securing devices and communications to the cloud and backend, risk assessment, and best practices.

Chapter 9, *Governance and Assuring Compliance*, covers assessing governance, risk and compliance, international compliance, consortia and emerging standards, government and public institutions, industry compliance, and determining the guidelines that apply.

Chapter 10, *Industrial Internet Use Cases in Various Industries*, describes summarized use cases in various industries and then provides more in-depth looks at manufacturing, predictive maintenance, asset tracking and handling, and environmental impact and abatement.

Chapter 11, *A Vision of the Future*, covers the possible impacts of maturing frameworks and applications, evolution in edge devices, networking, human machine interfaces and industrial robotics, and the applicability of blockchain and quantum computing in the future.

Appendix, *Sources*, provides a list of sources the authors used throughout this book that might prove useful in your own research.

In several chapters of this book, we apply what is learned to a supply chain optimization example that can be relevant in many industries.

What you need for this book

The book assumes that the reader possesses a basic IT and technology architecture background. There are no coding examples as that is beyond the scope of this book.

Who this book is for

This book is intended to be used by architects as they gather requirements, justify projects, and consider the components that they will include in the architecture of their Industrial Internet projects. Others in roles involved in defining these projects should also find this book to be of value.

Conventions

In this book, you will find a number of text styles that distinguish between different kinds of information. Here are some examples of these styles and an explanation of their meaning.

New terms and **important words** are shown in bold.

 Warnings or important notes appear like this.

 Tips and tricks appear like this.

Reader feedback

Feedback from our readers is always welcome. Let us know what you think about this book-what you liked or disliked. Reader feedback is important for us as it helps us develop titles that you will really get the most out of.

To send us general feedback, simply e-mail `feedback@packtpub.com`, and mention the book's title in the subject of your message.

If there is a topic that you have expertise in and you are interested in either writing or contributing to a book, see our author guide at `www.packtpub.com/authors`.

Customer support

Now that you are the proud owner of a Packt book, we have a number of things to help you to get the most from your purchase.

Downloading the color images of this book

We also provide you with a PDF file that has color images of the screenshots/diagrams used in this book. The color images will help you better understand the changes in the output. You can download this file from `https:/ / www. packtpub. com/ sites/ default/ files/ downloads/ ArchitectingtheIndustrialInternet_ ColorImages. pdf`.

Errata

Although we have taken every care to ensure the accuracy of our content, mistakes do happen. If you find a mistake in one of our books-maybe a mistake in the text or the code-we would be grateful if you could report this to us. By doing so, you can save other readers from frustration and help us improve subsequent versions of this book. If you find any errata, please report them by visiting http://www.packtpub.com/submit-errata, selecting your book, clicking on the **Errata Submission Form** link, and entering the details of your errata. Once your errata are verified, your submission will be accepted and the errata will be uploaded to our website or added to any list of existing errata under the Errata section of that title.

To view the previously submitted errata, go to https://www.packtpub.com/books/content/support and enter the name of the book in the search field. The required information will appear under the **Errata** section.

Piracy

Piracy of copyrighted material on the Internet is an ongoing problem across all media. At Packt, we take the protection of our copyright and licenses very seriously. If you come across any illegal copies of our works in any form on the Internet, please provide us with the location address or website name immediately so that we can pursue a remedy.

Please contact us at copyright@packtpub.com with a link to the suspected pirated material.

We appreciate your help in protecting our authors and our ability to bring you valuable content.

Questions

If you have a problem with any aspect of this book, you can contact us at questions@packtpub.com, and we will do our best to address the problem.

1
The Industrial Internet Revolution

Today, we often hear the terms **Internet of Things** (**IoT**) and Industrial Internet used to describe an area of emerging technological focus, an opportunity for many start-up companies and technology giants, and a skill set much in demand. We believe that incorporating sensors and intelligent *edge devices* into an information architecture is the latest stage in an evolution that has been progressing for some time and will continue to evolve in the future. So, we thought it is quite timely to write this architect's guide in creating Industrial Internet solutions. We also hope it will prove to be somewhat timeless and useful for many years to come.

The term IoT covers a wide variety of business and consumer devices and applications and business solutions where data gathered from those devices is analyzed. We have chosen to focus this book on the **Industrial Internet of Things** (**IIoT**), the industrial side of the IoT. We will describe use cases and reference architectures that include those for industrial manufacturing; manufacturers of consumer packaged goods; and other sectors such as healthcare devices, transportation, aviation and energy generation, transmission, distribution, and controls. Some of today's initiatives focus on manufacturing quality, preventive maintenance, and improved service efficiency. We will also explore transportation use cases and reference architectures including those that solve aviation, automotive, rail, and supply chain problems. Additionally, we will explore solutions in the oil and gas industry and in the intelligent buildings and cities area.

IIoT can be defined as a system of connected things, machines, computers, and people, enabling intelligent industrial operations using advanced data analytics for transformational business and societal outcomes. In this chapter, we will begin by describing how we arrived at the Industrial Internet generation to provide you with some context for all that follows. Since there are many types and definitions of architects today, we'll describe their areas of focus and roles next. We'll then briefly describe the remaining chapters of the book to help you understand how their architecture role might align to what we will cover in each chapter.

Though we wrote this book to serve as an architect's guide, we realize it will attract a more diverse audience. If you are a manager focusing on the implications of the Industrial Internet today, you should find many portions of the book to be of interest. Similarly, developers who want to understand why and how these projects are initiated and the reference architectures behind them should find much content to be of interest. We hope to close the gap between professionals who handle information technology systems and those who manage operations and the associated technology.

The authors work at some of the leading companies that provide products that address various requirements when deploying these projects. That said, one of our goals in writing this book was to create a non-vendor-specific guide that should be useful regardless of what technology footprint you use. We will share with you the practical knowledge we gained in helping our own and other companies and organizations adopt the architecture patterns and solutions that we describe.

This chapter will serve as an introduction to some of the fundamental concepts we discuss in the book and should provide you with some background if you are new to the Industrial Internet. The key topics are as follows:

- How the Industrial Internet evolved from the Industrial Revolution
- Why organizations are investing in IIoT solutions
- Some of the challenges to prepare for in the deployment of IIoT solutions
- Roles and responsibilities of the various architects and the roles tied to professional development paths

Cloud-based and technology platform providers, applications, and custom solutions

Most Industrial Internet backend development is occurring today on cloud-based solutions for reasons that we explain in this book. Typical platforms considered include **Amazon Web Services** (**AWS**), Google cloud, IBM cloud solutions, Microsoft Azure, and the Oracle cloud for the infrastructure. Organizations sometimes select the IoT platform or custom-develop and deploy IIoT solutions themselves, choose to deploy applications they purchase, and/or hire system integrator and consultant to help. IoT **Platforms as a Service** (**PaaS**) in the cloud and applications **Software as a Service** (**SaaS**) are growing areas of emphasis, with General Electric perhaps providing the most widely known IIoT solutions sold in this manner.

How today's Industrial Internet came about

Many organizations, including the World Economic Forum, describe the IIoT as being the fourth generation of the Industrial Revolution. The four generations have shared a common business goal such as running businesses more efficiently and producing goods and services more cheaply for stakeholders and consumers at large. They owe their existence to new capabilities created by inventions and advances in technology. In each generation, old manual jobs disappear, but new jobs and job types are created that operate at higher efficiency levels.

Today, pessimists point to the fact that many jobs will disappear during the age of the Industrial Internet. Optimists believe that because many new job types will be created, new jobs (albeit with different skills) will also be created. Time will tell if individuals whose jobs are displaced will be able to move into these new jobs, but many now feel that another revolutionary change is occurring. The future of work in the age of Industrial Internet is becoming a critical topic and connects it to the societal aspects of these innovative solutions. The term **Internet of People** (**IoP**) is sometimes used to remind us that people consume the benefits from the information that is extracted from data generated by people and/or the machines.

Earlier generations of the Industrial Revolution

Most agree that the first generation of the Industrial Revolution began in the middle of the 18th century. Let's go back in history to see how it led to the evolution of the IIoT today. The 18th and 19th centuries, which experienced the Industrial Revolution saw a transition from the manually intensive manufacturing processes to the mechanization of the manufacturing. This laid the foundation of the modern heavy industries. At the time, most people lived on farms and worked in agriculture. Factories were commonly located close to rivers and streams where they could be powered by water wheels, and there was usually much handwork involved. With the invention of the steam engine, factories could be located elsewhere. The power that was supplied to machinery by steam engines became more predictable, and more processes could be aided by machinery.

Great Britain experienced many technological innovations ranging from the first engine in 1712 by Thomas Newcomen to the steam engine in 1765 by James Watt to the first public railway line in 1825. The Industrial Revolution transformed manufacturing from the home and cottage industry level to a vastly more scalable level. With the introduction of railroads as a transportation alternative to river traffic and horse-driven carriages, faster travel between distant locations was enabled and provided a new means to deliver supplies to factories and products from them. This theme of decoupling the production facilities from the consumers can be seen in today's computing world where remote data centers can be decoupled from the information technology users. Over time, this Industrial Revolution led to a transition from human labor to the use of machines, spread over whole of Europe and to North America, leading to the industrialization of the world. Gradually, this led to consumerism as goods became available, accessible, and affordable.

The increased widespread availability of electricity through power grids and the invention of the assembly line in the first decades of the 1900s introduced the second generation of the Industrial Revolution. Once again, power became more predictable and the amount of space required for power generation in factories was reduced. Production became more optimized through assembly lines, and workers assumed new specialized roles. Motorized vehicles also appeared for the delivery of supplies and transporting finished products, thus enabling more variation in factory locations. We began an age of mass production as well as mass merchandising, which resulted in the creation of many additional, new kinds of job.

In the third generation, business computing was introduced and efficiencies were greatly improved. Mainframe computers became widely available with subsequent pricing adjustments, making them more affordable and hence more widely adopted in the 1960s. Still cheaper minicomputers and then personal computers followed. The Internet was in common usage for networking within companies and across the world by the 1990s.

The Internet evolved from a way for the military to connect and communicate and appeared in universities and then mainstream companies. The mid 1990s saw the transition from the military's **Advanced Research Projects Agency Network** (**ARPANet**) to the consumer Internet. In this wave, computers and servers connected across the world and then provided an information super highway for the people. This revolutionized how people interacted with each other and with the businesses leading to the growth of e-commerce and social media. New leaders emerged in this era, starting with **Information Technology** (**IT**) system providers, and companies such as Amazon, which started with online sale of books and went onto become a general-purpose e-commerce platform. Likewise, on the human interaction front, emails became mainstream and more interactive and rich multi-media evolved on the web. This led to the rise of Myspace, Facebook, Twitter, and similar social media platforms to essentially connect the people across the world. We refer to this as the consumer Internet.

Computing also became more accessible through improved software development tools and through business applications and tools that provided increasingly more intuitive user interfaces. Some refer to this as the beginning of the information age as line of business users could access and manipulate their data to measure and optimize their business activities.

While the consumer Internet focused on connectivity between businesses, consumers, the IT systems, and the computing devices such as servers, PC's, laptops, and emerging mobile devices, it largely ignored the machines from the Industrial Revolution. This led to a great divide between the machines for industrial operations and the traditional IT systems and set the stage for the fourth wave that we call the *Industrial Internet Revolution*.

The Industrial Internet can be defined as the connecting of industrial-grade machines and devices to networked computing devices with the goal of collecting the diverse data originating both inside the machine and the surrounding environment and processing or analyzing this data for meaningful outcomes. Such data originates in various forms and is often referred to as big data. The systematic organization and analysis of this data is referred to as big data analytics for industrial outcomes.

The Industrial Internet and IIoT are the industrial flavor of the IoT. While IoT refers to any physical object or thing connected to a network and the Internet, IIoT focuses on scenarios where the connected objects are primarily industrial in nature (such as manufacturing assembly lines, power generation equipment, or mass transportation vehicles). Thus, Industrial Internet is often used interchangeably with IIoT. There are three Ps important to an industry:

- Products (machines and assets)
- Processes (assembly lines and supply chain)
- People (human stakeholders)

The following illustration captures the interaction of these three Ps:

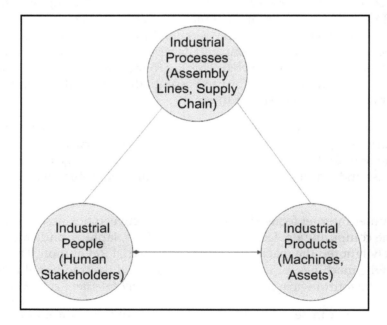

Industrial machines and assets have a long life, especially when compared to many consumer devices. The following table serves as a reference to highlight the difference of scale in usable life comparing various industrial assets to a smartphone:

	Industrial asset/product	Average life in years
1	Airplane	25
2	Automobile/car	10
2	Coal-fired power plant	40
3	**Heating, ventilation, and air conditioning (HVAC)** systems	20
4	MRI scanner	12
5	Oil rig	35
6	Smartphone	3
7	Water heater	9

Due to the long life and cost of ownership of industrial machines, it is important to provide ways to protect the investment in these machines over time. Thus, the optimization of field maintenance services is an integral part of the Industrial Internet. Service execution and service delivery platforms and applications are within the realm of the Industrial Internet architects, and this book will provide coverage to it.

The long life of industrial assets leads to two terms often used in the context of Industrial Internet solutions: greenfield and brownfield applications. A greenfield project refers to a scenario where a company decides to build a new infrastructure since it offers the maximum design flexibility and efficiency to meet a project's needs (an existing infrastructure limits the ability to change by its present design). From the Industrial Internet architecture perspective, the new infrastructure can add sensors to collect relevant data.

Brownfield projects leverage infrastructure that is already in use. The costs of starting up are usually greatly reduced with this approach, but it can be more difficult to modernize the infrastructure and incorporate the addition of sensors. Construction and commissioning times can be minimized using this approach. For Industrial Internet projects, brownfield systems can be retrofitted by adding external sensors to collect data. For example, external acoustic sensors might be added to the body of air compressors in a factory to do the harmonic analysis and determine air leaks in a brownfield project. Air leaks can cause wasted electricity in manufacturing plants where compressors are used to drive several pneumatic tools.

Some of the concepts we associate with the Industrial Internet today began to mature in the last few years. For example, in a world before widely available smart sensors, oil and gas exploration companies brought computers to the exploration sites, processed the data locally in relational databases, and transmitted the processed data and their conclusions back to their headquarters. Some referred to this as early *edge computing* on the remote computers. The following diagram reflects this type of deployment:

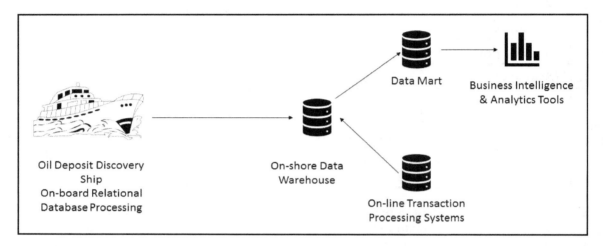

Data warehouses and data marts became common in most businesses. Batch-fed by **Online Transaction Processing** (**OLTP**) systems, they became the place to store historical data used to report on current trends and compare current data with past data through business intelligence tools. Of course, this footprint remains common today.

Predictive algorithms were also developed, tested, and deployed with increasing rapidity in certain industries and gained wider adoption over time. Some early use cases included understanding financial market investment strategies and insurance risk, and the prediction of the likely quality of expensive manufacturing processes to better optimize the production.

Each generation became shorter. Moving from the first generation of the Industrial Revolution to the next was a matter of centuries, but the subsequent generations took half the time of the previous change. This implies that future generations may come at a faster pace, and while we are embracing the Industrial Internet, we need to be prepared for the possible next generations as well.

Why is it time for the Industrial Internet?

In 2010, the IoT and Industrial Internet became familiar terminology. The World Economic Forum and others declared this to be the next generation of the Industrial Revolution. As in previous generations, several technological advancements came together to enable a new class of solutions and applications, changing business models and capabilities.

Sensors began to be mass produced at ever decreasing costs. As price points, size, weight, and power requirements for sensors decreased, engineers began to create device designs that included them in anticipation of being able to gather useful data on device status as soon as it became feasible. Since smart sensors can also be programmed and updated, they can evolve and become more "intelligent" over time. For example, inclusion of such smart sensors in automobiles led to rapid advancements in the development of autonomous vehicles.

The sensors themselves most often transmit semi-structured data in a streaming fashion. Coincidentally, analyzing mass quantities of semi-structured data became possible a decade earlier through development of NoSQL data engines (and Hadoop specifically) to solve the problems of Internet search optimizations and recommendations. Next generation platforms holding exabytes of data are deployed today by companies in the search engine business.

Exabytes

Depending on when you read this book, the exabyte could be a new term to you. An exabyte is a unit of data storage equivalent to one quintillion bytes. A more common reference is that it is equivalent to one million terabytes or one thousand petabytes. In case you were wondering, the next bigger unit of scale you might hear about is the zettabyte, which is 1,000 exabytes. The amount of data that sensors can produce is driving us to define solutions with new data storage units.

The development of new and innovative software solutions became more viable for start-ups and smaller organizations as cloud-based platforms became available (mostly eliminating an expensive upfront investment in infrastructure). The cloud also enabled faster time to deployment and elastic scalability that was difficult in classic data centers.

The cost of networking and bandwidth reduced over this time to provide ubiquitous connectivity for the IIoT. Some of the connectivity options and technologies used include **Radio-Frequency Identification** (**RFID**), Wi-Fi, **Bluetooth Low Energy** (**BLE**), and 2G/3G/4G with 5G on the horizon.

The growing popularity of open source software data management offerings and development tools also helped minimize early costs. Today, as the Industrial Internet has matured, we see many integrated solution footprints and applications that rely on underlying open source components.

The following diagram represents a common architectural pattern often seen in Industrial Internet implementations and is called a **Lambda architecture**:

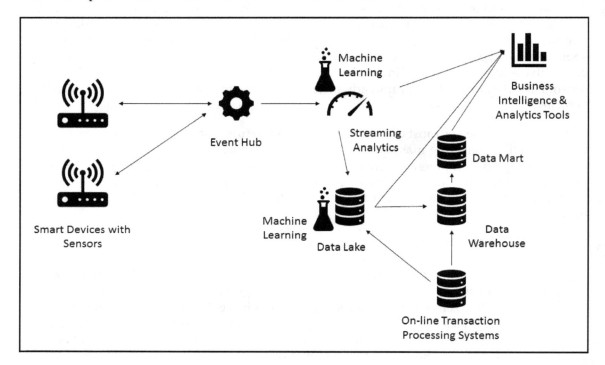

The illustration shows streaming data feeds from smart devices. The streaming analytics engine analyzes this feed in real time and will sometimes have machine learning algorithms deployed to process the data. The data lake pictured is most often a Hadoop cluster and is designed to load and store massive amounts of data of all types. As in the previous generation, traditional data warehouses and data marts are batch fed. Business intelligence tools are shown pointed at the data mart, data lake, and streaming analytics engine in our illustration.

We'll describe these components in much more detail in subsequent chapters as we lay out the data and analytics architecture. Obviously, there is also a lot more detail in the information technology platform architecture, which we'll cover as well.

New manufacturing technologies are also now employed in Industrial Internet solutions. Robotics in manufacturing became common in industries where the cost of labor was high, such as in the automotive industry, around the turn of this century. The robotics that were deployed improved the consistency and quality of the products produced and helped to contain costs. The addition of intelligent or smart sensors to newer generations of these devices enabled more functional and flexible capabilities. The wider applicability and growing usage of robotics also led to decreases in their pricing, helping drive further adoption.

Many manufacturers and companies that design products are now experimenting with 3D printing. 3D printers enable the manufacturing of products and components anywhere; such a printer is deployed and accessible via a network. Such technologies are often referred to as additive manufacturing. The ability to print spare parts on demand for industrial machines can have a profound positive impact on the supply chain ecosystem, as the cost of such additive manufacturing continues to decrease.

Artificial intelligence (**AI**) and machine learning are also enabling more intelligent devices. As devices become self-learning, they can react to changing situations in real time. We'll discuss these topics and other emerging technologies when we explore what is likely to occur in the near and more distant future in the last chapter of this book.

These new capabilities are causing companies to rethink the value of their data and the kinds of businesses they are competing in. Many are facing new and non-traditional competition from other industries and are evaluating *digital transformation* strategies that sometimes include new strategies for monetizing their data assets. Some are becoming data aggregators, selling data to other companies and subscribers that find it useful.

The following diagram summarizes the four generations of the Industrial Revolution we described:

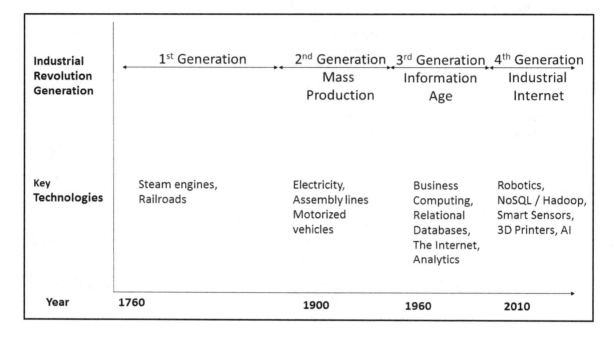

Industrial Revolution Generation	1st Generation	2nd Generation Mass Production	3rd Generation Information Age	4th Generation Industrial Internet
Key Technologies	Steam engines, Railroads	Electricity, Assembly lines Motorized vehicles	Business Computing, Relational Databases, The Internet, Analytics	Robotics, NoSQL / Hadoop, Smart Sensors, 3D Printers, AI
Year	1760	1900	1960	2010

Challenges to IIoT

As always seems to happen when a new generation begins, there are some holdover problems from the old generation as well as problems introduced by the new architecture. One carryover from the previous generation is the need for projects to be driven by line of business requirements, not by IT. As it was earlier, projects will usually stall when IT-initiated proof of concepts do not really solve problems that the business needs and wants to address.

In Industrial Internet projects, architects and IT must also sometimes work with engineering designers who are specifying the types and locations of sensors in devices to assure that data needed for the proposed solution can be gathered. Similarly, these teams need to work together regarding networking requirements given the amount of data that might be transmitted. Continuous data gathering from equipment operated in industrial settings is key to enabling maintenance and field services-related solutions.

The mixture of semi-structured and unstructured data and the variety of data management solutions needed introduce complexity and the need for new skill sets that an organization might not possess and face difficulty in finding. Further adding to the complexity is the rate at which data is transferred over networks arriving in the data management engines and the data volumes that must be managed in them.

Of course, device and data security must be maintained throughout the ecosystem. Software and firmware updates that are pushed to intelligent sensors and devices must be secure and successful, or denied. Data transmitted to cloud-based solutions must meet or exceed industry-relevant certifications and country data sovereignty and privacy laws.

External threats can exploit vulnerabilities in under-protected Industrial Internet systems and thereby cause harm to the organization owning the assets and the associated business processes. Such concerns led to an increased focus on solving these security risks and adopting the emerging standards.

The architect's roles and skills

If your company or organization is like many, it defined many roles and job titles for its architects. Most often, the roles we will describe in this section reside in the IT organization. That said, linking these projects to business needs and requirements is critical as we previously noted. We'll describe the process to do that later in this book.

Many look to **The Open Group Architecture Framework** (**TOGAF**) as a place to begin to define the skills an architect must possess. TOGAF describes characteristics needed to define a business architecture, application architecture, data architecture, and technical architecture. As cloud-based computing has gained popularity, some of the architecture considerations and emphasis have changed a bit. Today, the following roles are the typically defined ones for each architecture type:

- **Business architecture**: This architecture includes the business strategy and goals, business processes, organization, and governance that are primarily driven by the lines of business and provides documentation for the business justification for projects
- **Application architecture**: This architecture maps the relationships between identified-needed business processes and the application footprints, the interactions among applications, and how the applications are to be deployed (such as defining cloud-based SaaS strategies)

- **Data architecture**: This architecture defines the appropriate logical and physical data structures aligned to business needs and the most appropriate data management platforms (choosing among relational databases, NoSQL databases, Hadoop, graph databases, and other options)
- **Technology architecture**: This architecture defines software, server, storage, and networking solutions (including cloud-based PaaS and IaaS strategies) in response to technical requirements

The TOGAF definitions became the basis for defining the role of the **Enterprise Architect (EA)** in many organizations and a certification process. An EA could become certified by demonstrating skills in each of these architecture areas. In truth, many of today's EAs have strong IT technology backgrounds because of their heritage but are weaker in other areas.

Because of the unbalanced skills often present in architects, many organizations designate specialists for each architecture area. So, they will have business architects, application architects, data architects, and technology, infrastructure, or cloud architects. An organization will sometimes also have a chief architect who serves as the lead strategist and participates in strategic planning across the different specialties.

The growing realization of the importance of secure data and data centers in always delivering a trusted and timely picture of true business state has caused many organizations to create the role of **Chief Security Officer (CSO)**. Security architects or cloud architects with strong security backgrounds are sometimes part of the team. They bring skills in defining authorization, authentication, and encryption architectures, and a knowledge of secure networking designs and options. They also have knowledge of industry and country mandates, as well as security certification standards that must be adhered to.

In the crowded C-suite alphabet soup, a relatively new entrant is the CDO or Chief Digital Officer. CDO has also been used for Chief Data Officer. However, in the context of the Industrial Internet, the Chief Digital Officer often plays a pivotal role. A CDO is the leader who helps a private company or a public organization drive digital transformation initiatives to achieve well-defined outcomes.

Digital transformation can be defined as the change associated with the conversion from traditional and often analog business technologies to digital ones using one or more of the modern computing paradigms involving data, analytics, mobility, social media, or cloud computing. A simple example of the digital transformation of business in the public sector setting is the use of automated toll machines communicating with automobile transponders to process tolls on highways, thus eliminating coin-operated or human-operated tool booths. The transponder is a good example of a thing.

CDOs are appearing in more and more companies. Examples include leaders of IIoT projects and initiatives at General Electric (William Ruh) and ABB (Guido Jouret). CDOs will sometimes have the title of Vice President - Digital. Regardless of the exact title, the person in the CDO role is often closer to the business operations than the traditional **Chief Information Officer (CIO)**. Such an individual can have a natural promotion progression to President of an operational division or CEO.

CDOs usually have a strong architecture background. In fact, a career path we have seen is evolution from one of the architect roles defined by TOGAF to chief architect and then CTO and finally CDO or Vice President of Digital. Thus, IIoT is introducing new career paths for architects.

The architects and similarly skilled individuals responsible for the Industrial Internet are increasingly becoming part of the CDO organization as opposed to the CIO organization. Such digital organizations are often tasked to help break the barriers between **Operations Technology (OT)** and IT. This convergence of IT and OT is key to the full realization of the value of the Industrial Internet. This idea of the convergence of IT and OT systems into IIoT systems in visually represented in the following illustration:

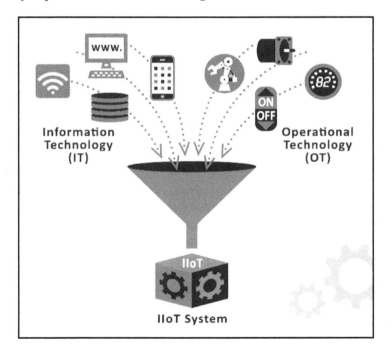

This implies that the organization needs to hire and develop skills based on these new demands. In some cases, companies are developing Digital Leadership Programs to groom professionals from the lines of businesses who are skilled in OT and pairing them with more traditional enterprise IT skills to accelerate the delivery of the Industrial Internet, inside and outside their organizations.

The traditional **Systems Integrator** (**SI**) and professional services companies are creating digital and IoT practices. They are creating reference architectures and building proof of concepts to showcase applications for Industrial Internet. As these organizations increase the number of Industrial Internet architects to implement these IIoT solutions, we will likely see the emergence of new kinds of training and certifications.

Architectural approaches for success

In this section, we will look at the need for an Industrial Internet-centric architectural approach to be successful in delivering the business outcomes. Just as civil engineers and building architects use blueprints to incorporate best practices in their work in a reusable way, reference architectures for IT systems have been extensively defined and used to prevent the reinvention of the wheel again and again.

Here, we will focus on reference architectures for IoT and more specifically on emerging reference architectures for the Industrial Internet and IIoT projects. To fully understand such reference architecture, a familiarity with system design principles, enterprise architecture, security frameworks, and networking architecture will be highly useful.

Reference architectures for the Industrial Internet

Reference architectures for the Industrial Internet can be very useful in facilitating the communication between the architects and the stakeholders in industrial manufacturing domains, including plant managers, field engineering managers, service professionals, business managers, and others. The solutions tend to address very specific business problems such as determining fuel efficiency and when engine maintenance is required. IT-centric architecture frameworks are less useful for understanding how the convergence of OT and IT will provide a means to achieve the business outcomes expected from the Industrial Internet solutions. However, there is a need for the reusability of this underlying IT architecture to scale the lessons that are being learned broadly.

Architects refer to the reference architecture and use it as a template as they capture the requirements. They design the specific implementation of the architecture and can convey a consistent understanding to internal and external stakeholders. Thus, interoperability, security, and other requirements are addressed upfront and do not become an afterthought.

Reference architectures lay the foundation for best practices and the reuse of the architectural patterns. As per the US **Treasury Architecture Development Guidance (TADG)** publication (`http://pubs.opengroup.org/architecture/togaf8-doc/arch/chap28.html`), the definition of a **pattern** is *an idea that has been useful in one practical context and will probably be useful in others*. The structure of the pattern can include some of the following elements:

- **Name:** Easy-to-remember nomenclature
- **Problem statement**: Description of the challenge to solve
- **Context:** The current state where the pattern could be applied
- **Forces:** The internal and external drivers and constraints; this could include the regulatory landscape as well as the societal implications
- **Solution:** The details of how to solve the problem at hand
- **Resulting context**: The outcomes and the trade-offs
- **Examples:** Sample applications
- **Rationale:** The *why* and the detailed explanations
- **Related patterns**: How this pattern is similar or related to others
- **Known uses**: Where this pattern is in use

Throughout this book, we will see the evolution of and use of architecture patterns in the context of the Industrial Internet. For example, there are different patterns for gateways and edge architecture. New cloud-based architecture patterns continue to be introduced.

The **Industrial Internet Consortium (IIC)** has recognized the need for the reference architecture and has published the **Industrial Internet Reference Architecture (IIRA)**. This three-tier architecture provides different view points targeted at the different stakeholders. IIC defines the reference architecture as the output of the application of architecture principles to a class of systems. This is used to provide guidance as the architects analyze and solve the common architectural concerns. The resulting IIRA then provides a template for use in the concrete architecture of Industrial Internet systems.

IIoT projects and architecture solutions can be extremely complex. A proven approach to solving complex problem design is to decompose it into its subsystems. So, to further accelerate the adoption of the Industrial Internet and enable delivery of the desired business outcomes, similar analytics, security, and connectivity frameworks are provided by IIC.

The multi-tier IIoT architecture

Next, we will take a look at the tiers of the architecture and how they interact to produce the desired system behaviors. In subsequent chapters of this book, we will provide guidance on how to simplify the design and analysis of the subsystems and foster their reusability.

The most commonly used reference architectures for the Industrial Internet and IIoT have three-tiers: Edge tier, Platform tier, and Enterprise tier. The commonly used definitions of the three tiers are as follows:

- **Edge tier**: The Edge tier collects data from the deployed machines (the sources of data) using various connection types. The architectural concerns for the Edge tier can include the nature of sensors and the machines or devices where data is being collected from, their location, governance scope, and the type of network connection, as well as the storage, transmission, and the computing needs for the collected data.
- **Platform tier**: The Platform tier receives, processes, and forwards data and control commands from the Edge tier to the Enterprise tier and vice versa. It can provide structures for data ingestion, data stores, and asset metadata, and can store configuration data and provide non-domain-specific services such as data aggregation and analytics.
- **Enterprise tier**: The Enterprise tier can implement domain-specific applications, decision support, and business intelligence systems, and provide user interfaces to human consumers of the information.

Let's take a quick glance at the following diagram depicting the tiers mentioned earlier:

Edge Tier	Platform Tier	Enterprise Tier
Sensors, Machines, Industrial Assets, Factory Assembly lines connected via Gateway device	Infrastructure, Data Store, Asset Management and Analytics Capabilities	Business Applications, Domain Specific Rules, Customer Interactions

Data Flow / Control Flow (between Edge Tier and Platform Tier), *Data Flow / Control Flow* (between Platform Tier and Enterprise Tier)

The providers for Industrial Internet platforms and solutions decide what functionality to provide and which components to configure in each of the tiers. General Electric often uses the terminology *get connected*, *get insight*, and *get optimized*, which requires all the three tiers to fully realize outcomes from Industrial Internet. A more detailed review of typical IIoT platform strategies and solutions will be covered in subsequent chapters.

A security framework for the Industrial Internet

Industrial accidents can cause devastating damage (as witnessed at Fukushima, Chernobyl, and Bhopal) with large-scale damage to the environment, injury, or the loss of human life. As we enable software-based systems to increasingly interact with operations of critical infrastructure, there is an increasing need for robust security frameworks for the Industrial Internet.

The IIC has defined an **Industrial Internet Security Framework (IISF)**. The IISF is a collective work product of security experts from companies such as ABB, GE, Intel, RTI, as well as academicians from JHU and UPenn. It was reviewed by professionals from Oracle, Microsoft, and IBM to name a few. Such cross-company initiatives prove that security frameworks and best practices cannot be over-emphasized for Industrial Internet.

The purpose of IISF is to provide a point of view on the security-related architectures, designs, and technologies, and identify procedures relevant to trustworthy Industrial Internet systems. IISF describes the security characteristics, technologies, and techniques needed to address security concerns and gain the assurance that system trust worthiness is achieved.

Apart from the traditional concerns of hacking and theft of information, resiliency is a key concern for Industrial Internet systems. IIC defines resilience as the condition of the system that allows it to be able to avoid, absorb, and/or manage dynamic adversarial conditions while completing assigned mission(s), and to reconstitute operational capabilities after casualties.

For example, a smart thermostat controlling the HVAC system in a building could receive a command to raise the building's temperature by 50 degrees Fahrenheit in the next hour. It is known that the building was operating in a normal temperature range for the human occupants in the building. The resilience built into the system would prevent a sudden rise in temperature and would either create an alarm for this command or include a reliable human in the loop of the decision making before acting.

This kind of system is called a **Cyber-Physical System (CPS)**. According to the **National Science Foundation (NSF)**, CPSs are *engineered systems that are built from, and depend upon, the seamless integration of computational algorithms and physical components* (`https://nsf.gov/funding/pgm_summ.jsp?pims_id=503286`).

Future research and advances in CPS will enable capability, adaptability, scalability, resiliency, safety, security, and usability that can be used for the benefit of Industrial Internet systems. CPS technology will drive innovation and competition in the industrial sectors such as agriculture, energy, transportation, building design and automation, healthcare, and manufacturing.

A connectivity framework for the Industrial Internet

Connectivity is at the heart of making IIoT projects functional. Interoperability among the tiers and to devices must be planned for.

IIC released the **Industrial Internet Connectivity Framework (IICF)** to deal with such architectural considerations; this is a result of contributions from professionals in several large companies, including Cisco, Ericsson, Nokia, RTI, GE, Samsung, AT&T, and SAP. The IICF links the different elements of the rich and diverse landscape of the Industrial Internet and defines an open connectivity reference architecture. IICF enables architects to evaluate and determine the suitability of a connectivity technology for their systems and solutions.

The IICF answers commonly asked by architects about connectivity in the different layers and their functions for Industrial Internet systems. It describes the architectural characteristics and design trade-offs at each layer, commonly available industry standards for these layers, and the categorization and evaluation of the relevant connectivity technology. As we dig deeper into the connectivity issues for Industrial Internet systems, in upcoming chapters, you will learn about connectivity frameworks often used in manufacturing such as **Open Platform Communications Unified Architecture** (**OPC-UA**), developed by the OPC Foundation. OPC-UA is a **machine-to-machine** (**m2m**) communication protocol commonly used for industrial automation.

The industrial data analytics framework

The industrial data analytics framework describes dig data analytics management systems on Industrial Internet systems data, which often take the form of the following data:

- **Relational data**: This format is best suited for metadata of assets and things, and as it captures the system configurations and relations to enterprise data systems. Commonly used relational database systems are Oracle, Microsoft SQL Server, IBM DB2, MySQL, and PostgreSQL.
- **Time series data**: This is a series of discrete data points in time order, often equally spaced in time. For industrial assets and sensors, this may be the bulk of the data. Such data is often stored in historian software that records the historical information and trends about industrial processes. NoSQL databases are also used to manage this type of data.
- **Object related data**: This form of bulk object storage is best suited for images, blobs, and other unstructured data. Examples of this type of storage are Amazon S3, Microsoft Azure blob storage, and Scality that can be deployed on-premise.

To run industrial analytics on such a variety of data formats, real-time and batch capabilities are required. The ability to orchestrate multiple analytics workflows is also required.

The stakeholders for analytics can be data scientists, analytics developers, architects, as well as **subject matter experts** (**SMEs**). The following diagram illustrates the typical life cycle of the development of industrial analytics:

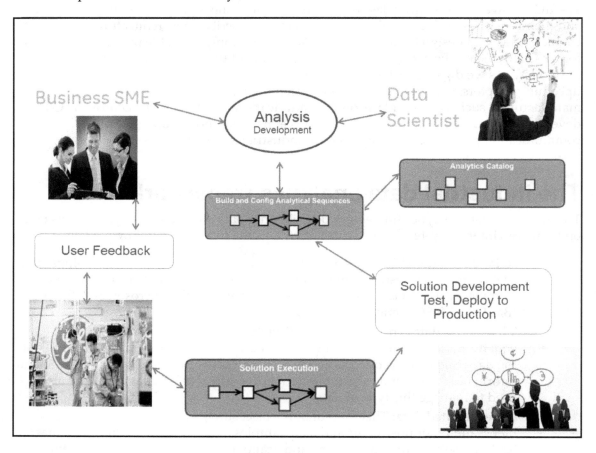

This is an iterative process and suitable for agile development. An important characteristic of the industrial analytics is the ability to not only pull the aggregated and summary data to the analytics but also to be able to push down the analytics to near real-time data feeds. This is due to the extremely large data volumes that devices transmit and the frequent nature of these transmissions.

In subsequent chapters, we will talk about such near real-time analytics technologies and discuss the emergence of the NoSQL database and Hadoop-based data management solutions fundamental to solving these problems. Architects of Industrial Internet solutions must embrace skills in industrial analytics and new data paradigms to be able to design effective solutions.

Cloud and user experience considerations

The frameworks we've described provide some of the background material you will need. However, other areas are less well covered because they are relatively new (cloud computing) or not typically in the domain of architects (user experience).

Architects are typically very comfortable defining on-premises systems and translating that knowledge into *public cloud concepts*. IaaS is a form of cloud computing that provides virtualized computing resources for enterprise and Industrial Internet systems in the form of operating systems, servers, storage, and, networking. They can also choose PaaS which also delivers data management systems, tools, and the management of those components, or SaaS that provide an even more complete solution. We will further discuss the business and technical trade-offs of each in the next couple of chapters.

That said, architects must make key design decisions that span the on-premises and Public Cloud paradigms. They must consider where the data is stored and who it belongs to. The compliance and regulatory landscape often becomes a key consideration for the architects. As with any solution, they must consider who has access to the data and under what context. We'll provide much more guidance here later in the book.

As data is collected and analyzed to turn insights into action, the user experience, or UX, assumes importance. It is important to remember that UX Design refers to the **User Experience Design**, while the more understood UI Design stands for **User Interface Design**. An industrial worker on the factory floor or a field service technician working on overhead power lines has a very different expectations when interacting with the environment and the device they use to deliver *actionable* tasks.

Business strategy framework for the Industrial Internet

While architects often confine themselves to technology challenges, in the realm of the Industrial Internet, business considerations go hand in hand. IIC provides a business strategy framework that illustrates the major areas that should be of interest:

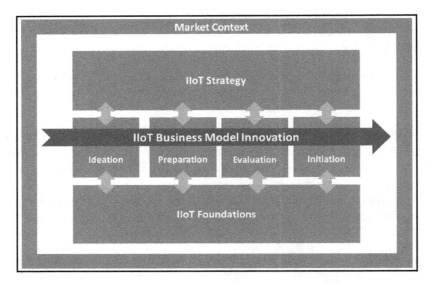

Industry analysts agree that the IIoT is experiencing explosive growth, and emerging leaders in companies, such as the CDOs, are being tasked with driving strategies. Architects must sharpen their business acumen and have an opportunity to groom up for future digital leadership roles.

Areas where architects can broaden their contributions to their companies will include, but not be limited to, the following things:

- Understand the competitive landscape and help define their company's role
- Understand new market dynamics and pressures introduced by IIoT
- Understand new business models, the value chain, and partnerships/alliances and continuous reevaluation of the same within their company
- Evaluate the societal impact of the Industrial Internet

Summary

This chapter served as an introduction to some of the fundamental concepts we will discuss in the book and provides you with some background if you are new to the Industrial Internet. After reading this chapter, you should now understand how the Industrial Internet evolved from the Industrial Revolution and why organizations are investing in IIoT solutions. You should have also gained a better understanding of some of the challenges to prepare for in the deployment of IIoT solutions. This chapter also explained the roles and responsibilities of the various architects and tied this to their professional development paths.

We'll continue our journey in the next chapter by further exploring how various roles will interact and how we can begin to define our Industrial Internet architecture in a way that will ultimately lead to a viable project. You will also learn about different architecture viewpoints and their impact on the design of your overall IIoT solution.

2
Architectural Approaches for Success

The previous chapter discussed the historical foundations and evolution of IIoT from the Industrial Revolution. We looked at the challenges as well as the reasons driving companies to invest in IIoT solutions. We looked at the various roles and their respective responsibilities, as IIoT solutions get designed and rolled out. In this chapter, we'll delve deeper into the IIoT architect's role and cover the following topics:

- How different viewpoints impact the architecture and design of the IIoT system
- Various architectural patterns and concerns
- How the design process flows from ideation to PoC to deployment
- Security concerns for each viewpoint and their impact on the system

Architectural framework

Architectural framework IIoT systems comprise connected systems of machines, or industrial systems, exchanging data, analysis, and actions to improve production and performance, and reduce defects or failures. Vast quantities of data are collected, analyzed, and transmitted at a rapid rate to consuming systems or components, where further analysis and actions may occur. An architectural framework therefore becomes necessary to guide the design of the system and ensure all stakeholders' expectations are considered. Specific concerns of each stakeholder are described and organized into appropriate types of models (model kind). The various model kinds of each viewpoint are consolidated and organized, while resolving concerns, into an architectural view for the respective viewpoints. The architectural views of the various viewpoints in turn form the architecture framework:

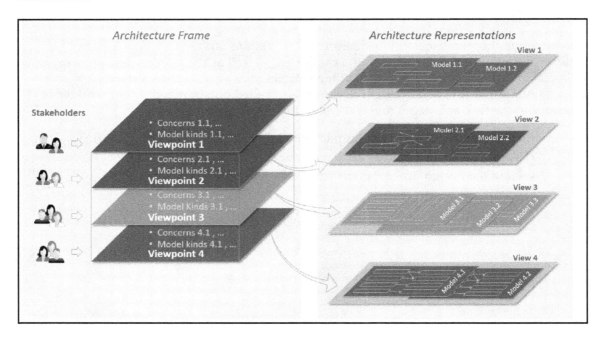

Figure 2.1: Architectural framework

As there are many factors for system architects to consider, it is useful to follow a common framework to organize topics of interest (concerns) and further the clarification, analysis, and resolution of concerns. A common framework such as the **Industrial Internet Reference Architecture** (**IIRA**), as published by the IIC in the paper *The Industrial Internet of Things Volume G1: Reference Architecture (IIC:PUB:G1:V1.80:20170131)*, can provide a basis for this analysis, and the systems architects can expand upon it with their specific requirements. This standards-based reference architecture defines a common vocabulary and definitions, and can aid in the evaluation and resolution of concerns. It eventually guides the development of the IIoT system, and provides a reference for subsequent communications and documentation.

Architectural viewpoints

Many disciplines and viewpoints need to be considered in architecting an IIoT solution, and the various stakeholders from each viewpoint can have intertwining concerns spanning the lifetime of the system.

Let's discuss the following typical viewpoints and how they interact with each other:

- Business viewpoint
- Usage viewpoint
- Functional viewpoint
- Implementation viewpoint

The business viewpoint maps business strategy to capabilities and identifies opportunities to achieve additional value thru IIoT. The business viewpoint identifies the capabilities that become the driver for the usage viewpoint, which deals with how the system is used. The usage viewpoint guides the life cycle of the project, including design, development, implementation, deployment, and the sustaining engineering. The functional viewpoint defines what the system does, and breaks it down into its functional components. Finally, the implementation viewpoint determines and defines the technologies and components needed to implement the usage and functional viewpoints. These viewpoints form *Figure 2.2: Architecture viewpoint hierarchy*:

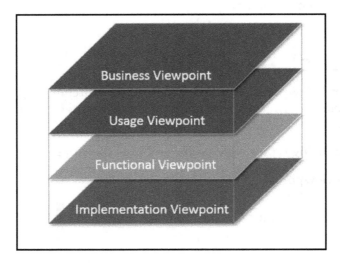

Figure 2.2: Architecture viewpoint hierarchy

In architecting an IIoT system, it is vital to consider security at every level and in every component, and how they interact. Each viewpoint has its unique security concerns, which are introduced next.

Business viewpoint

The *business viewpoint* addresses the business concerns and expectations to be considered in defining the business value the IIoT needs to address. The business viewpoint begins with the stakeholders for each viewpoint, and identifies their vision and values for the project and the company. The vision determines the business direction and describes the future state of the organization. The vision is reflective of the values of the stakeholders and the organization, and may play a role in the perception of the IIoT system.

The business viewpoint defines the key objectives of the system, as expressed by senior business and technical leaders, in keeping with the vision and values. Key objectives describe the expected outcomes from the system, and should be measurable and time-bound, for example, 10% cost savings within 2 months.

Fundamental capabilities define the system's ability to perform major business activities and are not concerned with how the system will be implemented or what technologies will be used. The key objectives and fundamental capabilities ultimately determine the framework for the usage activities and system requirements (*Figure 2.3: Business vision and value driven model*).

The business viewpoint also defines the fundamental success criteria on which the resultant IIoT system will be evaluated to determine if it meets the key objectives. This is represented in the following model diagram:

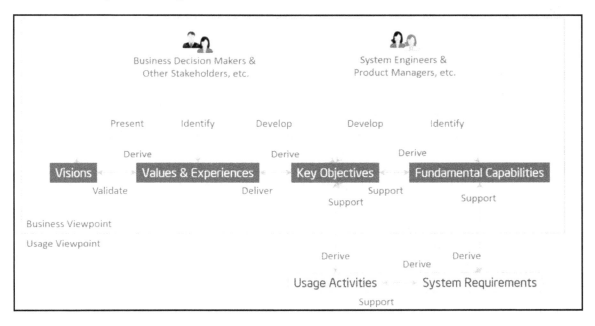

Figure 2.3: Business vision and value driven model

Security considerations for the business viewpoint

Regulatory and compliance mandates pertaining to privacy, data protection, critical infrastructure protection, access to sensitive information, safety, and so on. must be followed regardless of the cost.

Business value pertains to ensuring that the physical and intellectual assets of the business are shielded from intrusion, leaking of sensitive information, malicious use, or any other potential threat that could damage the business or its customers and business partners.

Usage viewpoint

The *usage viewpoint* identifies the users, parties, and roles of the IIoT system, and how they will interact with it. The usage viewpoint describes the coordination of activities throughout the system and its components, or how the system will be used; it becomes the input for the system requirements, and guides the design, deployment, operations, and evolution of the system.

The usage viewpoint is primarily concerned with executing tasks. Tasks are performed by parties who assume operational roles and do the work of the system. Roles consist of capacities and privileges to execute tasks or functions in support of specific activities. A party is any autonomous agent, either human or automated, whose job it is it to execute tasks and perform activities. A party must assume an appropriate role to execute the tasks required for the corresponding activities. A party may be assigned to one or more roles, and a role may be assumed by more than one party.

Tasks are defined within the context of a role. A functional map describes the functions and functional components mapped to the task. For example, a task analyzing temperatures may map to functions to analyze temperature data and aggregation functions to return the values for average, highest (maximum), and lowest (minimum) temperatures. An implementation map describes the implementation components necessary to execute the tasks. It also describes how a task's associated role(s) map to system components and operations.

Tasks may be combined in a coordinated fashion to perform an activity. Activities are sets of tasks required to perform a process in an IIoT system and are frequently executed repeatedly. An activity consists of a trigger, which initiates the activity, a workflow to control the sequence of task execution, and constraints, which define the boundaries of what the activity can do and preserves system characteristics such as data integrity.

Activities do not need to be described in detail initially, but should at least be described in the abstract, as potential activities are important in the design phase to define the requirements of the system.

The usage viewpoint ultimately drives the detail requirements, design, implementation, deployment, and sustaining engineering. An experience framework helps define how the desired human IoT experience maps to key usages and capabilities required to deliver the usage and experience:

	IoT Experiences	Key Usages	Potential Capabilities
1	Improving People, Culture, and Practices	• Empowering Individual and Aggregated Behavior Change • Enabling Decentralized Decision Making	Pattern identification, predictive & prescriptive analytics, data collection and visualization, data monitoring & alerting, incentive systems, crowdsourcing platforms, preference & recommendations engines
2	Growing the Business	• Uncovering New Revenue Opportunities • Capturing Lost Revenue	Legacy to open protocol transformers, smart data pipe, edge analytics, cloud analytics
3	Enhancing Oversight	• Regulatory Compliance • Connecting Dots and Breaking Down Silos	Systems for data logging, storage and verification, data integrity checking, algorithms for compliance assessment (standards/ BKMs), redundant backups, failure mode analysis, oversight mechanisms, data integrity guarantees
4	Managing All Kinds of Assets	• Asset Identification • Asset Tracking	Unique asset ID assignment, databases linking ID to asset, Method for interrogating ID (NFC, RFID, network broadcast), methods for communicating location (GPS, local positioning systems, relative proximity (RSSI)), inventory management systems
5	Optimizing System Performance	• Predicative Maintenance and Reducing Downtime • Effective Distribution and System Stress reduction	Identification of "weak links" in system performance, predictive and proscriptive maintenance algorithms, diagnostics and recommendations systems for repair, augmented reality at point of service, intelligent, interactive, situation sensitive repair instructions, remote worker communication, proprietary to open protocol translation
6	Minimizing Threats, Mitigating Risks	• Accuracy of Alerting • Improved Trust in Systems and Processes	Full security across the signal path, real time analysis and alerting, threat identification, malware detection, intrusion detection and remediation, trusted execution environments.

Figure 2.4: IIoT experience framework

In this framework, each IIoT human-value experience is mapped to its key usages and the capabilities required for the usage. Focusing on usage sets the level of detail required for the use case.

The usage scenario approach can be used to:

- Identify current and future use cases and ensure the IIoT experiences are satisfied for the respective use cases
- Ensure coverage across the human-value experience for IIoT deployments by creating key usage scenarios that map to those values
- Provide guidance to bridge usage scenarios to the architecture framework

The experience framework allows the technical framework to be tracked back to key value experiences. Storyboarding each usage facilitates the definition of the usage requirements. Each pane in the storyboard has a detailed story with insights into what is happening, and can aid in identifying the entities, relationships, data sharing, and analysis needs. This decomposition exposes the architectural needs for each scenario.

Security considerations for the usage viewpoint

Following are the security considerations for implementing the usage viewpoint:

- Security monitoring continuously collects security-related data from events or activities, and analyzes it for security risks
- Security auditing collects, stores, and analyzes security-related information
- Security policy defines the usage and constraints for each user, role, and component
- Cryptographic support management stores, manages, grants, and revokes secure credentials, and provides global key management

Functional viewpoint

The functional viewpoint begins to categorize and organize the tasks and activities of the solution into corresponding functional components, and describes how data flows between them, and in the physical system. Here, we will begin to define the integration of the IT world with the OT world, with the goal of increased local collaborative autonomy and increased system optimization, through global orchestration of sensor data collection and analysis. This creates a dichotomy as IT and OT each have a different focus, and they each have far-reaching impacts. A functional domain definition attempts to address these architectural concerns. The functional architecture definition begins by identifying specific functions in the system and their specific requirements. These functions are categorized by the IIRA as follows; however, they may require some customization or additional domains may be required, depending on the use case and industry:

- Control domain
- Operations domain
- Information domain
- Application domain
- Business domain

Control domain

The control domain consists of functions performed by industrial control systems and are typically performed in closed loops, for example, constantly reading temperature and pressure and opening a valve when they exceed a defined limit. *Figure 2.5, Control domain functions*, represents a typical control domain; however, the specific functions may vary depending on the industry and system.

The control domain typically consists of sensing functions and actuation. The sensing function reads data from sensors and may span hardware, firmware, device drivers, and software elements. The actuation function writes data and controls signals to an actuator to perform an actuation.

The third important function in the control domain is communication between the sensors, actuators, controllers, gateways, and other edge systems. Latency, bandwidth, jitters, reliability, and resilience can interrupt or delay communication and decrease **Quality of Service (QoS)**, and must be considered in the architecture design, especially in critical systems. It may be appropriate to use APIs to expose a set of connectivity services, which may include additional connectivity features, such as auto-discovery.

Entity abstraction defines a virtual representation of the sensors, actuators, controllers, and respective higher level systems, and models the relationship between them, as well as providing a context from which to interpret and understand sensor data.

Modelling attempts to interpret and correlate data gathered from sensors, peer systems, and controlling systems into states, conditions, and behaviors. Models may simply interpret sensor readings, such as a time series of temperature readings, or may be complex artificial intelligence models. Models involved in local control systems are referred to as edge analytics, and are usually used in real-time applications when decisions must be made rapidly in local control systems and where it is impractical or expensive to send raw sensor data to a central processor for processing. Other functions may be employed to prepare data for analysis, including filtering, cleansing, transforming, and persisting.

Operations management of control systems is enabled by the asset management function. Asset management includes configuration, policy enforcement, system controls, and other life cycle operations.

An executor carries out control logic according to control objectives. This may be a sequence of actions applied through actuation and may involve interactions with peer or higher-level systems. Control logic may be straightforward, as in simple set-point algorithms to adjust room temperature, or they may be sophisticated, employing advanced cognitive and learning capabilities:

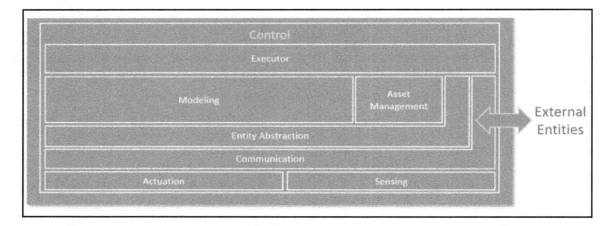

Figure 2.5: Control domain functions

Operations domain

The operations domain includes the functions responsible for operating the systems in the control domain, with a focus on system-wide optimization, rather than local operations, taking a more holistic approach than traditional plant- or component-level operations. By focusing on operational efficiency across the business, new opportunities emerge for added value in the business domains. *Figure 2.6* illustrates the operations domain supporting multiple customers:

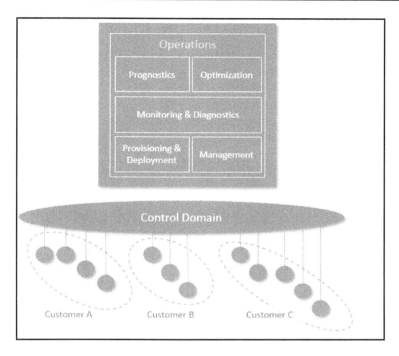

Figure 2.6: Inter-dependent operation support functions

Let's understand the operation of each function illustrated in the preceding diagram:

- **Provisioning & Deployment**: These functions performs configuring, on-boarding, registering, retiring, and tracking of assets. They also communicate with assets at the individual asset level and across fleets of assets, and must be able to function regardless of the environment.
- **Management**: These functions enable asset management centers to propagate commands across control systems and to the assets, and likewise allow the assets and control centers to respond.
- **Monitoring & Diagnostic**: These functions assist operations personnel to respond to problems rapidly. By performing real-time monitoring of the asset health, problems can be detected early or even predicted before they occur.
- **Prognostics**: This analyzes historical data against current conditions and predicts outcomes, usually by identifying problems before they occur.
- **Optimization**: These functions are concerned with improving asset reliability and performance and ensuring they operate at peak efficiency.

Information domain

The information domain consists of functions concerned with gathering data predominantly from, but not limited to, the control domain. However, while the control domain monitors data in real time, analyzes it, and applies rules to perform local control of systems, the data gathered in the information domain is stored, or persisted, and transformed for analysis. It could also be applied to machine learning, potentially discovering deeper intelligence about the overall system and operations.

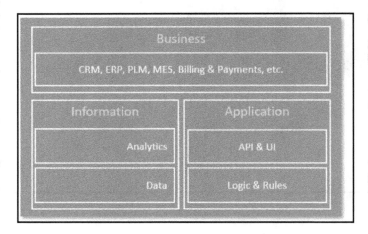

Figure 2.7: Functional components of the business, information, and application domain

Data functions consist of ingestion, data quality, syntax, or formatting; that is, date formats, semantics, or context transformation, data persistence and storage, and data distribution.

IIoT data is typically generated and transmitted in online streaming mode, and the data is processed as it is received to provide real-time and near real-time analytics and feedback. Data collected in locations lacking sufficient connectivity may be collected and accumulated locally, and can be processed in offline batch mode.

The information domain also deals with data governance, including security, privacy, access control and rights management, and resilience. These functions may involve data replication, backup and recovery, snapshotting, and so on. Big data systems incorporate data replication as a fundamental part of their architecture, and are useful for inexpensive storage and the processing of very large data sets.

Analytics encompasses functions for data modeling, statistical and trend analysis, classifications, machine learning, data science, and other advanced processing. Analytics may be applied to data at rest in batch mode or on demand or on streaming data in motion, as it is received. Batch mode analytics are typically performed for consumption by the business domain, while streaming data analysis is typically performed for the operations and control domains.

IIoT systems typically generate large volumes of data at high speed. The volume and granularity of the data can quickly overwhelm networks, storage systems, and databases. Therefore, raw data can be stored on big data systems, and data that is known to have value for the business or operations domain can be extracted, typically as aggregated summaries, calculated **key performance indicator (KPI)**, or snapshots. As there may be undiscovered value in the raw data, big data systems can store and process very large data volumes and can be analyzed and mined by advanced analytic tools and data scientists for insight into the operations.

Application domain

The application domain consists of application logic, or functions, for performing specific business functions and is concerned with high-level, global, or system-wide functions, not detailed control logic, which is the purview of the control domain. The application domain consists of logic and rules for executing functions, activities, and interfaces. The interfaces include APIs, which expose the application functions for other applications to consume, and **user interfaces (UIs)**, which enable humans to interact with the application.

Business domain

The business domain encompasses supporting business processes and procedures. These could include traditional business applications, such as **Enterprise Resource Planning (ERP)**, **Customer Relationship management (CRM)**, billing systems, scheduling, and so on, and other business and industry functions. The incorporation of the business domain in IIoT systems enables a more robust, cross-system analysis to be performed.

Cross-cutting functions and system characteristics

The business, usage, functional, and implementation viewpoints bring together the requirements and concerns of their respective stakeholders, and help provide a framework for developing the IIoT architecture. In general, the business viewpoint determines the mission and the boundaries for the usage viewpoint, ultimately driving the requirements for the functional and implementation viewpoints. In turn, the functional and implementation viewpoints may influence or impose limitations on the business viewpoint. For example, if the business viewpoint requires that field engineers must react immediately to certain events, in all conditions, then the usage viewpoint may determine they need heat-proof, waterproof, shockproof devices with unlimited connectivity to receive the information. The business viewpoint may then determine it is not cost-effective to provide all field engineers with such devices.

Cross-cutting functions support activities across the functional components and cut across the generic IIoT system capabilities. These enabling functions include data management, connectivity, and analytic capabilities.

System characteristics are system-wide properties required to manage the interaction of the parts of the IIoT system. System characteristics focus on how the system works rather than what the system does from a functional or business perspective. These functions are typically only noticed by end users when they fail. These characteristics include security, privacy, scalability, safety, resilience, and reliability. These interconnected characteristics contribute to the trustworthiness of the system. Trustworthiness also depends on how well the system characteristics are integrated into the functional components and their interactions. Basically, trustworthiness is dependent on the weakest link; for example, privacy cannot be protected if security is weak. *Figure 2.8* illustrates the relationship between functional domains, cross-cutting functions, and system characteristics.

A strong architecture incorporates cross-cutting functions and system characteristics while also ensuring the proper functioning of the fundamental capabilities:

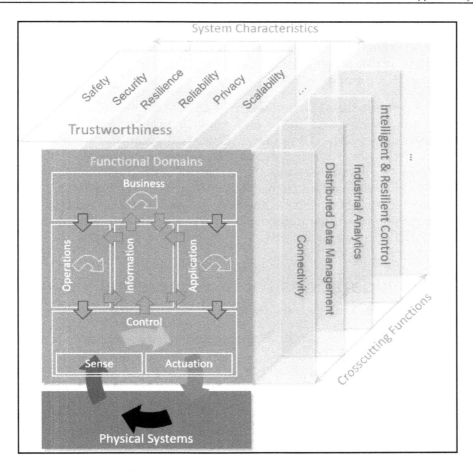

Figure 2.8: Functional domains, crosscutting functions, and system characteristics

Computational deployment patterns

The Industrial Internet encompasses many topologies of assets, and sensor and computational distributions. Traditional control systems typically disperse computational power close to the physical systems, in the network periphery, and are performed at the controller level. Traditional data centers perform centralized computations. The Industrial Internet requires a combination of both of these. Smart sensors and devices perform dispersed computations to enable localized control and decision making, while concentrated computation placed throughout the network supports higher-level decision making.

Network connectivity is critical for communication between the periphery and the concentrated capabilities. Concentrated computational capabilities enable a wider and deeper spectrum of analytics using data integrated throughout the industrial system, including traditional applications data.

The placement of computational capabilities in relation to the periphery requires architectural choices to be made. If the assets are high in number and widely dispersed to remote areas, a strong peripheral computation capacity is necessary, especially if latency, local control, and resilience are critical. Functions performing higher-level computations that incorporate data from multiple systems, but do not depend on strict latency requirements, can be performed by a concentrated computational capability. Generally, IIoT systems use a combination of peripheral and concentrated computational patterns. Distributed computational concentration is most resilient, while concentrated computation has the potential for more robust analytics.

Security considerations for the functional viewpoint

Following are some of the security consideration for the functional viewpoint:

- **Security audit**: To collect, store, and analyze security-related information.
- **Identity verification**: In communications, it protects the integrity of communications within the IIoT system.
- **Cryptographic support**: This involves software and hardware for encryption and decryption.
- **Data protection and privacy**: This protects sensitive and personal information, both at rest and while in transit. Data protection requirements are defined by a security policy, and should be in keeping with organizational and regulatory requirements.
- **Authentication and identity management**: This ensures users only have access to the functions and data for which they are authorized.
- **Physical protection**: This enforces security policies to prevent tampering and unauthorized observation.

Implementation viewpoint

The implementation viewpoint is the manifestation of each of the previous viewpoints. The business viewpoint ultimately drives the selection of technologies, with considerations for costs, time constraints, business strategy, regulation, and the vision for the future.

The implementation viewpoint describes the ultimate structure and distribution of the system components and how they are connected. The required interfaces, protocols, and behaviors are defined. Functional components defined in the usage viewpoint are mapped to implementation components.

IIoT implementations typically follow established architectural patterns, including the following:

- Three-tier architecture
- Gateway-mediated Edge connectivity
- Edge-to-cloud
- Multi-tier data storage
- Distributed analytics

Three-tier architecture consists of Edge, Platform, and Enterprise tiers. The functional domain determines the component requirements of the three-tier architecture, and the components generally map to the functional domains, or viewpoint, as in *Figure 2.9, Three-tier architecture*:

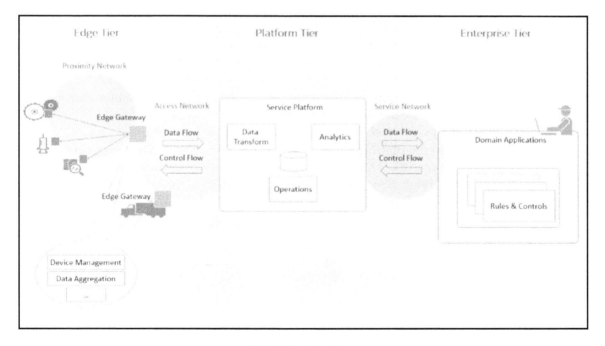

Figure 2.9: Three-tier architecture

Each tier has a specific role corresponding to the usage viewpoint, and they are connected via three separate networks:

- The **Edge Tier** collects data from the edge nodes across the proximity network. Device-specific processing and control may occur in the **Edge Tier**, depending on the application.
- The **Platform Tier** receives and processes data from the enterprise tier to the edge tier, via a service network, and from the platform tier, via an access network. The platform tier performs management functions for the devices, and the detail and consolidated data can by queried or transformed for further analysis.
- The **Enterprise Tier** receives the data and integrates it with data from other systems, to perform analysis across business silos. The enterprise tier may also execute control commands on the edge or platform tier.

 The functions depicted in *Figure 2.9* indicate the primary function of the tier, but are not exclusive to that tier. The same functions are implemented in each tier according to the usage within the tier level.

The tiers are connected by different types of network as follows:

- The proximity network connects sensors, devices, assets, control systems, and other components in the edge nodes. The edge nodes are typically grouped into clusters and bridge to a wide area network via the edge gateway or hub.
- The access network connects the edge- and platform-tier and enables data and control flows between them. This could be a corporate network, a 4G/5G network, or a private network on the public internet.
- The services in the platform tier connect to each other and to the enterprise tier via a service network. This can be a private network over the public internet (or the internet), and enables enterprise grade security between the end user and the services.

The three-tier architecture maps the components to the functional viewpoint (*Figure 2.10*). The edge tier encompasses the control domain, and the platform tier contains aspects of the information and operations domains. The information tiers provide services to each other in support of the functional domain, completing the end-to-end activities:

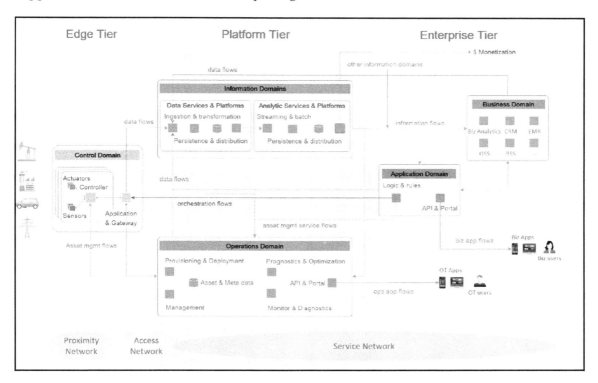

Figure 2.10: Three-tier architecture mapping to the functional viewpoint

Gateway-mediated edge connectivity and management defines the bridge between the edge nodes and a wider network, where the wide area network cannot access the edge nodes directly. An edge gateway in the edge node can perform local operations and controls. It may also be used to manage devices and serve as a conduit for aggregated data. This localization of control both reduces the complexity and enables the scaling up of assets and the network. Devices can be managed, and data can be aggregated by the edge gateway, thus enabling local control:

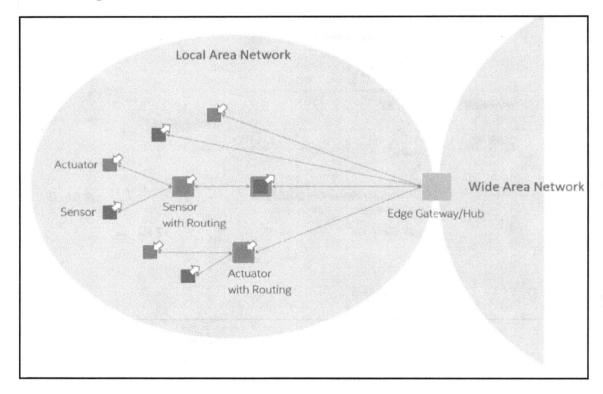

Figure 2.11: Gateway-mediated architecture pattern

The local networks may follow the hub-and-spoke topology, where the edge gateway acts as the hub for a cluster of edge nodes and to the wide area network, and the hub connects directly to each edge node. A mesh, or peer-to-peer network, follows the *hub-and-spoke* topology, but some edge nodes have routing paths to other edge nodes or the edge gateway. In both topologies, the edge nodes are isolated from the wide area network and are only accessible through the edge gateway.

The edge gateway supports the following:

- Local connectivity
- Network and protocol bridging
- Local data processing
- Device and asset control and a management point
- Site-specific decision and application logic

The Layered Databus architecture pattern is commonly used in IIoT systems, as it enables systems to directly manage interactions between remote applications, including control and edge analytics. Peer-to-peer communications across the systems layer can be secured, and the inherent low latency minimizes delays between the transmission and receipt of data, as illustrated in the following architecture of Layered Databus:

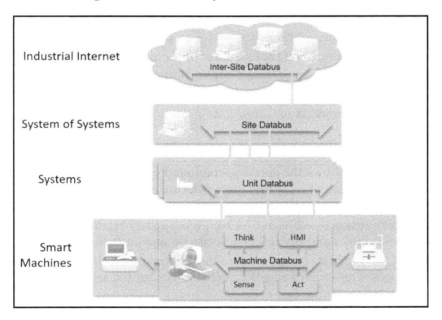

Figure 2.12: Layered Databus architecture

Low-level systems in this architecture pattern provide the local control and automation for smart machines, using databuses. Databuses are used in the higher level systems for monitoring and supervisory control.

A databus uses a common schema to communicate between endpoints. Each layer of the architecture employs its own databus, employing a schema specific to the endpoints in that layer. Adapters cross-match the data models between layers and can also be used as an interface for legacy systems or components using different protocols. This architecture facilitates operational monitoring, device management, provisioning, as well as applications and subsystems.

As data is collected at the lowest levels for local control, it is generally filtered and summarized for higher level systems that control a broader set of functions. A publish-subscribe model is used for communication of data and information, wherein applications on the databus publish their data output, and the consuming applications on the databus subscribe to the data they need. With the publish-subscribe model, components can share large volumes of data quickly.

Benefits of the layered database architecture include the following:

- Extremely fast delivery times for device-to-device integrations
- Scalability for integrating thousands of end points and actuators
- Automatic discovery of data and applications
- Extreme availability
- Isolation of subsystems

Additional architectural patterns include the following:

- Edge to cloud follows the gateway-mediated edge connectivity pattern; however, it is assumed that the wide area network can access the devices.
- Multi-tier data storage involves multiple types of storage tiers, with older data in a slower or less accessible archive tier, more current data in a capacity tier, and data needed for rapid operational decisions in a performance tier.
- Distributed analytics brings analysis and decision-making to the edge tier close to the devices. This creates additional challenges for the security of the devices as well as the data traffic.

Security considerations for the implementation viewpoint

End-to-end security includes securing both IT and OT realms and their integration points.

Securing legacy systems includes securing legacy endpoints, systems, and data transmission in order to minimize the risks of an attack on the older systems. Each architectural pattern has its own unique sets of risks and areas to secure, including end points, information exchange, management and control, and data distribution and storage.

End-point security embeds security in the devices itself, enabling them to protect themselves while disconnected from any central security management systems. Information exchange security protects communication and data exchanges, ensuring that the data remains private and authentic.

Data and analytics

IIoT solutions rely heavily on the use of advanced analytics on the data collected from the operational systems. This data is often merged with the data from the enterprise systems. Typically, the volume of data from the operation systems may far exceed the data from the latter source. Let's take an example of data from aircraft. According to Aviation Week, a modern generation aircraft can generate over one terabyte of data in a cross-country flight. Modern generation aircraft can have more than 1,000 sensors, including about 300 in the jet engine alone (http://aviationweek.com/connected-aerospace/internet-aircraft-things-industry-set-be-transformed).

This poses several kinds of challenges for the data and analytics design in the case of IIoT systems. Here are a few considerations:

- **Storage of data**: The sheer volume of data that can be generated by recording all the sensor readings at the rate of even 1/16 of a second makes it hard to store all the data on board an aircraft, for a single flight.
- **Transfer of data**: Due to the very high cost of secured communication channels between the aircraft and ground systems, it is not feasible to transfer full data with wireless, while the aircraft is in flight. Thus, only summary data in the range of a few kilobytes is transferred via the wireless medium. The bulk of the data collected on board the aircraft is transferred once the aircraft lands.
- **Data semantics**: The data that is collected from the aircraft at the airport must be decrypted and assigned meaning. In addition, engineering units must be added to this data before it is useful for any meaningful analysis.
- **Data volume**: Once the data from the single aircraft is collected for one flight, it must be sent to a big data store to allow its use with prior data for the same aircraft or engine. Such big data systems can quickly reach to petabytes or more, as data from the whole fleet of aircraft is collected, even say for 90 days.

- **Challenges for analytics**: Due to the nature of sensor data and its sheer volume, the data scientists face several challenges in coming up with meaningful analytics. They cannot pull large amounts of data where the analytics process runs in the server's memory and needs to load all the data for analysis. An example would be a Java program trying to cycle through terabytes of data. Instead, the computing paradigm shifts to near-data analytics as shown in *Figure 2.13*. On the right-hand side, we can see that big data systems such as Hadoop allow the analytics process to run near data, alleviating the need to pull large amounts of data into memory:

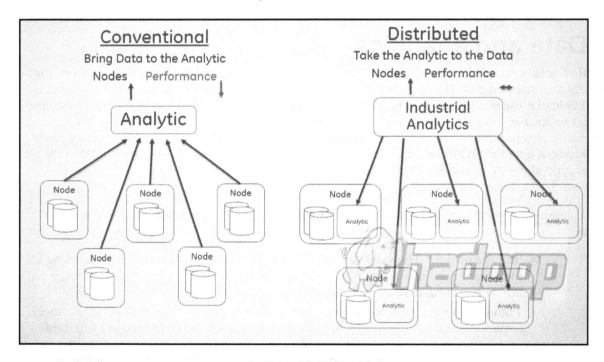

Figure 2.13: Challenges for analytics

- **Merging OT and IT data**: We discussed how to handle a large amount of operational or sensor data using the near-data analytics paradigm. However, the IT systems or enterprise data, for example, who owns this aircraft or the prior history of this engine, will often reside in relational systems. It is not easy to merge OT and the IT data in a meaningful way. To achieve the full potential of IIoT systems, it is important to bring all the relevant information or the enterprise context of the data in one place before it is fed to the analytics engines.

- **Multiplicity of Analytics languages**: Finally, most mature organizations have a proliferation of languages and tools for advanced analytics. Commonly used languages and environments may include, C/C++, Java, Matlab, Python, R, and so on. Thus, the analytics platform for IIoT systems should ideally be able to deploy analytics and analytical workflows that are written in these common languages.

Data management

IIoT solutions collect potentially huge volumes of data, typically at high velocity, and can also include data from traditional or legacy systems. This integration of data can consist of time series data from sensors and device data, including logs, and structured and unstructured data. Structured data is typically data from traditional enterprise or departmental software applications with known predefined data structures, or schemas. Unstructured data includes data with unknown or irregular and varying structures. These can include text from social media and digital images. Integrating these data sources can be challenging, but also can provide the basis for more effective monitoring, identification of problem areas, targeted and timely responses, and more effective analysis and decision making.

IIoT data management activities include the following:

- Reduction and analytics
- Publish and subscribe
- Query
- Storage, persistence, and retrieval
- Integration
- Description and presence
- Data framework
- Rights management

Here, the usage and functional viewpoints should provide guidance. IIoT data management needs to provide the users with information, analysis, and cross-functional insights that would not have been available in traditional applications where data may be stored in functional silos and unavailable for cross-functional analysis.

Analytics and advanced data processing

Each viewpoint will have unique analytic requirements. Engineers and front-line managers' analytic needs may be more functional in nature and may include real-time stream analysis, anomaly detection, and prescriptive analytics, that is, predicting when a part or machine needs maintenance. Middle and upper managers representing the business viewpoint may only need the aggregated data or calculated key performance indicators, as well as data from ERP, CRM, or other enterprise or departmental systems.

Advanced analytics involves the application of statistics and machine learning to analyze trends, make predictions, and provide dynamic feedback in real time. Advanced analytics can be categorized as follows:

- **Descriptive analytics**: This analyzes what has happened and what is happening, and is typically used in historical reporting and operational dashboards
- **Predictive analytics**: This applies statistical models and machine learning to predict outcomes and understand trends
- **Prescriptive analytics**: This recommends or automates a course of action for achieving a goal or desired outcome through simulation

The goal of advanced analytics is to improve, or supplement, decision making or component operations by applying use case-appropriate analytic algorithms, such as clustering and regression analysis. Visualization of the analysis is a crucial factor for human decision making and can help provide a level of confidence in the resulting decisions.

Integrability, interoperability, and composability

There is no marketplace or vendor from which to purchase a complete IIoT system. IIoT systems are assembled or composed of many components supplied by many vendors. To successfully integrate components into large systems, components must have the following characteristics:

- **Integrability**: This is the ability to communicate with each other using compatible signalling and protocols
- **Interoperability**: This is the ability to exchange information with each other based on this interpretation of semantic context and common conceptual models
- **Composability**: This is the ability to interact with any other component, be re-combined to form new behaviors, and interpret the intention of the received messages

Connectivity

Central to the functioning of any IIoT systems is ubiquitous connectivity. Connectivity facilitates interoperability, integration, and composability among the endpoints.

An information exchange infrastructure enables technical interoperability, or the ability to exchange bits and bytes, and is a prerequisite to syntactic interoperability, which is the ability to exchange information using common protocols.

Connectivity is made up of two functional layers:

- The *communication transport layer* is the mechanism for carrying messages between endpoints, providing technical interoperability
- The *connectivity framework* facilitates syntactic interoperability between endpoints, typically using common data structures and schemas

A data services framework cross-cutting function builds on the communications and connectivity frameworks to facilitate syntactic interoperability

Intelligent and resilient control

With advances in data management and interoperability, connectivity, and analytics, new generations of control systems are emerging, enabling optimal automated control of devices and assets. The control function in IIoT systems tends to be distributed on the periphery, rather than a centralized control. The distributed control must be intelligent and resilient, and capable of responding rapidly to a changing environment. The control system needs to sense, interpret, and react in the context of maintaining and optimizing operations. This intelligence relies on models that consume data from sensors and devices, make assumptions, and deliver control decisions within the confines of the actuator's capabilities, as the model understands them. If the IIoT system understands the models at work in the controller and how the decisions are being made, the connected devices and systems can anticipate the controller's actions and take actions to improve the outcome, including prescribing alternative methods.

As IIoT systems are deployed in all kinds of environments, it becomes likely for network connectivity to be periodically unavailable. In the event of connectivity loss, a resilient system limits the data loss to disconnected endpoints and can continue operation. When the connection is restored, any data updates that were blocked by the disruption can be transmitted. Placing the control capability near the devices being controlled reduces the dependency on the network and centralized computing capabilities, resulting in a more resilient control system. Because control devices generally do not generate large data volumes, they do not require high bandwidth.

Security concerns arise with intelligent and distributed control systems. Each endpoint or device is vulnerable to both physical and electronic assaults. The firmware of devices deployed in IIoT typically includes features to protect the device, and system, from malware and other intrusions. However, just as you need to update the virus protections on your laptop, the firmware may require updates as security vulnerabilities are discovered. As it is prohibitive to replace the physical chips or boards in potentially thousands of devices, a mechanism to push out automatic security updates is necessary. Unfortunately, manufacturers of many devices have been slow to adopt automatic security update features, or they stop providing updates once newer models are released.

Dynamic composition and automated interoperability

IIoT systems encompass and connect a diverse and distributed array of systems, components, and networks that utilize a variety of protocols, and are expected to scale and deliver end-to-end services safely and securely.

The IIoT system must respond to changing environments and evolving technologies and standards without interrupting service. This requires adaptable methods of composing services where components can be integrated dynamically at run time, which is not possible with point-to-point connections. A flexible system requires semantic interoperability that supports many-to-many connections where connections are indirectly linked by metadata, not statically connected. The metadata enables the separation of the system capability and control, or what the capability or service does from the infrastructure and implementation, or how it does it.

The physical composition of a service is interpreted at run time by referencing the information model, which maps to the physical components of the requested service. The mapped connections and their corresponding policies and transformations are discovered and integrated at run time. This loose coupling of service capabilities and component connections enables automatic interoperability and policy-based optimizations, and can dynamically adapt to new components and compose and reconfigure network resources.

Using PoCs to evaluate design

The PoC enables the demonstration of technical feasibility to deliver business value for an IIoT solution. A PoC is carried out on a smaller scale than a production system, giving the project team this opportunity to work out technical issues at a reduced cost and risk. It also provides an ecosystem for the various viewpoints to discuss and form an agreement about the business values and technical solutions.

Scope definition

The scope for the POC must be clearly defined and agreed upon. The success and eventual acceptance of the IIoT solution is not only dependent on the technology, but on how well the solution fulfills the business goals. Therefore, the business viewpoint is the predominant factor in defining the scope. The PoC should focus on demonstrating the business value, not necessarily the technology itself. In the early stage of defining the scope, stakeholders and managers from all viewpoints bring their concerns and desired business outcome and agree to a few ideas or use cases. Formal evaluation methods, such as score carding, can be utilized to develop more detail. The use cases can then be refined to formulate the high-level requirements and success criteria.

The high-level requirements enable the project team to evaluate the investment requirements, risks, and potential impact on the organization. A cost versus benefit estimation can be performed at this point for the projection of **Total Cost of Ownership (TCO)** and **Return on Investment (RoI)**, which will guide the stakeholders in prioritizing the projects. Once a use case is selected for a PoC, a time frame, project team, and success criteria should be defined before proceeding.

Business case considerations

The TCO is further divided among the various parties in the ecosystem, based on their expected returns. The organization should also consider its potential performance without initiating the project and how it will share the costs of the generic, or common, capabilities.

Business cases need to consider how the project will impact the individual parties, stakeholders, departments, and so on the as well as the wider business impact, including operations and competitiveness. IIoT projects have the potential to create reusable assets that should be considered in the cost/benefits.

It is important not to underestimate the costs. Cost calculations need to consider integration costs with existing systems, design, prototyping, testing, and certification. Another consideration in IIoT is the continuing operating costs of the infrastructure.

Since business cases and value projections generally make certain assumptions, which should be documented for each business case calculation; this will facilitate calculating changes to the ROI in the event of changing parameters.

A thorough risk assessment should be performed, considering technology, implementation, execution, and operational risks, in addition to business risks.

Solution definition

With an agreed-upon scope and use case, the project team can begin the process of defining the solution and selecting technologies to be used. The solution definition focuses on the system usage and the functional viewpoint. In addition, the information domain guides the data and analytic requirements for the solution.

The solution definition describes the market segment and business value, the current situation from an IT and OT perspective, the challenge, and the proposed solution. The solution definition also maps the functional requirements to the cross-cutting functions and system characteristics, security being the most important.

A gap-fit analysis is useful to identify existing capabilities and gaps that need to be filled. In addition to identifying the gaps, the capabilities should be categorized as to what is common (platform foundation), and what is one-off (use case-specific).

Here is an outline for defining a solution definition:

- Solution introduction
    - Describe the current situation from an IT and OT perspective
    - Describe the challenge
    - Propose the solution, or use case description
    - Identify the application domain: industry, line of business, functional
    - Identify dependencies
- Business viewpoint
    - **Business vision**: Business perspective of the overall system, defines the *why* and *what* of the use case, and provides the criteria for validation.
    - **Market segment**: Defines the target market the use case is addressing.
    - **Business value**: Economic, societal, commercial, and good-will benefits. The value answers the *why* question from the business vision.
    - **System objectives**: Key objectives from the business viewpoint, as pertaining to the use case.
- Describe the context, or target environment
    - **Technology**: Required technologies, existing technologies, legacy systems, integration requirements
    - **Regulatory**: Compliance and regulatory requirements, export restrictions, and so on
- Usage and operational scenarios
    - Description
    - Participants and actors
    - Stakeholders and concerns
    - Pre-conditions
    - Workflow
    - Post-conditions

- Key capabilities:
    - **Data**:
        - **Physical properties**: Monitoring and action
        - **Volume and velocity**: Size and speed of the expected dataset processing
        - **Aggregation**: Aggregation requirements for communications and analytics
        - **Variability**: Anticipated growth, shrinkage of the data volume
    - **Computations**: Processing and computations required
    - **Communication**: Network details, scale, and connectivity requirements
    - **Performance**: Varies with the domain (for example, sensor readings per second)
    - **Interoperability**: Entities, actors, systems integrations required for the use case
    - **Accuracy**: Error tolerance and level of uncertainty
- Key characteristics
    - Security, trust, and privacy
        - **Reliability**: Level of robustness and failure prevention
        - **Resiliency**: Level of fault-recovery capabilities
        - **Behavioral**: How the system behaves and interacts with humans or other systems
- System requirements
    - Challenges and risks
        - **Business challenges**: Business model, competitive factors, regulations, and so on
        - **Technical challenges**: Performance, scaling, maturity, and unknown factors
        - **Implementation challenges**: Interoperability, testing, updating, and system migrations
        - **Regulatory challenges**: Government-mandated privacy, security, control, permissions, and so on
        - **Deployment challenges**: Integration, politics, and so on

Building the PoC

To build the PoC, the implementation viewpoint prescribes selection and deployment within the scope of the project.

Most IIoT systems share a common platform that provides the basic processing, network, and operating systems needed by the IIoT services. The platform foundation could be performed by cloud solutions such as hosted databases and big data services, and **infrastructure as a service (IaaS)**.

The IIoT platform's connectivity management services provide services and functions to connect devices and sensors to a network and manage the communications between them. Development, deployment, and application management are provided by application-enabled services. The following services, illustrated in *Figure 2.14*, are commonly shared across applications in IIoT systems:

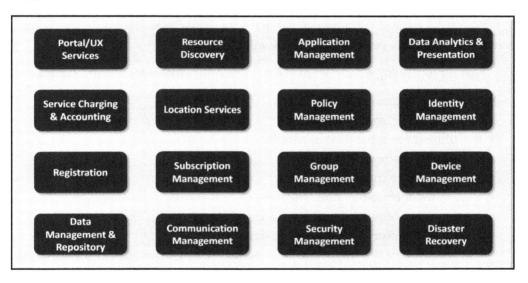

Figure 2.14: IIoT platform service functions

The tactical and strategic concerns of the architectural viewpoints are mapped to formulate strategic platform considerations for each viewpoint. These considerations should also be factored into platform-selection criteria. Platform investment decisions should consider specific requirements, market opportunities, long-term roadmap, and other factors.

The IIoT world brings into play a myriad of various technologies, including hardware and software. If market and competitive demands are critical, internal execution capabilities need to be examined. Organizations may find it necessary to augment technology and expertise from outside sources. Whether the components will be built, bought, or shared, engineering, software development, integration, or network consulting services may be necessary to augment the project team. The Industrial Internet is quickly becoming a fluid ecosystem of complementary and competing technologies in which organizations cooperate and partner on some projects and compete on others.

Various commercial technologies may be available to fill the identified use case gaps; therefore, build versus buy decisions may need to be considered. Building a solution in-house presents benefits and risks. In-house development enables the solution to exactly fit the requirements; however, it may require extensive man hours, and new skill sets that are not available internally. Consideration should also be given into how the solution will be maintained and upgraded if only a few engineers or developers understand the internal workings of the components. The inclusion of a commercially available technology reduces development time and mitigates skill shortfalls. Adopting an already proven technology reduces the risk, and best practices may be available.

When evaluating technologies and third-party partnering, many factors are considered:

- Enterprise alignment and synergy
- Opportunities from partnering
- Fulfillment for capability shortfalls
- Fulfillment for resource shortfalls
- Solution's fit to the requirements
- Cost of the technology and support
- How is it implemented and how does it integrate with existing systems
- How is it monitored, managed, updated?
- The technology roadmap, and how do future upgrades impact the IIoT systems
- What level of support can the vendor offer
- Availability of skill and expertise in the technology
- Security and privacy protections meet legal and organizational compliance requirements

There is a growing trend in IIoT towards the use of shared resources. Cloud services are an example of shared resources, where some of the infrastructures and software are *shared* in a hosted environment. Infrastructure, data storage, analytics, and applications are readily available as cloud services. Cloud service prices are based on subscription and usage, and may allow you to forego large expenditures and setup time for the required servers and software.

Open source technologies are another example of shared resources, with a seemingly endless supply of offerings, from operating systems to machine learning tools and solutions; however, reliability, and sustainability should be thoroughly studied. The sharing of commodity platforms and systems allows the PoC project team to spend more time and energy developing new and innovative technologies that have the potential to contribute directly to the organization's competitiveness.

Prototype scale

PoCs sometimes need to improvise or cut corners to fit within the prescribed time frame existing infrastructure, and cost constraints. Some features, processes, or data may need to be improvised or simulated. The solution definition should specify which corners can, or will be, cut, and which features and characteristics of the PoC must be demonstrated and proven.

The PoC may require infrastructure to be deployed. It would be cost-prohibitive to include all potential data sources for a PoC when the eventual IIoT system will collect data from hundreds of locations and thousands of devices. A few representative locations and devices, or simulated data, can be enough to demonstrate the business value. A representative demonstration of technologies under consideration and integrations must be selected. All viewpoints need to be addressed in the prototype, including their corresponding security concerns.

For some PoCs, a small-scale working model or prototype of the IIoT system can be developed. This enables the project team to simulate and evaluate the IIoT system and allows users and stakeholders to experience the capabilities at first hand. For example, in a system that will collect and process data from an aircraft engine, a physical prototype of the engine, sensors, and data collection can be modeled.

Evaluate/modify

The primary purpose of a PoC is to validate the requirements and capabilities of the system and its ability to deliver business value, and provide a basis for feedback and improvements. The PoC enables the project teams to identify flaws in the design, limitations of components, and other areas for further development, without major investments. The PoC process also provides a foundation and ecosystem for better understanding of the requirements and the feasibility of the solution.

In evaluating a PoC, the project team records observations, findings, measurements, and feedback and evaluates the PoC against the requirements and success criteria. The capabilities can be mapped back to the usages and human-value experiences to validate that the technical capability meets those expectations, and document where they fall short or miss entirely. At this stage, the requirements may need to be clarified or reconsidered. The project team can then make necessary modifications to the PoC and repeat the evaluation process. The valuation and modification stage is iterative in nature and may require several rounds of evaluations and modifications.

Production scale

Following the PoC acceptance and approval for the project to move forward to production, the architecture from the PoC must be scaled for production. A production-scale system will include significantly more end points, network connections, data objects, and data volumes. Additional data-management features may be necessary to control network usage. Memory resources are scaled to facilitate advanced analytics against larger data sets. The network must be resilient enough to support the many different components, programming languages, operating systems, resource constraints, and platforms in IIoT systems.

The choices made for connectivity, or architecture patterns, and distributed intelligence, drive deployment issues. Usually, development and testing are performed in separate environments from production, or deployment environment. The memory footprint, CPU, and other environmental variables and resource constraints can vary in the different systems. In IIoT, the framework should support all platforms in both the development and deployment environments.

Architecture

The choice of an architecture pattern drives many of the deployment problems. Edge devices must be secure, wired networks need to be installed. Wireless systems require certain levels of signal strength and reliability. While Ethernet and wireless deployments are well-established technologies, IIoT topologies can present new challenges, that is, the more reliable mesh networks are more difficult to integrate into the network.

Components

Edge devices and gateways have embedded software, or firmware, that is inherent in their design, but may require periodic updates, most particularly for security, but also for performance, bug fixes, or other concerns. The network, and architectural pattern, needs to enable access for upgrading of components without physically accessing the device and be adaptable enough to incorporate new protocols, as well as backward and forward version compatibility.

Continuing engineering

No connected system is static or complete. Changing conditions, both technical and business-related, can require changes, updates, and extensions to the system. User applications may be updated, as well as the OS, networks, drivers, and so on. A periodic feedback process helps ensure continuous improvements and continuing cost reductions.

Summary

This chapter set the foundation of the architectural approaches for designing a successful IIoT project. You learned about the different architectural viewpoints that are needed, from business considerations to the implementation stage. You then learned about the data and analytics considerations of an IIoT project. Finally, we looked at how to get started using PoCs.

The next chapter will focus on business requirements gathering. The traits that an architect must focus on for IIoT project requirements gathering differs from those for traditional IT projects. The chapter will cover how to align with the right business leaders. Furthermore, you will learn how to estimate the cost of the IIoT projects to help justify the ROI.

3
Gathering Business Requirements

In working with companies defining Industrial Internet projects, we have consistently found that the line of business leaders can articulate what information they need to run their portion of the business. They also usually understand what their competitors are up to, and have a vision of how their business must compete now and in the future. So, they have the *business viewpoint* that we described in the previous chapter.

That said, the line of business leadership hasn't always understood what technology could do for them in helping fulfill their business needs and vision, especially as they consider projects of this type for the first time. So, they need some help in establishing a *usage viewpoint*.

Of course, if the leadership you are working with are unconcerned about competitive threats and have fallen behind in their understanding of business changes that are occurring, the company has bigger problems than technology alone can solve. When IT or technology consultants bring Industrial Internet solutions to business leaders who are unaware of these new threats to their business, there is likely to be little real interest. The odds that they will see innovations driven by an Industrial Internet technology project as useful and something they will want to fund are greatly diminished.

Fortunately, in many companies, lines of business leaders are aggressively seeking ways to optimize old business models, create new business models, and gather new sources of information to help drive these efforts. They have a good notion of the sort of data that they need and understand the state of the data that they currently have.

When such companies are focused on innovation, we often find that business leadership no longer sees their IT organization as their only option for a deployment strategy when they want to invest in Industrial Internet solutions. The availability of cloud-based platforms and solutions brings new options. It can be relatively easy today for a line of business to work with a systems integrator to deploy a cloud-based solution. This tactic is often followed when business leadership has found IT unresponsive to their rapidly evolving business needs.

In companies where IT is part of the innovation process, they are close collaborators with the lines of business. There are typically ongoing joint meetings and planning sessions. Some companies create centers of excellence to speed up this process.

A unique role is sometimes created that is focused on the gathering of business requirements. Referred to as business architects, these people help lead the definition of future business technology solutions. They provide an important bridge to more technical architects within IT and share business requirements with them while providing guidance on how to make sure that technical proposals stay aligned with the business solutions envisioned.

The process we will describe in this chapter to gather business requirements is one that we've led in many organizations. We've also observed many organizations using similar processes independently of our involvement. Over time, we've refined our own techniques based on the lessons we've learned ourselves and from others.

As we take you through the process in this chapter, we'll describe the following major steps:

- Preparing for business discovery
- Gathering **critical success factors** (**CSFs**) from various business stakeholders
- Capturing potential business benefits if the solution is built
- Uncovering the KPIs needed to run the business
- Gaining an understanding of the skills of the business users and analysts
- Evaluating existing and proposed data sources
- The value in building early mock-ups or PoCs
- Prioritizing the stages in the build out of the project(s)
- Building the business case
- Selling the project

We'll provide you with examples of the collateral that is built and shared using this approach. For those of you deep in IT and technology, this might seem to be beyond your area of expertise and out of your comfort zone. However, if you are concerned about reconnecting IT with potential business sponsors or spending less time on dead-end projects that go unfunded, this approach will help you.

We also have some important pointers before you start this process to put you into the right mindset. Technology folks sometimes have the mistaken belief that business leaders and analysts expect you to know everything about their business. They realize you don't. They are coming to you for advice on how to align their requirements with potential technology solutions. So, our pointers are as follows:

- Spend most of your interviews with business folks listening to their needs
- Don't jump to solutions--in fact, push back if they ask you to propose solutions before you have gathered enough information and instead seek more details about the business drivers and needs
- Don't raise objections when they describe what they want to do (such as it will be too hard or expensive or that you are too busy); if they've heard similar objections from IT in the past, you must try to overcome that perception
- Don't be surprised if they start sharing the most significant issues that they face after you've gained their trust and proven that you are truly listening and documenting their input
- Don't be afraid to ask what the potential business benefits will be if a solution is built
- Ask if they have already implemented workarounds to get the information needed to make the business decisions being discussed, and don't criticize those techniques

In a sense, you are playing the role of a detective. Gathering clues and piecing together what is really happening and what is needed to solve business problems is your focus at this stage.

Initial business discovery

After some initial preparation, you will begin the business discovery with a series of interviews with relevant lines of business leaders. In this section, we'll focus on proper preparation and then uncover critical success factors, their potential impact on the business, and the KPIs that are needed to measure success in meeting business goals. We'll also gather the monetary value in revenue to be gained, or the cost of, savings in solving the problem that they identified.

We typically jot down a lot of free form notes during this process. We will guide the conversation in the direction of the information that we need to fully understand the problem. We will then summarize what we found interviewing key stakeholders in each line of business (LOB) using the following template:

Key Stakeholder (LOB)	Critical Success Factor	Key Performance Indicators	Revenue / Savings Impact	Ranked Priority

Each line of business interview with a key stakeholder can usually be conducted in 90 minutes to 2 hours. Later, we will go back and validate what we found with them and capture additional information that we might have missed.

Prioritization usually takes place after we've validated what we've found. We will then better understand the requirements and potential stages of the project, as well as the potential business benefits and risk.

Next, we'll cover the process in more detail and take you through an example.

Getting ready for business discovery

If you have primarily focused on technology in the past, you might not be fully comfortable with the notion of leading business discovery. With some experience and confidence gained, you might soon find yourself talking with people who can provide funding for Industrial Internet projects, such as the following:

- **Chief Financial Officer (CFO)**
- President or Vice President of one of the business operating units
- **Chief Executive Officer (CEO)**
- Members of the Board of Directors

You might not fully understand the sort of conversation needed to advance an IT project from an idea to a funded business solution. You must first gain an appropriate level of business understanding so that you can ask the right questions during discovery and find compelling potential projects.

We've used the following useful techniques in preparation for business discovery interviews in the past:

- Research recent company annual reports, quarterly financial statements, and other news, paying especially close attention to the problems that are identified and the needed changes that are described by senior executives
- Research posted jobs on job sites for roles in the departments where you plan to interview leadership, as these can give clues as to where investments in new skills are occurring
- Research recent annual reports, quarterly financial statements, and other news provided by the company's *competitors* and pay especially close attention when they describe their business challenges and provide guidance on their innovative strategies
- Read publications that describe new and emerging business strategies, such as those published by the Harvard Business Review, the Wall Street Journal, McKinsey & Company research, and other forms of business research
- If you have junior-level contacts in the lines of business, get their views on the business challenges they face and what they believe the leadership's strategies to be

This might seem to be a bit excessive to some of you. Unfortunately, our experience is that many in technology roles are often unaware of the emerging business trends impacting their business or what the company's business leaders are planning to do next to address their biggest challenges. This is time well spent.

Gathering CSFs

It is likely that the company and its lines of business have mission statements and clearly stated goals. These are sometimes stated in annual reports and during industry analyst briefings. You might not have paid attention to these in the past, but they are extremely useful in understanding the critical success factors that could help define a project.

CSFs are the most important goals that must be achieved to move the business forward in fulfilling its mission and strategy. Each line of business will have unique CSFs in describing how they will help the company reach its goals. That said, there are some general business-related questions that you can ask regardless of the line of business to tee up interesting dialogues. Those questions include the following ones:

- What are your key business initiatives that are currently at the top of your priority list?
- How do these business initiatives align to department goals and deadlines for execution?
- What business problems keep you awake at night (regardless of where they are on the priority list)?
- How do you measure success in your line of business and how does it align to your compensation (since compensation often drives behavior)?
- Is taking on risk in driving new business initiatives personally rewarded and something you gravitate towards?

After asking some questions that are general in nature, we will focus on specific business initiatives that the business leader has in mind. To provide an example here, we will explore a typical business goal that we find present in many Industrial Internet companies across many industry verticals, the optimization of the supply chain.

Supply chain inefficiency can cause several bad outcomes. Finished products might be under produced, and those that are produced might not meet quality standards. Products might be late in appearing in the market. Marketing promotional budgets might be misspent on products that are in short supply. Inventory could be wasted and factory or distribution center floor space could be inefficiently utilized.

The impact to a company's financial health can be huge. When these kinds of supply chain problems occur, you might hear about them on a company's quarterly financial earnings call.

Since supply chain inefficiencies can cause problems that must be addressed in several lines of business in a company, you should interview the impacted business leaders. Some of the questions you might ask of business leaders in product manufacturing, supply chain management, and finance could include the following ones:

- VP of Product Manufacturing:
    - Do you have specific examples of supply chain inefficiencies that impacted production?
    - What was the measurable impact to production?
    - What would be the impact if you could eliminate 10 percent of these inefficiencies?
- VP of Supply Chain Management:
    - How quickly can you identify problems in the supply chain today?
    - What are the typical steps that you take to remedy the situation?
    - What would be the impact if you could identify these problems in 10 percent less time?
- Chief Financial Officer:
    - What is the impact on the company's financial results caused by supply chain inefficiencies today?
    - How quickly do you realize when there is a problem in the supply chain that impacts production output?
    - If you and Product Manufacturing and Supply Chain Management could remedy the problems identified by them in 10 percent less time, what do you think the impact would be for production and the company's financial statement?

You might notice a few things about these questions. The questions are stated in ways that will directly impact the business stakeholder being asked. They also postulate that a new solution will not fully eliminate the supply chain inefficiency problem, but will begin to reduce it. Being conservative in approach is often viewed as sound business logic.

We are also trying to get an idea as to how big the problem might be, and the value of a potential solution to the stakeholders in the last questions we've posed, within each line of business. This can help us understand the potential business impact and whether our stakeholder might see so much value that they will want to become a project sponsor.

In this example, each line of business leader has a different view as to the CSFs related to supply chain efficiency, based on how it impacts their piece of the business as well as different views on additional revenue and potential cost savings. None of this should be considered as unusual.

The CSFs and the financial impacts they identified were as follows:

- VP of Manufacturing:
  - The factory should operate 24X7 at maximum capacity, thus yielding $10 million in revenue from additional products that are produced, and savings of $5 million associated with misspent wages, benefits, and other costs that must be paid during factory downtime
- VP of Supply Chain:
  - All necessary product components should be available just in time for manufacturing, yielding a $5 million savings in storage of parts and elimination of rush orders of parts in short supply
- Chief Financial Officer:
  - Production should able to match product demand yielding $15 million in revenue from the additional products produced and $2 million saved on marketing products that are not currently available and $2 million saved in using secondary suppliers to fill necessary parts gaps

Next, we will look at gathering KPIs, and some of the KPIs that were identified as needed by these stakeholders to effectively run the business.

Gathering KPIs

A KPI is a measure that enables an organization to determine the current state of the business and the progress being made towards business goals. The business leaders you are talking to will be familiar with the importance of such metrics, given that they likely already manage their business using some of them in spreadsheets or dashboards.
Your goal is to identify specific KPIs that will help the business leaders deliver the CSFs that they identified in our interview. The KPIs are usually gathered when the CSFs are identified.

Why we must talk to senior business leaders

We've seen technology folks, particularly in IT, insist that they know what the business wants without a need for interviews. While they might have knowledge of the most important CSFs, when the discussion turns to the potential business benefits and the KPIs needed to run the business, they often begin to realize that appropriate line of business interviews and discovery makes sense (especially when it becomes clear that there are many follow-up questions). Of course, we always keep IT in the loop regarding what we are discovering.

Let's look at the KPIs that might be identified in our supply chain optimization example. We'll view them in the form that we presented earlier, which is now partially completed:

Key Stakeholder (LOB)	Critical Success Factor	Key Performance Indicators	Revenue / Savings Impact	Ranked Priority
VP of Product Manufacturing	Factory operating at maximum capacity 24X7	Production up-time, unit goals, units produced, parts backlog	$10 m in additional product produced, $5 m saved in factory down-time	
VP of Supply Chain Management	All needed components delivered JIT	Parts delivery goals vs. on-time, parts inventory, parts in-transit	$5 m saved in storage of excess parts, rush order cost for parts supply	
Chief Financial Officer	Maximized revenue from production meeting demand	Unit demand forecast, units produced, unit production rate, parts inventory, revenue gained vs. predicted	$15 m in additional product produced, $2 m saved in misspent promotions, $2 m saved in secondary suppliers	

We've left the priorities column blank for now, as this is a discussion we'll have with all three lines of business present. During a follow-up meeting, we will first summarize the CSFs and KPIs we've documented and validate that we haven't missed anything during these interviews.

Do we think we will have a business case for a project? At this point, we are encouraged. The revenue and savings impacts are in the millions of dollars. If these impacts were only in the tens of thousands of dollars, we would rightly be skeptical that the project would be able to demonstrate a positive return on investment once we figured out the costs of procurement, development, deployment, and ongoing management of the solution. These CSFs were all related to the supply chain inefficiency problem and a single project. You might find a much more varied set of CSFs present when you perform discovery across a diverse organization that will lead to several unique projects. Regardless, the approach used is the same.

From data sources to KPI delivery

We'll often use our initial discovery to understand how information should be delivered in a useful manner to the line of business. We obviously don't want to deliver raw data to a business person who won't be able to figure out what to do with it. We might propose something as simple as delivering an alert via text messaging or e-mail when a certain critical threshold is reached. Alternatively, we might suggest dashboards or business intelligence tools with drills to detail capabilities. We'll explore more closely the evaluation of business skills present and matching those skills to the functions that must be delivered by the application domain in the next chapter.

At this point, we do want to evaluate the availability of data sources that will enable us to produce the needed KPIs. Lines of business leaders who currently use similar metrics are usually aware of primary data sources and the quality of data being accessed today. These business leaders and their analysts can also provide insight into external or non-traditional data sources that will prove valuable and that might not be accessible today. IIoT projects introduce many such non-traditional data sources, such as the data coming from smart devices and sensors. As this data is of a streaming nature and not formatted like transactional data, this introduces new data management requirements in an organization that might be only be familiar with loading data into relational databases (where the data fits neatly into rows and columns). Where new kinds of data are being sought, it usually makes sense to bring IT into the conversation, as well.

To document these requirements, we will create simple data flow diagrams that show data sources, intermediate steps, and the KPIs that are to be delivered. During this discussion, we will further gather detail on the KPIs needed and how they should be presented. The following diagram reflects such a diagram that could be created for the VP of the supply chain in our example:

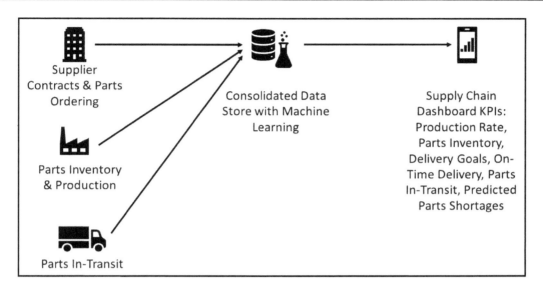

The data flow diagram shows that the supply chain dashboard provides a view of current production rates, the parts inventory, parts and product delivery goals, on-time delivery rates for parts and products, the status of parts in transit, and indicators of predicted parts shortages. This data comes from a consolidated data store that pulls source data from the supplier contracts and parts ordering system, the parts inventory and product production system, and the parts logistics management system that is tracking where parts are in transit. Machine learning is pictured here as it is used to predict parts shortages using predictive models that will be developed.

To further evaluate the value and viability of the proposed solution, mock-ups of the dashboards might be built and shown to line of business sponsors to confirm that the dashboards will deliver the information needed in a usable format. A prototype might be built to demonstrate the value of machine learning in predicting parts shortages in our supply chain example, using previously gathered data sets during shortages that impacted the business. Such data is needed to train the new model. We might be able to deliver some early business benefits using our prototype that will help us, and the lines of business, appreciate the full potential value of the project.

Prioritizing the building of solutions

You might think that organizations will always prioritize how Industrial Internet projects are built based on the potential ROI of each stage, deciding to start with a stage that will generate the most ROI over the lifetime of the solution. In fact, the order in which these stages occur is usually more complex and sometimes dependent on company culture. Some of the criteria we have seen used for prioritizing potential project stages to pursue first include the following:

- **ROI:** The stage with the greatest ratios of business benefits to costs over the lifetime of the project is selected as the first projects to pursue
- **Business benefit/competitive threat to the business**: Some companies put much greater weight on the business benefits of potential stages that address a competitive threat where they believe an immediate response is needed
- **Executive backing:** C-level backed Industrial Internet initiatives might always take precedence, regardless of their apparent ROI or business benefits
- **Cost:** Some organizations closely control costs to the degree that funds are limited to start any new project or project stage, regardless of the potential ROI
- **Time to completion :** In many organizations, the lines of business have short attention spans, so proof of value of a project must occur very quickly, perhaps in the initial stage
- **Risk:** When some companies determine that a project is very risky because new ground is being broken or they believe additional data security problems are being introduced, they will back away from proceeding no matter how great the potential ROI is
- **Skills required and organizational match/mismatch:** Some organizations will shy away from projects when required skills are in short supply internally, or are difficult or expensive to acquire externally
- **Availability and quality of data:** The lack of stable data sources (due to changes in source applications) or clean data from sources might cause a stage of the project to be delayed or de-prioritized
- **The innovation factor:** In some organizations, a stage that is believed to be particularly *innovative* or *cool* might be prioritized over more mundane project stages that could generate more ROI
- **Prerequisite stages:** Some stages must be executed prior to later stages that build a upon them and will receive higher prioritization as a result

Sometimes, organizations prioritize the building of project stages based on just one of these criteria. More commonly, several criteria are considered in combination. For prioritization to be effective, all stakeholders' views should be included in the process. A collaborative planning session might be held with the stakeholders to establish the prioritization.

Let's look at the three stakeholders' ideas for the project that will deliver the KPIs needed by each in our supply chain efficiency improvement example. In the company considering this project, the three criteria used to determine the prioritization of stages to pursue are business benefits, cost, and time to complete. We will collaborate with our stakeholders to rank their stages that each identified (across the top of the following table) with the criteria evaluated (the left-most column):

Key Stakeholder (LOB)	Product Manufacturing	Supply Chain	Finance
Project Benefits	2	3	1
Project Costs	1	3	2
Time to Complete	1	3	2
Total:	4	9	5

Top priorities are ranked as **1** followed by the second (2) and third (3) priorities. When we total the rankings, the lowest number indicates the top priority stage of the project. In this case, we would recommend that the product manufacturing dashboard be delivered first if we follow this prioritization.

There are situations where ties occur between project stage priority totals and only one can be funded at a time. In that situation, a vote might occur among all interested parties, or another evaluation criteria might be added to serve as a tie breaker.

We can now complete the form we introduced earlier in our supply chain example. The form will serve as a useful summary when we explain to others the reasoning behind our project stage priorities and our plans for solution implementation. The completed form is as follows:

Key Stakeholder (LOB)	Critical Success Factor	Key Performance Indicators	Revenue / Savings Impact	Ranked Priority
VP of Product Manufacturing	Factory operating at maximum capacity 24X7	Production up-time, unit goals, units produced, parts backlog	$10 m in additional product produced, $5 m saved in factory down-time	1
VP of Supply Chain Management	All needed components delivered JIT	Parts delivery goals vs. on-time, parts inventory, parts in-transit	$5 m saved in storage of excess parts, rush order cost for parts supply	3
Chief Financial Officer	Maximized revenue from production meeting demand	Unit demand forecast, units produced, unit production rate, parts inventory, revenue gained vs. predicted	$15 m in additional product produced, $2 m saved in misspent promotions, $2 m saved in secondary suppliers	2

Building the business case

At this point, we believe we have a business case, but haven't gathered enough details regarding the costs of design, deployment, and management of the solution, to know for sure. As we formulate the other aspects of the architecture in subsequent chapters, we will be able to better assess the scope of the effort and then can begin to gather more accurate cost information. We can plug those costs into the model we will describe here. Benefits are also speculative at this point and will be until the project moves into production. However, if line of business leaders think that the numbers are realistic, that is good enough for now. We should gather a current business baseline so that we will be able to compare it to the benefits we achieve through our project implementation later.

The costs and benefits will continue to accrue as we deploy various stages of the project. We'll provide an illustration of this later, in the section of the chapter showing our supply chain project rollout timeline.

Costs we need to consider can be categorized as solution development and implementation (usually the greatest cost item), underlying infrastructure, and ongoing operations, management, and support. These costs can be associated with each of these major component locations in the IIoT technology footprint:

- Backend infrastructure (data center if on-premises or in the public cloud)
- Networking from the edge devices to the data center
- Edge devices (smart devices containing sensors)

We'll begin exploring costs by first looking at the backend infrastructure cost models.

Components of backend infrastructure cost models

How the backend infrastructure relates to how costs are tallied is heavily dependent on the deployment scenario used. Traditional on-premises backend infrastructure cost models for IIoT projects include the following:

- Software licensing and support
- Computer servers and maintenance
- Disk storage and maintenance
- Networking (in the data center)
- Data center power and cooling (and data center expansion if needed)

We will break the software costs into applications, middleware and data management, operating system, and virtualization layers. Each of these have licensing and support costs in the on-premises model. This breakdown will help us explain the components included the subscription costs of the various public cloud-based offerings:

- **Infrastructure as a Service** (IaaS)
- **Platform as a Service** (PaaS)
- **Software as a Service** (SaaS)

We will illustrate the on-premises model using the following diagram:

Applications
Middleware & Data Management
Operating System
Virtualization
Servers
Storage
Networking
Data Center Power & Cooling

An IaaS deployment in the public cloud includes server operating systems, virtualization software, computer servers, disk storage, networking, and other data center costs (including maintenance) in the subscription price models. This is illustrated by the following diagram's shaded areas:

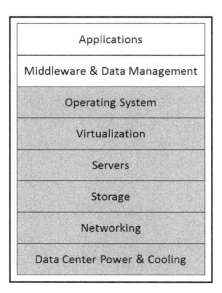

In IaaS, organizations follow a w model for middleware and data-management software, and for applications software, or sometimes a *pay as you go* model. They also pay maintenance to those software vendors just as they would in the on-premises model. PaaS deployed in public clouds additionally includes middleware and data-management software licensing and support (including maintenance) in the subscription costs. So, we will illustrate that here by adding middleware and data management as a shaded area to our previous diagram:

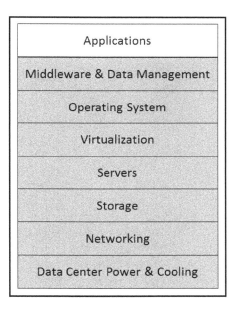

SaaS solutions also includes applications in the subscriptions. These applications can include the specific applications and application logic required for the Industrial Internet solution, as well as modern business applications that become closely linked to, and part of, the project. So, the entire diagram appears shaded as pictured here since all backend infrastructure costs are included in the subscriptions:

Applications
Middleware & Data Management
Operating System
Virtualization
Servers
Storage
Networking
Data Center Power & Cooling

The way that an organization accounts for costs can impact whether on-premises or cloud-based solutions are chosen. Some prefer to purchase data center infrastructure since they can account for such purchases as Capital Expenditures, or CapEx. CapEx is defined as the acquisition of permanent assets in a non-recurring manner, where the benefits accrue over a lengthy time and the assets can be amortized or depreciated.

CapEx has been particularly favored in organizations that receive budget increases and approval through governing bodies (such as in utility companies where rate increases are reviewed by government commissions). Many regulated companies continued to deploy their latest solutions on-premises even as cloud-based deployment strategies were becoming popular in other industries.

Cloud-based subscription models fit into the **Operational Expenditures (OpEx)** model for cost accounting purposes, and many companies find this better aligned with how they run their business. It is noteworthy that cloud-based solutions have also experienced significant subscription price decreases over time as the major public cloud providers gain benefits from massive scale and repeatable footprints deployed around the world. Such price fluctuations in a beneficial direction further align with the OpEx strategy for cost accounting.

About on-premises cloud solutions

As this book was being published, several public cloud providers had begun offering the same cloud software stack on platforms designed to be deployed in traditional data centers. While these share some similarities in cost models to public cloud IaaS, PaaS, and SaaS solutions, there are some differences that impact cost. The power, cooling, and data center space must be provided by the company hosting the solution. Local networking is also the responsibility of the hosting company. The servers, storage, and networking are less elastic since they must be pre-installed in anticipation of future growth (if on-demand growth is to be provided). They are typically not shared among multiple companies. Since platform growth is guessed at, the growth typically occurs in larger cost increments than in a public cloud-based solution, where shared resources are available and added on-demand. So, such on-premises cloud deployment strategies tend to be higher cost than deploying in public clouds.

Smart device and networking costs

Now, we will turn our focus from costs associated with the backend infrastructure to the costs of smart devices and networking outside of the data center. Smart devices that contain sensors continue to decline rapidly in price as the sensors in them grow in functionality but become cheaper and more power efficient. Smart devices range from off-the-shelf (more expensive initially, but requiring much less customization) to completely customizable kits (cheaper initially as piece parts, but requiring extensive development and time to build a solution at higher costs).

How the devices transmit data also impacts cost. The type of network transmission impacts power consumption (and battery life when not solar or otherwise powered). The various networks deployed today support different data upload and download rates (and packet sizes) at different pricing levels. At the time this book was published, the following were the options most often evaluated for networking smart devices to data stores in the cloud or on-premises in current and future implementations:

- Cellular (3G, 4G, LTE-Cat M)
- Bluetooth Low Energy (BLE)
- Bluetooth Smart (Bluetooth 4.0)
- Zigbee
- Wi-Fi (and HaLow/802.11ah)
- **Low Power Wide Area Network (LPWAN)**

In addition to networking from devices, many organizations also define networking from their cloud-based infrastructure to existing on-premises systems or other cloud-based solutions that serve as data sources. Third-party providers of **Multiprotocol Label Switching** (**MPLS**) networks are contracted to provide this service. Many can also provide network exchanges to move data among the various public cloud offerings available today.

Estimating implementation costs

As you probably noticed, there are many varied skill sets associated with these projects. Most organizations get their first real look at project costs by engaging systems integrator to come up with development and implementation estimates. Some work with specialty firms for various parts of these projects. Getting several estimates and taking a close look at the implementer's skills is always a great idea.

One cost that is often overlooked is the cost of training. Training costs can particularly impact for the following personnel depending on the deployment style and strategy selected:

- Data scientists and business analysts
- Data management administrators and specialists
- Security administrators and specialists
- Systems or cloud administrators
- Network administrators
- Device and infrastructure support

Training related to how the deployment will be utilized and supported will help ensure long-term success.

Documenting future benefits

Documenting believable future benefits that will be realized because of the project is a key step in building the business case. Earlier, we discussed gathering estimates of potential revenue gains (top line growth) and/or monies saved (bottom-line cost savings) during the initial discovery process. During this phase, we need to re-explore the validity of those assumptions and think about how those benefits will accrue as the project rolls out. Industrial Internet projects can enable a company to enter new markets where they face different competitors than historically encountered. Though substantial new revenue might be anticipated, such gains could be harder to quantify given a lack of experience in how the new market operates.

Emerging market opportunities often need to be addressed early and quickly for the company to attain a significant market presence. Since time to market is an important consideration, public cloud-based solutions are often chosen, since they enable rapid spin up of new computing resources and improved elasticity when compared to traditional on-premises IT procurement and installation. The cloud-based deployment model enables the organization to achieve business benefits faster. The resources can also be shut down faster and with less impact if anticipated benefits are not realized.

In most organizations, business leaders provide an initial best guess as to revenue gains and potential savings over the life of the project. Capturing their most optimistic and pessimistic views of potential benefits during discussion is recommended, as these can also be used when selling the project.

Ideally, the project can still be justified even if the most pessimistic predictions come true. Providing such predictions will give senior leadership additional confidence to fund the project. Noting more optimistic predictions than the best guess can provide support that the best guess is a reasonable projection.

Financial justification of our supply chain project

We will now apply cost models to our supply chain efficiency example, and then align those with benefits achieved as we determine return on investment at various stages of our project. In this example, we'll first compare the costs of deploying a solution using an on-premises backend infrastructure with one that includes deploying the backend infrastructure using a PaaS model.

Note that the numbers we present here are not meant to be specific to a vendor (though we hope you find them broadly representative and that they provide you with guidance as to how you might create similar models). Some of the cloud vendors provide useful TCO modelling tools and other pricing tools to help you understand the costs of deploying your backend infrastructure on their cloud offerings.

Traditional on-premises cost models are well understood. The models include price of hardware acquisition, software acquisition, networking and data center costs, and support. Subscription models are a bit more complex in PaaS deployments, as subscriptions are priced using various metrics that the cloud vendors determined align to utilization of the offering.

Pricing is generally reflected on a per month basis in PaaS. Pricing can vary across data center regions due to differences in electricity rates, staffing costs, and other factors. This could be one factor you consider when selecting a region to deploy in. You might also select a region based on other criteria, such as proximity to your on-premises location or the region's ability to meet data sovereignty requirements.

Some of the typical PaaS data management, data loading, and access-related components in IIoT projects and their associated metrics that you would need to define to gather costs include the following:

- **Hadoop compute engine**: Number of nodes, cores/node, hours of activity
- **Hadoop data lake storage**: Storage volume, read transactions, write transactions
- **NoSQL database**: Storage volume, utilization units
- **Relational database data warehouse**: Storage volume, utilization units
- **Extraction, load, and data transformation tools**: Number of activities and length of time that data movement occurs
- **Data egress**: Volume of data moved out of PaaS cloud
- **IoT hubs**: Number of messages per day
- **Authentication (directory and multi-factor)**: Number of users

Analytics and business intelligence components and related metrics include the following:

- **Data lake analytics**: Analytic utilization units, length of time utilized
- **Streaming analytics**: Analytic utilization units, length of time utilized
- **Machine learning tools**: Number of seats, length of time experiments occur
- **Business intelligence tools**: Number of sessions per month
- **Data catalog**: Number of users

Some of the core backend infrastructure components and metrics include the following:

- **Virtual machines**: Platform instance size, number of VMs, length of time available
- **Networking**: Port speed, data plan (metered or unlimited)
- **Support**: Most basic developers, standard, or extended / professional

With that as background, let's now compare on-premises backend deployment costs versus PaaS in the cloud for our supply chain efficiency example in a very simplified model.

Large-scale storage and compute is often needed in IIoT projects. These are major factors that drive configurations and costs. Here, we estimate that we are going to need about 80 terabytes of storage in the Hadoop cluster and about 20 terabytes of storage in a data warehouse to store and analyze the data coming from our smart devices. The following table compares the two backend deployment options that include the key components required over a 3 year period:

	On-Premises Data Center	Platform as a Service in a Public Cloud
Compute (Hardware, Software, Electricity)	$849,366	$282,744
Storage	$399,360	$221,184
Data Center Networking	$162,730	$180
Data Center Build Out	$76,405	$0
IT Labor	$103,411	$52,252
Total Backend Infrastructure	$1,591,272	$556,360

The PaaS option appears to be more cost effective in this example. We need to add several important additional cost items that we will assume to be the same here (for simplicity), regardless of whether or not we deploy the backend infrastructure on-premises or using PaaS. The items added include the cost of the smart devices (pre-assembled and in hardened containers), data transmission costs (based on the amount of data transmitted over time and the networking charges associated with the data volume), and the cost of custom development that includes implementation and training.

We have summarized these costs in the following table:

	On-Premises Backend & Devices	Platform as a Service Backend & Devices
Devices (500 smart devices deployed)	$500,000	$500,000
Device data transmission costs	$90,000	$90,000
Total Frontend costs	$590,000	$590,000
Total Backend Infrastructure costs	$1,591,271	$556,360
Custom Development costs	$2,300,000	$2,300,000
Total Costs over 3 years	$4,481,271	$3,446,360

We have consistently seen that deployment of Hadoop clusters (including procurement and set up of servers and storage) takes most IT organizations 6 to 8 months. For purposes of this exercise, we'll assume the total benefits achieved by building the IIoT project with the backend deployed either on-premises or as PaaS will be the same, but the benefits associated with the PaaS backend will begin to accrue 6 months earlier.

You might expect us to deploy the project stages in the order of the priorities we outlined earlier in this chapter. Based on those priorities, we'd begin with the product manufacturing solution, followed by the finance solution, and then the supply chain management solution. However, many of the benefits to be gained are directly attributable to solving supply chain issues, so we'll start that portion of the project sooner than might be expected.

The following illustration shows when key investments are made, when project stages are started, and the total costs and benefits accrued after the first 3 years using an on-premises backend deployment strategy:

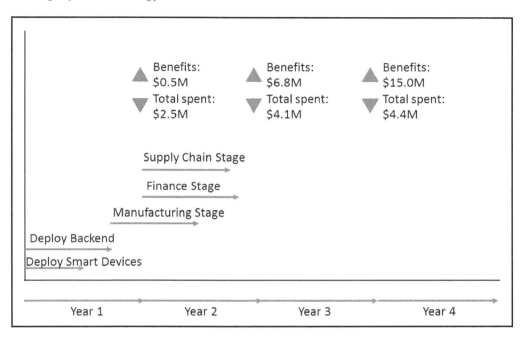

This diagram is aligned with our earlier logic indicating that about 8 months are needed to procure and install the new backend components (including Hadoop and other software, and related servers, storage, and networking) in the on-premises data center. At that point in the timeline, work on the manufacturing stage of the project can begin on the production systems.

In the PaaS environment, we simply configured the needed backend server, storage, and software components on our cloud-based platform. This can take place within days. Thus, development work on the backend production systems can start much sooner.

The following diagram shows how delivery of the project could progress using a public cloud-based PaaS backend:

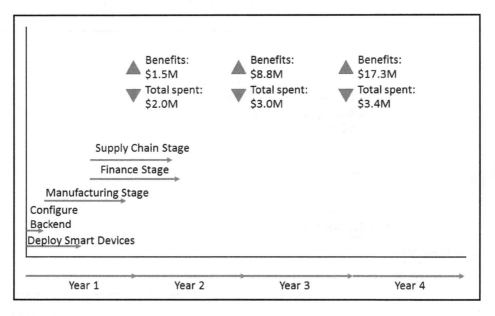

When comparing the two timelines, we can readily see the impact of deploying using the PaaS backend strategy. Since the backend platform is more quickly configured in the cloud, full development begins sooner (and more development spending begins earlier). However, much less platform money is needed up front, and significant business benefits begin to accrue much earlier.

In many ways, early benefits are even more important than the cost difference between the two (although the cloud-based approach is also less expensive during the timeline that is illustrated). Early attainment of significant benefits helps ensure that the value of the project is seen quickly. This can help guarantee that funding will remain in place for the project as it continues to roll out.

Net Present Value (NPV)

 The value of money fluctuates over time. NPV is calculated by a formula that adds the initial investment outlay to subsequent cash flows that are discounted based on prevailing rates of return on money over time. These formulas are often used by financial analysts to determine the viability of potential projects as they seek to understand when a positive return on investment might be expected while considering the changing value of money.

The benefits in our example are quite spectacular and might not be fully believed by financial reviewers, even if backed up by our line of business sponsors (though we did get the numbers from them in our earlier discovery). So, we might choose to go back to the sponsors and suggest that we use more conservative numbers that can more easily be defended if there are any doubts about their validity.

Selling the project

Now that we've compared the costs and benefits for a couple of our deployment options and understood how quickly the business benefits will accrue, we are ready to sell the project internally to obtain funding. The level at which we need to sell usually depends on how high the estimated cost of the project is and how the company delegates the decision-making process. Given the large investment that is often required in Industrial Internet projects and the high visibility that they can have, we will assume that you will need to present your findings to a senior-level business audience, and possibly to the CEO and Board of Directors.

This type of audience is typically not interested in the technical details of the project. They instead want to quickly understand what the project will deliver in business benefits (in a summarized manner), the potential return on investment and cost, the time span of the project, and when they will see the first benefits delivered. Keeping in mind that the person or people you are delivering this information to are extremely busy and might be called away during a scheduled meeting, you must deliver this information within the first 5 minutes of the discussion. You might not get a second chance anytime soon.

If you have held their attention so far; next, you should note the business executives and sponsors who provided you with the business objectives and critical success factors. This will help establish the business credibility of the plan and can also demonstrate broad support for the project. You can then describe the CSFs and goals and the measurable benefits and outcomes that each expects.

Your senior-level business audience will want to understand how the project will roll out. You should provide a summarized time line showing project stages and the incremental costs and benefits like the previous diagram we provided in this chapter. You might also use this part of the discussion to describe the prioritization process used to determine the sequence of the project roll out.

Though you might be more interested in the architecture behind the project and how you will extend the capabilities of your infrastructure well beyond what is currently possible, the business executive will likely want to spend little time considering this. Any architecture drawings should be simplified and used to illustrate data flow and analysis through the major components, and how the information will be delivered to business decision makers. You might want to show a few typical dashboards to visually support what the project promises to deliver.

No project is without risk. The business executives will likely ask you what the major risks are and how you are mitigating those. Be prepared with a list that shows how you plan to respond and overcome each risk that you have identified. Some of the risks you might identify and typical mitigation steps could include the following:

- Shortage of business analysis skills
  - Mitigated by training plans and easy-to-use self-service tools
- Shortage of appropriately skilled IT individuals with IIoT experience
  - Mitigated by the training of staff, engaging systems integrators and consultants to fill skills gaps, and leveraging managed cloud providers
- Concern about the robustness of the infrastructure
  - Mitigated by a development and testing plan for the rollout of new features and capabilities--this might also include high availability and disaster-recovery plans with testing procedures to measure speed and recoverability
- Anticipated need for additional smart device intelligence over time
  - Mitigated by enabling an ability to push software updates to the devices in a secure and reliable manner

- Massive data growth caused by a growing number of devices, their growing sophistication, and the addition of other data sources needed for analysis
  - Mitigated by an agile and elastic infrastructure that can quickly be scaled larger to meet these needs
- Concern about exposure to hackers and other security risks
  - Mitigated by a well thought out security plan and rollout plan that includes data protection, authentication, monitoring and automated response to threats, and auditing
- Cost of the project(s)
  - Mitigated by incremental and fast return on investment and an agile development and deployment strategy

Finally, during the presentation, you should summarize the next steps that must occur to kick off the project.

Of most importance, you should ask for the funding and indicate why funding must be approved now. Be prepared to defend the immediate need for the project if the executive asks: *What will happen if we do nothing or delay a decision?*.

Summary

This chapter provided guidance on gathering business requirements. It shared lessons learned and provided direction on how to facilitate this critical stage of developing, justifying, and gaining funding for an Industrial Internet project.

You should now understand the importance of preparing for business discovery so that the sessions with business leaders are compelling. You should also understand how to gather CSFs from business stakeholders that will drive a need for our projects, the capturing of potential business benefits, and how to discover the KPIs that serve as metrics used in running the business.

You should recognize that we will need to match the skills of our business users and analysts to the solution we propose so that the solution will be useful and the project will be successful. We evaluated existing and proposed data sources so that we can deliver the needed KPIs. We might build a mock-up or PoC at this point to demonstrate the potential value of the project to the business leadership.

We also covered steps you should take as you get into the details of the implementation, including prioritizing the build out of the project(s), creating a timeline, and the further refinement of costs and benefits. As we discussed in the various deployment strategies that might be considered in Industrial Internet projects, we noted some of the trade offs associated with various cloud-based and on-premises backend infrastructure options that you should consider.

A business case can then be built using financial modeling techniques that are the accepted practice within the organization. We used the business case and our project timeline to clearly show when payback occurs.

Finally, the project must be sold to business leadership. You should now understand the essential information you will need to present to gain approval.

In the next chapter, we'll explore the five functional domains in Industrial Internet that the IIC defines as control, operations, information, applications, and business. We will also discuss how we will use the business requirements that we gathered in the process outlined in this chapter to help us define the right functional requirements for our infrastructure solution. We will do this as a prelude to the deeper exploration of the applications, data and analytics, and technology components and architecture that we will cover in later chapters.

4

Mapping Requirements to a Functional Viewpoint

Industrial Internet projects are being deployed to address the ever-changing business needs. Many businesses are encountering new threats from traditional and emerging competition. They often find that competitors posing the biggest threats to their business are gathering data from smart devices and sensors, analyzing it, and building innovative solutions that enable new business models. The competitors building these solutions gain new business and technical skills and adopt agile development methodologies, enabling deployment of more flexible solutions in faster increments.

In the previous chapter, we used business and usage viewpoints to gather requirements and the justification for new projects needed to counter these competitive threats and improve business processes. In this chapter, we will take a functional viewpoint to understand the capabilities we will need in our architecture to deliver a solution. The following diagram illustrates how the functional viewpoint fits in this process as defined by the IIC:

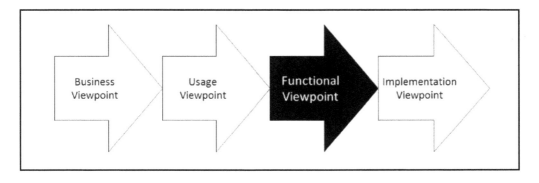

As with all viewpoints, we might need to revisit earlier viewpoints to re-validate the information we previously gathered. Here, we would do this to fill in gaps that we discover in the business and usage requirements as we determine needed functional capabilities.

We'll frame our discussion in this chapter by describing the five functional domains deployed in IIoT projects as noted by the IIC that were introduced in Chapter 2, *Architectural Approaches for Success*. For each domain, we'll also link the domain's functionality to the requirements identified in our supply chain optimization project that was described in Chapter 3, *Gathering Business Requirements*. We will picture the five IIC domains here using the following illustration:

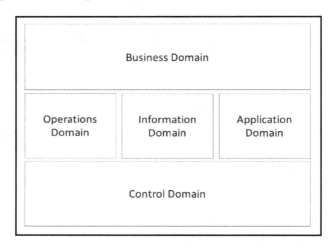

To provide additional clarity, we'll match each domain's functionality to the primary components where the functionality will be provided in our solution. As we discuss the application domain, we'll also provide some guidance on assessing skills in the lines of business, including their ability to use business intelligence tools and apply analytics. Finally, we'll consider the impact of all of this on the type of custom software development and integration environment we will need, to deliver this functionality in an agile fashion.

So, the layout of the chapter is as follows:

- The control domain
- The operations domain
- The information domain
- The application domain
- The business domain
- DevOps and the agile movement

Once we have defined our functional viewpoint, we will then be ready to move to an implementation viewpoint and explore the architecture at a deeper level in the upcoming chapters.

The control domain

The control domain denotes the functions taking place in edge devices that serve as industrial controls. These functions include reading data from sensors in the devices, applying rules and logic to create fine-grained closed-loop processing, and providing control over the physical system through actuators. The devices might be networked together or highly distributed and are most often distant from a centralized data store containing historical data gathered from the devices. In the Industrial Internet, they are connected via a network connection back to this central data gathering point.

The following diagram pictures devices in the *field* (in manufacturing plants, distribution centers, or on transit vehicles in our supply chain example), cloud-based data processing components, and business **on-line transaction processing** (OLTP) systems and tools. The typical primary components in the control domain are in the shaded area:

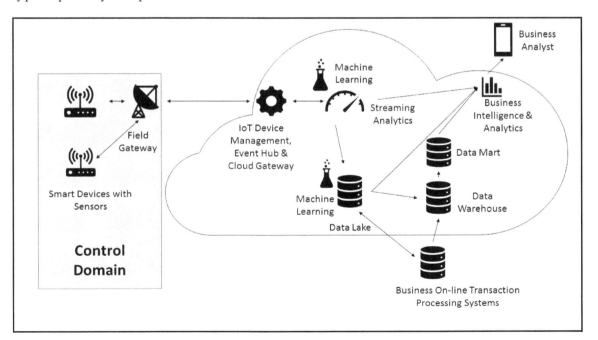

As described in Chapter 2, *Architectural Approaches for Success*, the IIC describes the essential functions in this domain as follows:

- Asset management
- Sensing
- Actuation
- Communication
- Entity abstraction
- Modeling

Asset management, sensing, actuation, and communication are basic functions that must occur in the edge device for it to be useful. Entity abstraction and modeling might take place in the edge device or in the backend infrastructure (depending on how *smart* the device is).

Understanding network requirements and careful planning here is needed to assure success. You would want to consider network reliability, message latency, and whether a persistent connection is required as you define the architecture for this domain. A benefit of deploying smarter devices is that they can operate on their own for periods of time even if the network to the backend infrastructure fails. Of course, smarter devices tend to cost more since they are providing computational engines and support additional functions.

SCADA applications

 The capabilities provided by applications in the control domain are sometimes referred to as **SCADA** or **Supervisory Control and Data Acquisition applications**. SCADA applications include the processes, systems, or machinery you want to monitor and control, the networking, and the network of smart devices and their interfaces that are provided.

Basic edge device capabilities

Not all edge devices that could be considered will align with our deployment strategy. We will need to specify viable devices consistent with our business goals, the functionality we need, and the rest of our architecture.

The control domain and the edge devices must be managed. Asset management functionality is needed for the on-boarding of devices, configuration of devices, setting policies, and deployment of system software and firmware updates to devices. The control domain receives direction from the operations domain (we'll cover the operations domain in the next section).

We need to assess the placement of sensors in our devices and the metrics the sensors can gather. These metrics must align with the data we need populated in our backend infrastructure, that will be used by the business community in making decisions.

Sometimes, our smart devices need to take immediate action (termed as providing actuation) as data is still being processed within the edge devices. These actions are typically critical tasks that would cause damage and safety concerns, or impact production or yield, if not immediately corrected.

Data is transferred from the edge devices to the backend infrastructure for analysis of many devices at scale over lengthy periods of time. The edge devices are directly attached or networked to field gateways that then use messaging protocols to send data to the backend infrastructure. Examples of typical messaging protocols include the following:

- **Advanced Message Queuing Protocol (AMQP)**
- **Message Queue Telemetry Transport (MQTT)**
- AMQP or MQTT over web sockets
- **HyperText Transfer Protocol (HTTP)**
- Custom protocols

Some field gateways can communicate using a choice of multiple messaging protocols. Others are limited to a single protocol. You will need to decide the protocol to be used prior to selecting the edge devices and field gateways. This is often driven by the protocol(s) that your backend infrastructure is set up to support. If you are going to deploy your backend infrastructure in a public cloud, the public cloud provider can provide you with a list of available protocols that they or their partners support for IIoT projects.

Communication is typically bi-directional (**device to cloud (D2C)** and **cloud to device (C2D)** when the backend infrastructure is in the cloud). The messaging that must occur at scale includes data transfer, requests for data transfer and replies, and device management. For example, the sending of messages to the cloud can trigger delivery receipts, expired message notifications, and device communication error messages. Understanding message volume and transfer rates is extremely important when evaluating functionality required in this domain.

In addition to selecting field gateways based on protocols, you'll need to look at other features of the gateways. These can include the networking and device connection options that they offer, environmental operating characteristics (such as the recommended temperature and humidity range), power requirements, and their processing power, memory, and storage specifications. The gateways should buffer data when the network is down and support data transmission retries. They are also evaluated on their ability to batch messages and support connection multiplexing for better messaging volume scalability.

Smarter edge device configurations

When dozens of sensors are present in the smart device and data rationalization at the source is required to push only the necessary data to the backend infrastructure, the ability to do entity abstraction in the control domain becomes one of the evaluation criteria. Sometimes, semantic representations are used to augment the data from the sensors and actuators.

Modeling refers to the ability to perform analysis of data within the control domain. This is sometimes referred to as pushing computational capabilities to the edge in an IIoT implementation.

These capabilities might be programmed into smart edge devices or into the field gateways where there is enough processing power, memory, and storage provided. **Software development kits** (**SDKs**) are typically available to enable these tasks and extend the management and servicing capabilities in the control domain.

Selecting sensors and edge devices

If you are defining a custom solution, you will need to choose sensors and/or the edge devices by matching required functional capabilities you need with those that they provide. Public cloud vendors are making these choices easier by maintaining catalogs of devices proven to work with their footprints and solution offerings.

Often, you will need sensors to gather specific kinds data. The device will transmit the data to the backend infrastructure to populate the KPIs needed to run the business. The device might also need to take immediate action based on incoming readings from the sensors. Examples of sensor readings that are sometimes gathered include GPS, touch, LED, light, gas, noise, proximity, air temperature, liquid temperature, weight, soil alkalinity, vibrations, image capture, motion detection, and chemical compound presence.

Devices can be categorized by their type. Some types you might choose among, include embedded PCs, prototyping devices, gateways, thin clients, industry tablets, mobile point of sales devices, security and surveillance devices, and wearable devices.

There are other considerations. You should check on the geographies where vendors support the sensors and devices and how their support models align with your deployment plans. You must consider their ability to connect to the network present and current messaging protocols in use, their I/O hardware interfaces, and how they align with any industry protocols and certifications that are required. You will also likely consider your skills in programming languages that the devices support (such as C, C#, Java, JavaScript, and Python).

If you are deploying solutions built on applications from an IIoT vendor, you will face less customization and have fewer choices. These solutions usually require specific mandated devices and gateways, thus simplifying the process, though you will have less flexibility in choosing components.

The supply chain optimization control domain

You might recall from Chapter 3, *Gathering Business Requirements*, that our stakeholders defined three critical success factors that are the motivation for our supply chain optimization project:

- Operating factories at maximum capacity (24x7)
- Delivery of all needed components (parts) to factories just-in-time
- Maximized revenue from production by meeting product demand

We've identified the KPIs that will enable the business to meet these requirements. They are required to gather data from the equipment (smart devices) that assembles the products and detects current production status. As these capabilities are embedded in our manufacturing equipment, we'll need to work with the equipment suppliers on a strategy for gathering the data and transmitting it. We will also want to explore with them the options that we have for taking immediate action if anomalies are detected on the production line.

We also plan to deploy other sensors and smart devices into our manufacturing facilities, distribution centers, and transportation vehicles. The vehicles deliver components containing tagged shipping containers. These sensors and smart devices will enable us to determine supplies on hand, their locations, and likely arrival dates of critical parts in transit, and understand the conditions the parts encountered while in transit.

The operations domain

The operations domain provides life cycle management of the control domain. The scope of management includes device grouping, authenticating and provisioning the devices for service, configuring them (including ongoing updates and applications), and monitoring changing conditions in devices for health, security, and remediation (including retirement).

As you might expect, the components underlying the operations domain overlap heavily with the control domain since many of the operations are pushed to the devices. We will illustrate this in the shaded area of the following diagram:

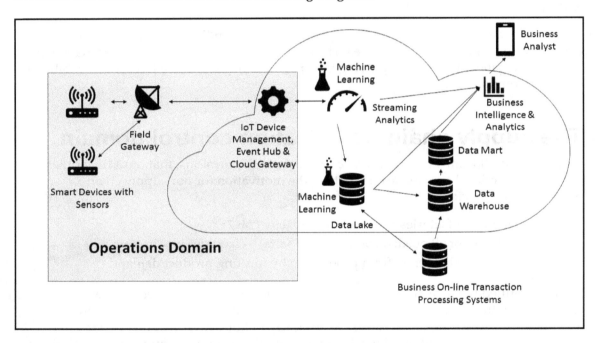

Management of millions of devices is possible today. The devices managed might have varying hardware, software, and messaging protocol characteristics. Identification, logging, and management of devices occurs in the cloud gateway or in an on-premises gateway if the backend infrastructure is not located in the public cloud.

Key management functions that should be provided, and that you should evaluate, include the following:

- Synchronization of properties between cloud and device *twins* when monitoring and responding to changes on the device
- Ability to take interactive device actions (referred to as **methods**)
- Broadcasting and scheduling of twin changes and methods at scale in the form of *jobs*
- Dynamic reporting of device status and health through queries
- Ability to perform firmware updates, rebooting, and factory resets of devices, and configuration management of device behavior
- Authentication of devices (typically using X.509 certificates)
- Support for secure and encrypted data messaging via AMQPS, MQTTS, or HTTPS
- IP filtering to reject or accept specific IP addresses

Device and digital twins

 Device or digital twins refer to a hardware agnostic approach to representing device input, device state, device metadata and device configuration. The use of device twins can shield management of the devices from underlying protocols and can be useful for testing device driven applications in agile development environments.

SDKs for devices, services, and field gateways are often offered as complementary to the management products in this domain. Custom software might be developed in the cloud or on-premises development environment, and then deployed to the device(s) using the capabilities we outlined in this section.

In our supply chain optimization example, many of these actions will be critical to the success of the project. To deliver value to the business, the infrastructure must be well managed and secure. When shortages of critical components or possible damage to those components in transit are detected, we must take appropriate actions to ensure production continues so that key optimization critical success factors can still be achieved. Periodically, we will issue software and firmware updates to the smart devices to improve their functionality and security.

The information domain

Though some data collection and analysis can take place in the control domain to actuate immediate responses in the edge devices, a much broader and larger data collection and analysis repository is established in the information domain. Here, data can be gathered from multiple control domain locations and from business domain data sources to enable better business operations decision making and to optimize business processes.

In our example, the information domain could be deployed adjacent to control domains in manufacturing plants and distribution centers or on mobile equipment or platforms. The information domain is more commonly established in a central repository in the public cloud or on-premises with the ability also to gather data from back-office business applications.

The following diagram illustrates the information domain in the public cloud as represented by the shaded area:

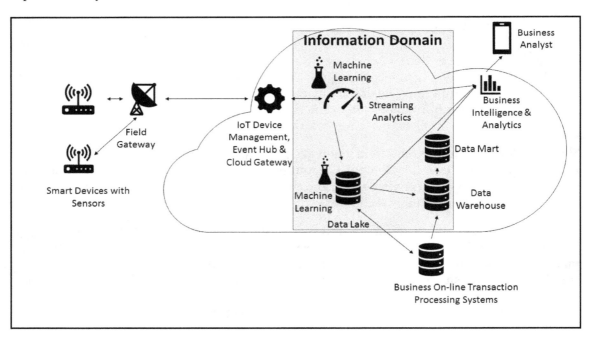

Several data-related operations take place in this domain, including the following:

- Data ingestion from sensors in the control domain and operations data sources
- Data quality and cleansing activities

- Data transformation (to rationalize data from various sources into common formats)
- Data persistence and storage
- Data cataloging establishing common metadata
- Analytics applied to data in motion and at rest
- Data governance

We will cover the architecture for the delivery of these capabilities in more detail in `Chapter 6`, *Defining the Data and Analytics Architecture*, but will introduce key components here that provide the necessary functions.

Solving information domain functional requirements

The complex nature of this domain causes us to gather many different functionality requirements. These, in turn, result in the evaluation of many diverse components. Among these components are the following ones:

- **Extraction, transformation, and loading** (**ETL**) and data factory tools
- Data catalog tools
- Data management systems (including NoSQL, Hadoop, and relational databases for data warehouses)
- Analytics and machine learning tools and engines for streaming and persistent data
- Compute and storage deployed in public clouds and/or on-premises

Functional requirements for data governance introduce the need for additional management strategies and domain capabilities. Among the capabilities that are assessed are the abilities to manage the following:

- Data encryption
- Access control and rights management
- Data resilience provided through high availability and disaster recovery strategies (including data replication, backup and recovery, and site duplication)
- Data retention

Let's now look at the functionality that is required in our supply chain optimization project and how the information domain will address these needs.

A supply chain optimization information domain

Our list of required functions in our example includes the following:

- This information domain could introduce a need for many skills that are not present in the company's IT organization. We'll need to assess the skills present and begin developing strategies to address those gaps. Typical options considered include skills development through training, hiring consultants to initially provide support, or leveraging the managed services offered by public cloud providers.
- Data will be ingested from sensors located throughout the manufacturing facilities and in transportation vehicles, and we will be gathering production, location, and temperature data every minute with transmission volume expected to reach 100,000 messages per hour.
- Some data cleanup will be needed prior to storage and analysis due to incomplete or corrupted transmissions that will occur.
- The equipment in the manufacturing plants is of various ages and from different vendors, so rationalization of inconsistent data formats will be necessary.
- The streaming nature of a significant amount of incoming data and the history we will need for more accurate analysis will influence our data management strategy toward inclusion of a Hadoop engine. We expect tens of terabytes of data to be gathered here, growing into the hundreds.
- As structured data from several existing systems in the business domain will be required as part of the analysis and there is already a data warehouse in place, we will include that in our design.
- Given data will exist in multiple locations. We'll create a data catalog to help business analysts find the data and understand its meaning.
- Alerting is needed if temperature extremes occur or there are anomalies in production that could cause safety concerns driving a requirement for streaming analytics to be part of the solution.
- We will be proactive in protecting our data and require procedures and careful monitoring of data access and encryption of all data.
- Because this system will be so critical to factory operations, we will include plans for high availability and disaster recovery in all key information domain components.

The application domain

This domain consists of the logic, rules, models, and user interfaces needed to address the business requirements that we gathered previously. The primary components that will comprise an application domain are illustrated in the following diagram:

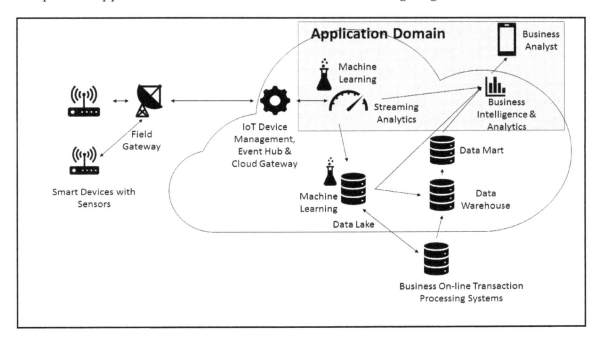

We will need to reference our discovery documentation and data flow diagrams for our project that were described in the previous chapter. We will also consider how information that is needed will be delivered to the business analysts and other users of the information. For this, we need to assess the skills present among our business users to ensure that we deliver the KPIs and related information in a usable form.

Assessing business analysts and user skills

Seemingly, everyone wants to be a data scientist these days and wants to put that moniker on their business card. Few are. On the other hand, many might not agree that the business should be managed based on data and analytics. How do we rationalize the variety of skills and attitudes present?

The goal of any project should be to deliver just the right amount of information to business leaders and others who might be impacted, at the right time and in the right form. Most of these people are not technical. Many do not understand statistics.

The kinds of analytics that might be delivered are sometimes designated as follows:

- Descriptive analytics telling us what happened
- Diagnostic analytics telling us why an event happened
- Predictive analytics telling us what will happen
- Prescriptive analytics guiding us on how to make an event happen

For people working with the data, the skills required are very different in these four categories. Analysts might simply view reports to see what happened. If the analysts want to explore why an event happened, they'll likely use business intelligence and analysis tools (probably accessible through dashboards). For predictive and prescriptive analytics, they will take on the character of a data scientist, developing applications that include machine learning algorithms.

Delivery of information to business folks making decisions should occur in a format that they easily understand. While some might want to view dashboards, non-analysts who simply want to get their job accomplished are more likely to want a text message or an alert telling them about a significant event and suggesting an action that might be taken.

In some situations, it can be desirable to take automated actions without the need for human intervention. Business logic could be executed within the smart devices because of machine learning predictions performed in the streaming analytics engine. For example, we might want to slow production in the plant automatically when we predict a likely shortage of component parts will occur. Business logic might also be executed within the business domain. We might initiate a shipment of component parts from a second distribution center if machine learning in our data lake predicts that the primary distribution center will run short of the needed parts.

By understanding our audience and their skills as well as their personal motivation, we can create the right user interfaces. Gathering best practices examples of actions taken in response to events, enables us to establish rules and build the business logic needed as part of our solution.

Gaining application adoption

We have seen some IT organizations struggle with gaining adoption of new analytics footprints. This should never occur if the right business sponsorship is behind the project and business requirements are well understood. Given that these projects can have huge business return on investment, it should come as little surprise that some organizations link compensation of their targeted users in the lines of business, to the metrics that are monitored in these solutions. Compensation is a powerful incentive to drive adoption.

The supply chain optimization application domain

The application domain for the supply chain optimization project will include the logic and rules that performs the functions needed to meet the CSFs. These include logic and rules for our example that do the following:

- Detect production uptime and rates of products being produced as well as pending parts shortages that will impact the ability to run the factory at capacity
- Track parts in inventory and parts delivery schedules and then determine if rush orders are needed or second suppliers need to be engaged
- Track product demand and adjust production rates and inventories as demand for the product changes
- Match product market promotions to the availability of finished products by location and market opportunity
- Alert the finance team when product revenue is impacted by supply chain problems

You might notice that these align well with the revenue and cost savings impact of the project that we identified in the previous chapter. Obviously, the infrastructure we are proposing will be capable of much more. For example, it might be used to enable smarter negotiations with suppliers, gain a better understanding of product quality and the implications of using certain suppliers, and provide better optimization of human and other resources needed to run the factories. However, consistent with our approach in the DevOps section of this chapter, we will manage scope with frequent delivery of improvements to the highest priority portions of the project, and then add new functionality based on continuing demand from the lines of business.

The business domain

In the business domain, we integrate our IIoT project data with data residing in our **Enterprise Resource Management (ERP)** systems, **Customer Relationship Management (CRM)** system, and **Human Resource Management (HRM)** system that run the business. The business domain data sources we will need will align with the business problem we are trying to solve. For example, key ERP modules providing data needed in our supply chain optimization project includes finance (including billing and payment), asset management, **Product Lifecycle Management (PLM)**, **Manufacturing Execution System (MES)**, work planning and scheduling, and **Service Lifecycle Management (SLM)**.

We will broadly classify those ERP, CRM, and HRM systems as **Business On-line Transaction Processing Systems**, as shown in the following diagram:

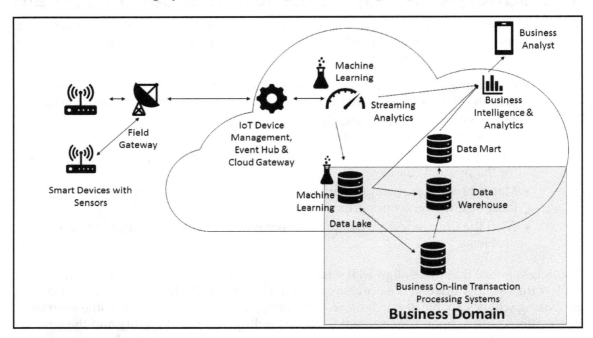

Each of these business systems provides specific functionality. We'll now explore how the data in each can be used to augment the supply chain optimization project that we've described:

- The finance module in the ERP system enables the core financial accounting of the business. It is also used to prepare estimates, send invoices, and accept payments. In our example, it will provide data regarding our financial relationships with our suppliers. This data is often paired with other supplier data (such as on-time delivery records) during contract negotiations. It also provides the product sales transactional data that we will use to understand demand.

- Asset management enables management of the purchase, deployment, maintenance, utilization, and disposal of inventory and equipment. In our example, it will provide us with the status of the inventory and is also an important source of logistical information.

- PLM defines a process of managing a product from its beginning to end of life, including engineering design, manufacture, service, and disposal. Our supply chain optimization project will require updates on product manufacturing status and servicing.

- On the shop floor, the MES is used to schedule, track, and document the processing of raw materials into finished goods. It enables material resource planning and provides metrics on production, equipment efficiency, and quality. These are some of the key metrics we want to track in our supply chain example.

- Work planning and scheduling applications are used in the arranging, controlling, and optimization of work and workloads during production and manufacturing while accounting for available plant and machinery resources, human resources, and materials. Optimization of production in our plants is something we hope to accomplish in our supply chain optimization example, so these metrics will also prove important.

- SLM is an application that tracks and manages our field service, including call center management, workforce management and dispatch, parts planning and forecasting, repair and reverse logistics management (returns), and contract management. Our supply chain will be called upon to build replacement component parts for our products based on failure rates that are tracked and predicted.

- CRM software helps us manage and interact with current and future customers with a goal of improving business relationships that will drive retention and sales. Our ability to ship products on time to our most valuable customers might be a metric that will be tracked as part of our supply chain optimization project.
- Finally, the HRM system is used in the hiring, training, management, and evaluation of employees. The ability of supply chain specialists to effectively manage the supply chain and get parts delivered just in time might be the evaluation criteria in determining their compensation. In that situation, there would be a HRM element in our project.

DevOps and the agile movement

Though this book is focused on architecture, we realize that many software developers engaged in IIoT projects will also be interested in the content we present in these chapters. Architects should also be interested in the software development methods that are presented here, as they impact the strategies used in delivering these projects. So, there are development functional capabilities to be considered (though IIC doesn't call this out as a domain).

Fast time to development and deployment is critical in most Industrial Internet projects. This requirement often drives organizations to take an agile approach to custom software development and integration. Many now follow a modern **DevOps** approach. It makes sense to develop software solutions using this approach in a public cloud. As we observed in the previous chapter, developing and deploying in a public cloud can reduce the time needed to obtain significant business value from our project.

When you observed the supply chain optimization project phases in the previous chapter, you might initially have thought that development and deployment would follow a traditional *waterfall* approach of gathering all project requirements, completing the design work, and then rolling out a finished solution. However, that is not what occurs when custom development cycles are embedded within these project phases.

Modern DevOps lifecycles tend to be highly iterative, collaborative, and incremental, producing new features and capabilities on an ongoing basis. This ensures frequent reevaluation of the project deliverables by development managers and the lines of business, and enables development to be redirected when new business requirements arise. The primary goal of agile development is to produce effective business solutions. Flexible teams and strategies are required to do this.

That said, one must still deliver an impactful solution within the timelines that we've outlined (and before the funding runs low or disappears). As less time is spent in planning and more time is spent on experimentation, solution delivery naturally becomes the focus when using a DevOps approach. So, rapid delivery of multiple iterations of the solution as it is developed are embedded within our project timelines and phases.

Agile approaches

The movement to more agile development approaches began in the 1990s. Several alternative methodologies to the waterfall approach were introduced at that time, including the **Dynamic Systems Development Method** (**DSDM**), extreme programming, and **Feature-Driven Development** (**FDD**). Formal definitions of agile and DevOps principles were created during the following decade.

As time passed, growing emphasis was placed on defining and building smaller components delivered in shorter time increments. Today, delivery of incremental improvements can appear to be nearly continuous, especially when compared to earlier methods.

A typical agile development cycle includes the gathering of new requirements, design, development, quality assurance testing, deployment, release, and tracking and monitoring. To speed development, some organizations use automated testing procedures and tools for quality assurance. Testing can occur at the component or unit level.

The following diagram illustrates this typical development cycle:

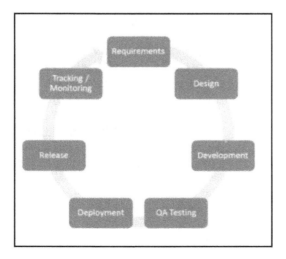

The cycle is shown as continuous since it repeats itself for each incremental building process. Development teams have taken to using tools such as Cloud Foundry and OpenShift as development and runtime environments in support of this approach. Classic development tools such as Visual Studio have evolved to support agile development efforts.

One of today's more popular approaches to agile development is called **scrum**. Since agile development is best performed when small teams focus on building the software components, scrum teams are usually limited to fewer than 10 members. Team direction comes from the product or project owner and scrum master. Software components are developed and delivered in sprints of short duration, usually of 1 to 3 weeks in length. The components are held in a version control repository such as GitHub and are continuously integrated together (with tools such as Jenkins) as they are being built.

Using microservices and containers to speed DevOps

The **virtual machines** (**VMs**) on hypervisors that include operating systems remain popular as deployment vehicles in public clouds and on-premises data centers. However, at the time of writing this book, many organizations were adopting development strategies that promised more agility and built upon previous SOA development skills.

Such skilled development teams now often build microservices, single function entities that can be executed on their own while having generic interfaces (such as HTTP) for integration. Though microservices can be deployed in VMs, they are most often deployed using containers. The container is used to provide scope insulation and establish the necessary dependencies among the microservices.

Containers include minimal operating system code as they use a shared operating system kernel, thus helping to reduce the size of the modules produced and speed their distribution. They communicate to the operating system via APIs, which become quite important when the security and data persistence services provided by the O/S are needed. Docker has gained in popularity and provides containers available in the major cloud vendor offerings. Most of these cloud vendors provide container services capable of managing Docker.

Containers, by themselves, are especially useful when building and deploying GUIs that require little in the way of stored data resources. When stored data is needed, container clusters are created, deployed, and managed using cluster managers. Popular cluster managers include Docker Swarm, Kubernetes, and Mesos. Multiple container clusters are deployed when multiple data repositories are needed to provide data for applications.

In addition to container configuration management, several other management tasks are required. These tasks include container service discovery and distributed configuration storage with dynamic scaling, container networking, scheduling of containers on hosts, along with cluster management of containers, hosts, services and interactions. Management of scheduling is handled through tools that provide orchestration (such as Ansible, Chef, and Puppet).

An IIoT development team's ability to use this approach and maximize the agility of custom solution development and integration will largely be determined by their familiarity with these technologies, their skills, culture, and organization. If such skill sets are not present but the approach is desired, systems integrators might be selected for design and implementation.

Of course, much custom development can be avoided if the desired Industrial Internet solutions are available as predefined, prepackaged, and pre-integrated applications. Though flexibility might be sacrificed, at the end of the day, the right approach is one that delivers business value to the company quickly and positions it for long-term success.

Summary

This chapter described linking the business and usage requirements gathered earlier with a functional viewpoint. You should now understand the functionality provided in the control, operations, information, application, and business domains. As we described the functionality, we provided guidance regarding the components in our solution that will be part of each domain and aligned the domains to the capabilities needed in our supply chain optimization project.

You should now also understand what an agile development environment is and why it is a preferred methodology in Industrial Internet projects. We described some of the approaches used to ensure that rapid delivery of solution increments occurs.

Now, it is time to turn our attention to the implementation viewpoint and architecture patterns. In the next chapter, we'll look at evaluating Industrial Internet applications to speed development and deployment of solutions. We'll describe their promise, what they are capable of, and how they can align with your functional requirements. We will also describe how to perform a gap analysis to determine how helpful an application might be, thus helping you determine whether to deploy an application or custom build a solution from scratch.

5

Assessing Industrial Internet Applications

Once the business requirements are gathered and validated, it is important to plan the implementation architecture of any Industrial Internet solution. At this stage, the various implementation viewpoints and the architecture patterns are evaluated. Build versus buy decisions and use of IoT platforms are considered. Since the Industrial Internet landscape is still evolving and transforming, it is important to consider current business needs, as well as a couple of years out, when assessing the applications. During the development of the implementation viewpoint, the technological needs of the different functionalities are assessed. The main stakeholders at this stage are the Industrial Internet architects, developers, and system integrators.

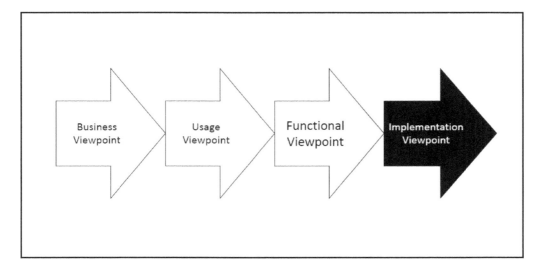

When the application implementation strategy is being formulated, it should be built on the previously documented viewpoints of the company. This will ensure that the functional expectations are met in the selected Industrial Internet application architecture landscape. Once the implementation viewpoint is developed, it should provide the architecture framework, including the topology, distribution of the different components, as well as how they are interconnected with each other. The stakeholders also expect details about the protocols selected for communication between the device/machine and the gateway and to the central system. The behavior and the properties of the involved interfaces must be detailed out as well. All these will help map out the implementation details with the business objectives and the functional characteristics of the Industrial Internet solution.

Architecture patterns for the Industrial Internet

A carefully selected architecture pattern represents an easy way to understand the abstraction of the IIoT implementation scenario. It allows reuse of best practices, alongside the flexibility to experiment with variations, within reason. We will look at the commonly used three-tier architecture pattern here. The three tiers are typically as follows:

- Edge tier
- Platform tier
- Enterprise tier

The edge tier is mainly used to gather the sensor and machine data from the edge nodes. It uses the localized or the proximity network. The architectural features of the edge network include the nature of the localized or proximity network. The distribution and the location of the devices are other considerations at this stage. Deciding whether all the data collected is forwarded to the platform tier or data aggregation or processing is needed may help design this edge tier and its processing and storage capabilities.

The platform tier can be in a private data center or in the private cloud. This tier receives the data, and ingests and organizes it before storing it in the appropriate data store. This tier may also be used to send the control commands from the enterprise tier to edge tier. The platform tier may aggregate, process, or analyze the data flows from the edge tier. Optionally, it may provide edge management capabilities for the devices and other similar assets in the edge. Often, querying and reporting on the data and the different kinds of analytics takes place in this tier.

The enterprise tier carries out industry domain-specific business applications and related decision support systems. This tier provides interfaces to the business end users, operators such as field service technicians, or the monitoring and diagnostics center operation specialists. The enterprise tier may often receive the data flows from the edge and platform tier. This tier could also originate the control commands to the platform tier and the edge tier.

In a general case, an implementation of the three-tier pattern in an Industrial Internet system will not prevent multiple implementations in each of the tiers. An example could be many instances of the edge tier due to different categories of the edge devices being connected to the platform tier in a heterogeneous solution. Even in such scenarios, the architecture pattern definition will represent each tier only once in each tier.

After looking at the architecture patterns for Industrial Internet, we will look at considerations for the building and implementation of software solutions. In the world of enterprise software, ERP, CRM, and **Human Capital Management** (**HCM**) applications are mature and are often referred to as packaged software. Common examples of ERP include Oracle EBS or Cloud ERP and SAP R/3 or business applications. The CRM world has seen Salesforce.com and Siebel CRM, which was acquired by Oracle. In the arena of HRM, PeopleSoft and Workday are common examples. The corresponding applications are emerging in the Industrial Internet area. One of the common application families today is **Asset Performance Management** (**APM**).

Build versus buy decisions

Companies can explore off-the-shelf software and platforms to get started with their Industrial Internet applications journey. Sooner or later, they will face the build versus buy decision.

 Commercial off-the-shelf (**COTS**) software or hardware products are ready-made and available for purchase or consumption by the end customer(s). Google Nest is a COTS product that is a packaged home thermostat and associated software solution for the home user.

The **World Economic Forum** (**WEF**) advised customers and technology adopters to first reorient or realign their overall business strategy to embrace and fully benefit from the latest developments in the Industrial Internet. In this process, they will need to identify their new ecosystem partners. They will need to determine whether they should join a partner's IoT platforms or develop their own. Companies in the initial stages of this Industrial Internet journey should identify the initial one or two pilot application avenues to pilot them in the next few months to get started and capture first-hand learning, irrespective of the COTS or custom route they choose.

In a Forbes article (`https://www.forbes.com/sites/chuckcohn/2014/09/15/build-vs-buy-how-to-know-when-you-should-build-custom-software-over-canned-solutions/#2841c7d2c371`), the benefits of a custom software strategy are defined with the following caution:

- Custom software is justified if it provides a competitive advantage relative to your competitors
- If building a large business, it can spread the cost of a proprietary system over many internal and/or external customers

Since many Industrial Internet needs and applications are still maturing, early adopters should decide where they want to end up on this spectrum of COTs and fully custom. There are both technological and business drivers as inputs to such decisions. The available technology such as the IoT platform which meets only a subset of the requirements for the initial set of applications may steer the company in one direction. There may be overlaying business factors such as a strategic move to reduce dependence on in-house resources for IT and software skills. In addition, there is a top-level mandate to adopt cloud technologies, as this is a route to reduce in-house dependence. The net result of the situation may be the adoption of the IoT cloud platform as the starting point and then building the application on top of it. This would result in a hybrid scenario, according to the following diagram:

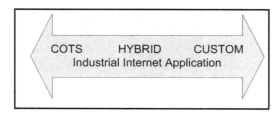

In the previous scenario, the IoT cloud platform is providing the PaaS layer. In this case, the company would use that as the starting point, and do a fit-gap analysis to see what the missing PaaS capabilities are may have to build on top of the underlying IaaS layer. Once the requirements are met at this level, the company can then build the SaaS to deliver Industrial Internet applications. Some IoT platforms may deliver SaaS applications as well. We will look at APM in the next section and use it as a basis of assessing Industrial Internet applications.

Asset Performance Management (APM)

APM applications can be delivered via public cloud (SaaS) or can be for on-premises use. In this context, APM will stand for **Asset Performance Management**, another common use of the term APM in the field of information technology and systems management. This term implies **Application Performance Management**. In that context, APM monitors and manages the performance and availability of software applications. APM's goal is to help detect and diagnose performance problems in complex application and software platform. This in turn helps maintain an expected level of service or the **service level agreement** (**SLA**) by the software services provider. We will not use APM in that context in this book.

APM is a set of applications that generally provide a capability for asset health maintenance, where an asset is typically a physical device or a machine, in an industrial setting. Examples of such assets can be wind turbines operating in a wind farm or locomotives for transportation of goods train. The category can be thought of as **monitoring and diagnostic** (**M&D**) for assets.

Gartner defined APM as a collection of the capabilities of data capture and ingestion, integration, visualization, and analytics, all working together, for the explicit purpose of improving the reliability and availability of physical assets. Gartner's definition of APM includes the concepts of condition-based monitoring, predictive forecasting, and **reliability-centered maintenance** (**RCM**). This definition ties well to one of the common goals of APM, which is to reduce unplanned downtime of the assets.

LNS Research has another variation of the APM definition (`http://blog.lnsresearch.com/what-is-asset-performance-management`). According to LNS, APM is regarded as an approach to managing the optimal deployment of fleet of assets with the business goal to maximize profitability and predictability in the operations. The operation goal could be to focus on real margin contribution by the specific asset. Instead of looking at the physical asset on the accounting basis, such as the market value or depreciated value, companies can see how the asset is contributing to their revenues and profitability by looking at how individual assets are performing--whether inventory or **Plant, Property, and Equipment (PP&E)**. This can allow the company to develop a vision of how they want to allocate resources and deploy the assets in the future. In this view of APM applications, it is not limited to a purely financial or even operational resource, rather one that cuts across functional lines. To realize this viewpoint of APM, it has to combine or connect to the best-of-breed **enterprise asset management (EAM)** software such as IBM's Maximo, with the need for near real-time information from production systems. APM has to use the power of the cross-functional data analysis and advanced analytics orchestration. Thus APM, broadly speaking, looks at the whole life cycle of an asset. This viewpoint of APM then enables organizations to make decisions that optimize not just their physical assets but also their operational and financial results while balancing the business risk.

APM applications can be used to monitor and prevent risk of the critical asset failure. APM applications often use analytics and data thresholds based on the properties and operating characteristics of the family of the asset or a specific asset. In more advanced APM applications, the operator may receive guidance for the optimal operating range and characteristics, in near real time. Likewise, an advisory could be related to repair versus sell or dispose decision for the asset or an expensive asset component.

The APM application would generally include capabilities to carry out the following activities:

- Provision the asset
- Capture the asset model, which will define the assemblies, subassemblies, components, and sensors
- Understand the relationship of the asset to the fleet and the whole network of assets
- Ingest data from the sensors and store it optimally
- Integrate other sources of data
- Design and/or deploy the analytics
- Create alarms and advisories based on execution of analytics and thresholds
- Display the visualizations of data and actionable items
- Optionally allow alarm disposition, case management, and trigger field services

Overall, APM applications will help reduce the total cost of ownership of the fleet of assets and improve the utilization, while balancing the risk to the company. This often results in lower unplanned downtime, reduced cost of maintenance, and better use of the scheduled maintenance windows. The following graphics shows how to balance a decision between preventive maintenance and scheduled maintenance cost for the physical asset to arrive at the minimum cost of replacement without compromising the business risk of operating the asset safely:

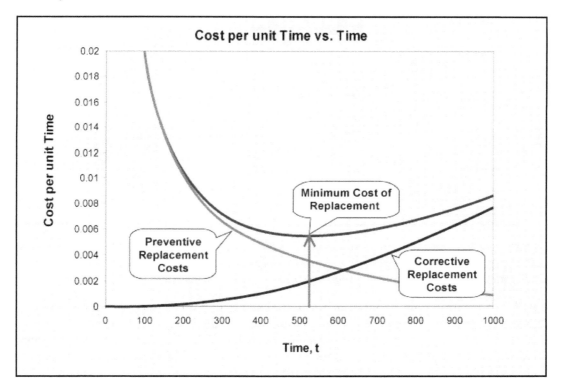

Source: http://www.reliasoft.com/newsletter/v11i1/asset_management.htm

The word *cloud* is a good representation of the common themes that accompany the APM. As a company is assessing APM, they should map their own requirements along these business themes while evaluating the capabilities and options for their APM suite.

The APM application used to monitor industrial assets like wind turbine can be built on the GE's Predix platform. It shows the three distinct tiers of the Industrial Internet platform. In this case, the industrial asset is a wind turbine operating in a wind farm, and it generates electricity. The wind turbine has sensors built in. Usually, the data from these sensors is collected via the control systems that are built in. Additional external sensors such as temperature, vibration, or wind speed can be retrofitted, when needed, to an existing asset. These, in turn, connect via a gateway device, in this case using the edge software called Predix Machine, to the Predix cloud via a secured means.

The Predix cloud understands the asset structure and its sensors and uses that information to store the data in a usable manner. This allows the analytics to consume this data easily. The business insights generated by these analytical applications such as predictive health monitoring alarms and advisories or operational guidelines can then be pushed to the enterprise tier for human consumption. Similar use case may apply to many other industry verticals such as energy (gas generator), healthcare (MRI machine), transportation (locomotive engine), or aviation (jet engine), but is not limited to just these types of industries. The following is the architecture of the GE's Predix platform:

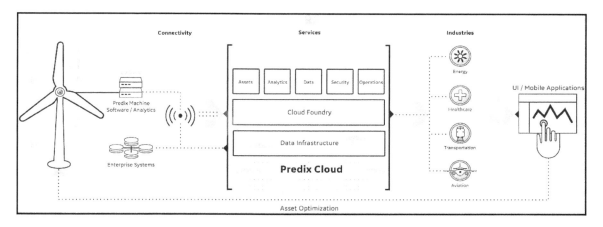

As Industrial Internet architects evaluate the application and its architecture, the end-to-end view from sensors to business applications provides a good perspective to help future-proof their decisions. The complete solution stack caters to both the edge and the cloud with the ability to connect to the existing enterprise tiers.

Assessing the analytics applications

While the APM applications may include the analytics framework, the architects would have to assess how this ties to the analytics application needs for the rest of the Industrial Internet and enterprise applications. The main categories of the analytics capabilities are as follows:

- Descriptive
- Diagnostic
- Predictive and
- Prescriptive

The following is an illustration of the categories of the analytics framework:

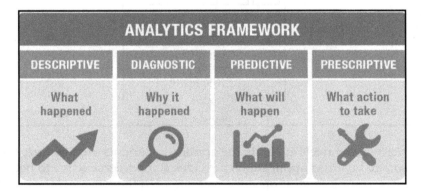

Source: http://blog.lnsresearch.com/understanding-big-data-analytics-in-manufacturing-comparing-splunk-seeq-sight-machine-monday-musings

Next, we will look at the details of the different kinds of analytics capabilities that are needed in conjunction with the APM to unlock its full business potential. Let's start with descriptive analytics.

Descriptive analytics

When the asset data is plotted as a line chart or bar chart, it is a simple representation of the description of the event. The accompanying figure shows the variation in the temperature of air, overlaying the different parts of the jet engine. In its simple form, this would be just a line graph without the asset. A slight variation can be a threshold to indicate that the value of temperature is above or below the expected range. APM often uses this form of descriptive analytics to alert an M&D center analyst when some asset behavior is drifting from the normal range. While this form of analytics is good for human-supervised scenario such as the M&D center, it may not often be high value addition, as it focuses on *what* happened, as it typically does not answer *how* and *why* questions.

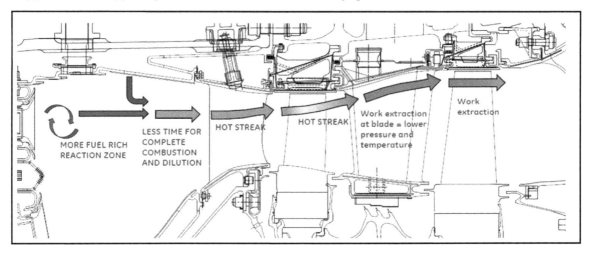

Source: Transportation Safety Board of Canada (`http://www.bst-tsb.gc.ca/eng/rapports-reports/aviation/2012/a12o0074/a12o0074.asp`)

Diagnostic analytics

Diagnostic analytics often helps figure out whether the alarm generated by the APM, using the descriptive analytics, is valid or not. Such analytics are often based on simple statistical models and relationships between the key attributes of the asset in context of the environment. In a human-supervised scenario, such analytics can help find the root cause of the problem and justify the action to take on the alarm.

The diagnostic analytics often help the M&D analyst to document *why did it happen?* For instance, in the jet engine case, if the temperature of the exhaust gas was above a certain threshold, the diagnostic analytics may help explain that pilot climbed to the cruise altitude at a faster than normal pace on a hot day. These analytics may involve drilling down to details, cluster analysis, and looking for other kinds of correlation. In this case, the correlation between the aircraft's climb rate and the exhaust gas temperature reveals the *why*.

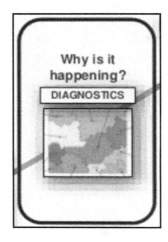

Diagnostic analytics

Predictive analytics

Predictive analytics is the basis of predictive maintenance. At this stage, we are using analytics to help answer, *what will happen next*? It can also be about predicting *when* it will happen. Let's go back to the airline engine example. If a pilot or an airline continues to climb to cruise altitude faster when operating in a hot geography, say Phoenix, Arizona in summers, then *what* is the expected impact to the engine say over a period of 2 years. Likewise, the airlines may want to predict *when* would be the right time to take the engine off the wing of the aircraft for servicing it, before it contributes to any unplanned downtime time.

Manufacturers and operators of the industrial assets often install sensors in equipment to capture the data that can be used for descriptive and then diagnostics analytics. Over time, they learn about the types of sensor data elements they need to analyze to act as the leading indicator of product problems or failures. This knowledge is then used to create the predictive analytics models. Once deployed, such models can indicate when failure is likely and what kind of corrective actions can be taken to prevent the adverse impact. Such type of predictive analytics is implemented within the APM suite of applications dealing with energy generation equipment such as gas turbines or windmills, or equipment in transportation such as jet engine and locomotives, a connected elevator, or escalator solution. In the health care space, the equivalent of predictive maintenance uses medical device data to help predict the onset of anomalies in an MRI machine.

The insurance industry is deploying IoT devices and collecting data for such predictive analytics applications to help answer the question, *what driving behaviors are most associated with a high risk of auto accident?*. This helps them predict the risk of the driver and come up with the right pricing or discount levels. The insurance is similarly evaluating other use cases of predictive analytics, such as what behavior patterns of the home owner reduces their chances of property and casualty claims.

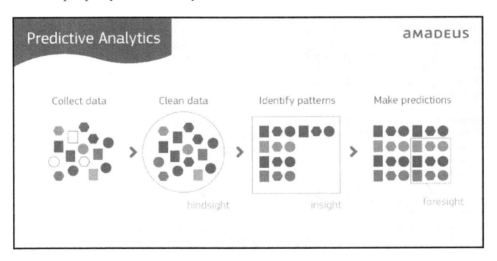

Source: Predictive analytics (http://www.amadeus.com/blog/07/04/5-examples-predictive-analytics-travel-industry/).

Prescriptive analytics

The prescriptive analytics is like a recommendation engine to help improve the outcomes. We are all familiar with the recommendations that Amazon provides for similar books to buy and Netflix that provides recommendations for movies to watch. Likewise, prescriptive analytics provides the models that decide what is the best course of action to take in an Industrial Internet setting and then informs or advice the human operator about it. Going back to the airline example, prescriptive analytics would provide guidance to the pilot and the airline on how best to take off and climb such that either the overall maintenance cost of the engine is minimized over its life time or the time interval between the major maintenance event is maximized.

Let's look at the scenario of the flight path optimization during the descend. In this example, the operation optimization module of APM is using some prescriptive analytics that is providing the recommendation for *how* to land while minimizing the noise and fuel efficiency of the aircraft engine. Such prescriptive analytics is relatively complex and requires advanced analytics expertise alongside the domain experts, in this case, the aircraft engineer, air traffic control personnel, and pilot.

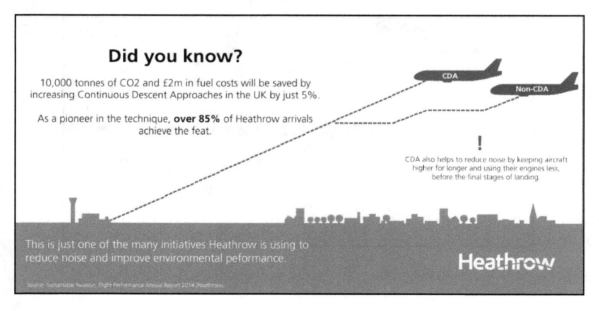

Source: Optimization of Flight Path Descend (http://your.heathrow.com/wp-content/uploads/2015/08/CDA-improvement.jpg).

We have so far looked at APM as an example of Industrial Internet application and how it is powered by the advanced analytics applications. Some may look at analytics content as part of the APM suite, while others may decouple the APM from the analytics content. In either case, APM must provide the framework for the deployment, orchestration, or workflow of the different analytics and execution of the analytics on the appropriate mix of data. Gaining a strong understanding of the APM applications and the different kinds of analytics helps the architects assess the applications and do the fit gap analysis relative to the business and functional needs.

Fit gap analysis

Here are some criteria that can be useful for the IIoT Platform and applications gap analysis:

- Completeness of the solution (edge and cloud)
- Different modes of sensing and actuation technologies, protocol support at the edge, edge analytics
- Privacy and security of the data and compliance
- Data ingestion and data store capabilities
- Analytics and workflow capabilities
- Applications availability
- Developer ecosystem and marketplace for services and applications

We introduced a generic supply chain optimization problem in the previous chapters. Here, we'll look at how this could apply to the manufacturer of cementing trucks. We will use a hypothetical case study of a company that manufactures and services cementing trucks, called **CEMENTruck Inc.**, for performing the fit gap analysis of the Industrial Internet platform and applications.

CEMENTruck's Main Product - Cementing truck

The following is an extensive list of points that we need to consider for our case study:

- CEMENTruck Inc., manufactures concrete-mixing trucks, which cost about $250K each
- CEMENTruck supply chain is facing the following problems:
    - Growing cost concerns and complexity in managing the fleet services
    - Loss of competitive footing
    - Reliability and throughput issues in the factories
    - Increased dependency on supply chain system and related ecosystem
- CEMENTruck's increasing dependency arises from the following:
    - Business partners such as distribution networks and repair shops sharing maintenance history
    - Suppliers - raw materials and parts performance
    - Multiple third-party vendor tools and equipment
    - Rising in-house IT costs in maintaining ERP, and data warehouse and analytics solutions with little demonstrable benefits
- CEMENTruck's executive leadership (board mandate) is keen to understand the following:
    - How to maximize operational efficiency of the fleet operations
    - How to address supply-chain management
    - How to prevent competition from after-market parts and services providers outside of their network
    - How to address IT/OT integration issues

We extract the functional requirements from this case study and then look at available options to meet these. Since the main product of CEMENTruck Inc. is a cementing truck, which is a complex asset, it fits nicely with the need for Industrial Internet platform and application. Since the company is responsible for the warranty, services, and parts, when the trucking fleets are in use in the construction sites, it calls for connected trucks. These connected trucks can then send the sensor, environment, and related data to the platform. The platform should provide the edge connectivity to the trucks and secure communication to the platform.

The need for monitoring the health of the trucks in the field and the ability to provide predictive maintenance calls for APM application. This can get them started with the descriptive analytics. As part of the gap analysis, the company would have to evaluate if the analytics needed to create meaningful alarms and provide diagnostics support is provided by the APM application provider of the needs to be custom developed. Very likely, the predictive and prescriptive analytics would have to be developed by CEMENTruck's internal resources. However, what they need to evaluate is how easily they can port their legacy analytics to this new platform. Hence, they would have to evaluate if the legacy analytics languages such as C/C++, Java, and .NET are supported in the new platform being evaluated. Consider the illustration of the practical Internet connected truck at `https://hbr.org/2014/11/the-internet-connected-engine-will-change-trucking`.

The alternative would be to rewrite these legacy analytics in the newer languages such as R, Python, Java, Node.js, or Go. In addition, multiple analytics may need to be orchestrated to create the end-to-end analytics workflow. An example of such a workflow for truck data could be the one shown here:

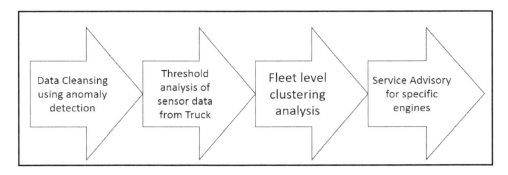

As we work through the fit gap analysis for the case study of CEMENTruck's requirements, we can see how the previous section of this chapter applies where we had reviewed the capabilities of the APM application and the different kinds of analytics that are needed to unlock the full potential of the IoT data. Let's now look at some of the elements of the platform architecture in the context of this case study. We noticed that the company wants to move away from in-house IT systems to free up internal resources from routine *keeping the lights on* type of technology work. This leads us to look at how the Industrial Internet platform is delivered to the customer. This leads us to look at the on-premises versus cloud-based architecture.

CEMENTruck realizes that when the cementing trucks are in the field and operating in customer premises or the construction job sites, they are outside the corporate network. This would make the use of public cloud delivered platform a good option. The trucks will need wireless connectivity to the cloud platform in a secure fashion. This is often achieved via a gateway device on the truck. The gateway device would have to be provided and secured by edge management software to allow the 12,000 trucks that could be potentially connected over the next year. From an architectural standpoint, it maps to the edge and the platform tier. Since the current enterprise systems run on premises, the platform tier on public cloud, would have to connect to the IT systems for the necessary IT/OT integration.

As we continue our fit gap analysis, we will now look at the manufacturing side and the tie-in to the supply chain system. Another important element is the field services execution and delivery applications. As the trucks are being manufactured in the factories of the company, there are reliability issues leading to challenges with the throughput. This leads to challenges with the supply chain as the company is not able to provide good visibility and demand forecast to the upstream suppliers. To alleviate some of these issues, the company should look at collecting sensor data from the manufacturing assembly lines, material movement status in the shop floor, and the quality data. Such capabilities are collectively referred to as smart manufacturing. We will take a deep dive into this application family later in this chapter.

Next, we will focus on the gaps in providing the vital link between the manufacturing to the field operations of the cementing trucks in terms of the warranty and maintenance services. We noticed that the company is facing challenges in being able to provide timely services to its assets, and this is a threat as third parties can enter the parts and services business. Once the trucks are connected to the Industrial Internet platform and APM applications start providing the predictive maintenance advisories, CEMENTruck would need a system in place for the execution and delivery of the field services. A gap that seems to jump out is a field service management solutions for the service technicians out in the field and the maintenance managers. We must explore such service applications to meet this gap. We will look at this class of application in the subsequent section of this chapter.

Brilliant Manufacturing

General Electric (GE) often uses the term *Brilliant Factory* for Industrial Internet applications primarily used to improve the efficiency of the manufacturing processes inside the factory. Brilliant Manufacturing is the enabling technology for brilliant factories. Brilliant Manufacturing enables manufacturers to make precise, real-time decisions through data-driven insights. These solutions are the digital technology behind Brilliant Factories. Another commonly used synonymous term, in the industry is smart manufacturing. Brilliant Manufacturing provides the link between the design, engineering, manufacturing, supply chain, distribution network, and field services into one connected and globally scalable intelligent system. It helps to collect and delivers equipment performance information to the right people in real time so they can make informed, accurate and quick decisions for optimized performance within the manufacturing system.

Next, we will look at the characteristics of the application suite that are needed to achieve the vision of the brilliant factory. The goal of the smart manufacturing applications is to increase the degree of control and optimization of the manufacturing floor machines and processes by the computers and augment the knowledge of the human operators by analyzing the big data from the sensors and the devices in relation to the known production plans and constraints.

MESes have been around in the industry for a while. MESes often work in near real time to enable the control of multiple elements of the production process such as material inputs, operators, machines in the assembly lines, and the support services. In short, MESes act as the control system for managing and monitoring **work-in-process** (**WIP**) on a factory floor. CEMENTruck would also need capability that provides plant-floor visibility of all work in process as the cementing truck is manufactured. Such applications can help eliminate the blind spots that **Manufacturing Resource Planning** (**MRP**) and MES may often have during the movement of the materials through the manufacturing stations. This would result in lower working capital and increased ability to adhere to delivery schedules of the trucks. This is turn may provide increased visibility and improved parts forecast to the suppliers of the parts and raw materials. The use of WIP management applications can help track the routes (the specific path based on the operations to be performed per the work orders) through the factory of the trucks.

CEMENTruck can also look at applications that can monitor the machine health and help improve the throughput. To accomplish this, some of the machines and the assembly lines may have to be retrofitted by sensors to allow collection of the relevant data. Coupled with the use of quality applications, this can help reduce scrap material rates and help with the cost control of material and process costs.

After looking at the fit gap analysis for the smart manufacturing related applications, we will now analyze the requirements for the field service technicians in order to carry out out their work smoothly and efficiently.

Field Service Management (FSM) application

We are familiar with the CRM applications such as Salesforce.com, Siebel, or Oracle Service Cloud. These are applications primarily for customer service and support for the sales or the call center professionals. When dealing with companies with complex and large physical assets, customer service is no longer restricted to call centers. There are field technicians who travel to the location of the assets or work out of the maintenance depots. To meet the needs of these calls of services, we need field services applications for CEMENTrack Inc. There are an estimated of five million field technicians in the US overall. Their primary job is to install, fix, and service the machines and equipment. CEMENTrack Inc. has about 300 field technicians.

The field service applications such as GE's ServiceMax offerings or Salesforce.com's field service **Lightning** typically provide capabilities such as management of field service delivery, including service contracts, scheduling of field staff, mobility, and knowledge base. The very nature of the field staff makes cloud delivery of such a field service application very attractive. It should include full support for mobile devices such as smartphone or tablets. An emerging area in field services is the use of **Augmented Reality (AR)** for providing additional assistance to the field service technician.

The following image illustrates the Augmented Reality for field service (http://exelerate. com.au/wp-content/uploads/2017/02/Augmented-Reality-Field-Service.jpg):

AR technology superimposes computer-generated images on a human user's view of the physical world. The resulting composite view can enhance the human experience for a specific task.

The following figure is illustrates the Augmented Reality for field service of a truck (`http:/ /www.digitalistmag.com/digital-economy/hyperconnectivity/2016/09/13/concrete- steps-towards-virtual-augmented-reality-in-enterprise-04470474`):

As CEMENTruck Inc. looks for an Industrial Internet platform and applications provider, it must evaluate how much of its needs can be met by a single provider for the following:

- Industrial Internet platform delivered as PaaS along with edge capabilities
- APM application with the ability to incorporate or create different kinds of analytics and its orchestrations
- Smart manufacturing applications
- Field service applications

The ability to provide multiple of these capabilities would alleviate or minimize the need for *systems integrations* for CEMENTruck Inc. Historically, in the IT and enterprise applications, companies have spent a larger fraction of their budget with the **system integrators** (**SIs**) than with the software provider. Carefully looking at how the variety of the Industrial Internet applications and capabilities are packaged and delivered by their providers can help to prevent this pitfall. Realistically, even after these broad capabilities are delivered by the platform and the application provider, the company would have to customize and enhance the out-of-the-box capabilities, as the business needs and the competitive landscape evolves over time. A good thumb rule it to strive for 80:20 rule, or look for *buy* option for 80 percent of the capabilities needed and be prepared to *build* the remaining 20 percent of the gaps in the capabilities.

Summary

We looked at the processes and the considerations of the assessment of the Industrial Internet applications. The architects need to look at the available options for the application infrastructure, platform, and the application capabilities. If the application is delivered as SaaS, then it minimizes the investigation for the underlying tiers, namely PaaS and the IaaS, since the SaaS provider makes those determinations. If the SaaS capabilities do not suffice for all the functional requirements, then the robustness and capabilities of the PaaS become important so that features to bridge the gaps can be *built* on it. Selecting an Industrial Internet applications provider who can help meet most of the broad buckets of capabilities, namely platform, APM, smart manufacturing, and field services application, helps reduce the excessive cost on the systems integration by the end user company.

The next chapter will focus on the information domain and include the data and the analytics architecture. Different data store technologies and architecture patterns will be discussed. These allow the sensor data to be stored in an optimized way so that analytics applications can easily access the relevant data structures. Concepts such as the Lambda architecture will be introduced to handle both the speed and the volume for analytics applications.

6
Defining the Data and Analytics Architecture

Now that we've considered some of the benefits of *buy* versus *build* by looking at what Industrial Internet applications can provide, it is time to take a closer look at the underlying architecture and considerations around key components. When we are deploying applications, much of this is under the surface. However, since you might choose to create a largely customized solution, and almost any IIoT deployment requires some degree of customization, understanding how to piece together the underlying architecture is required and is probably a big reason why you are reading this book.⌐

In Chapter 4, *Mapping Requirements to a Functional Viewpoint*, we described the information domain and the functional requirements it fulfills. You might recall that this domain delivers the metrics needed to run the business. Some of the functions that must be provided include ingestion and cleansing of data, data management, and data analysis through machine learning algorithms and business intelligence tools.

Here, we'll focus on the information domain components that must be part of our architecture. We'll also describe the roles of some of the tools and locations for processing analytics and machine learning inside the information domain, and at the edge (in devices and field gateways) in the control domain.

This chapter covers the following topics:

- Data and analytics requirements and capabilities
- The Lambda architecture and IIoT
- Analytics, machine learning, and analyst tools
- Early Industrial Internet applications and historians
- The speed layer in the architecture
- The batch layer in the architecture

As in the previous chapters, we'll describe how these components could be included in the architecture of the supply chain optimization example (CEMENTruck Inc.). By reading this chapter, you should gain an understanding of how you might include these components in your own architecture designs and solutions.

Data and analytics requirements and capabilities

Industrial analytics are unique in that the results of analysis often directly impact the physical world operationally, and can also have safety implications. Taking actions based on analytics could be harmful or undesirable. Since industrial analytics interpret and prescribe actions that interact with other sensors and components, there is also the potential for conflict. Therefore, it is important to fully understand the various information streams so that correct decisions can be made. The following are some of the unique requirements for consideration:

- **Correctness**: Industrial analytics requires a higher level of accuracy to avoid undesirable and unintended consequences in the physical world
- **Timing**: Industrial analytics must deliver results within their prescribed time horizon to satisfy synchronization requirements and ensure reliable, high-quality operations
- **Safety**: Strong safety requirements are necessary to safeguard workers, users, equipment, and the environment
- **Contextualized**: Industrial analysis is always performed within the context of an activity, and an accurate and complete understanding of the analytic results requires an understanding of the processes and the states of the equipment and peripherals

- **Causal-oriented**: As industrial systems have complex and causal relationships, the analytics must be modeled with domain-specific subject matter expertise linked to physical modelling and statistical, data science, and machine learning knowledge
- **Distributed**: Many industrial systems include hierarchical tiers and are distributed geographically, and each tier or subsystem might have its own unique analytic requirements requiring localized analytics (requirements for timing and resilience can result in the analytics being distributed and implemented close to the source of data, and to the target of the analytic result)
- **Streaming**: Due to the continuous execution or batch processing of industrial systems, most analytic data and analytic results will be streaming in nature so that the analytics will be applied to live data as it is generated or transmitted (traditional batch-oriented analytics might also provide information to improve analytic models and human decision-making)
- **Automatic**: To support continuous operations, streaming analysis and application of analytic outcomes must be automated, dynamic, and continuous
- **Semantics**: To properly understand the data and produce accurate analytic results, data needs to be understood in context, attributed at the source, and communicated to improve the accuracy (data that is inferred or taken out of context will result in uncertainty)

To glean useful analytic results, the architecture that is deployed should first efficiently collect data and then stream or store the data, or both, and then transform it for analysis. Robust data management is necessary to facilitate this process.

Successful analytics requires the pre-processing of the data. Pre-processing techniques that are utilized are driven by the type and format of the data being produced, where the data is produced, and whether the rate of data generation allows for it to be processed in batches or requires streaming processing. The volume and speed of data in IIoT can present several challenges.

Data management in IIoT systems involves incorporation of various tasks and roles from a usage viewpoint, along with the functional components of the functional viewpoint. The activities for data management include the following:

- Reduction and analytics
- Publish and subscribe
- Query
- Storage, persistence, and retrieval
- Integration

- Description and presence
- Data framework
- Rights management

Data reduction and analytics

IIoT sensors have the potential to generate a huge amount of raw data that possesses inherent value. Additional analysis is often required to gain important insights. However, it can be expensive and time-consuming to transmit such volumes of data over networks. The speed and volume of data can make some preprocessing necessary prior to transmission.

A variety of preprocessing techniques are typical. Data volume might be reduced through aggregation. Another method of data reduction is to perform sampling and then filter samples within the stream. Statistical and machine learning algorithms can be applied at the data source or edge so that only the analytic results are transmitted through the network. Moving these functions to the edge can substantially reduce network traffic.

Publish and subscribe

Publish and subscribe describes a reliable method for sending or publishing data by a person or process, at predefined intervals, to parties that have indicated an interest in the topic. These parties are called **subscribers**. The publisher and subscriber do not necessarily know about each other. A broker is used to filter and distribute the data. Data collected at the edge might be published to a consolidation and aggregation tier.

Publish and subscribe methods enable scalability for many data sources and consumers, and there is a reliable flow of management services to the devices. Broker operations can be run in parallel, and caching and intelligent routing can be employed to improve scalability. For extremely high volumes, clustered broker nodes can distribute the load using load balancers.

Query

A query enables the filtering and selection of data. Queries can be executed against a dataset by a user, by an addressable device (through web sockets), by an application, or through analytical, reporting, visualization, and other tools. Query results can be pushed to a gateway to provide a data source for higher level brokers.

Query models are typically one time or continuous. A one-time query involves selection of data in response to a request, while a continuous query produces a stream of data. One-time queries are used to return a single result set and are well suited for the publish-subscribe data pattern. Streaming data returns data in real-time or at prescribed intervals and can be used in tracking and monitoring real-time analytics and machine learning.

Storage persistence and retrieval

IIoT systems typically generate huge quantities of data that needs to be processed and/or stored for record keeping, post-processing, and analysis. There can also be regulatory or audit considerations as to what types of data must be recorded and preserved, and for how long.

Stored time-series data produced by devices might be used for replaying events or simulating scenarios. Time series data might be persisted by a historian, deployed using a NoSQL database or Hadoop-based system, or archived by the historian to a relational database or other data management system.

Integration

The components and applications in an IIoT solution produce varied data specific to their respective functions. This data was traditionally retained in their respective silos in field locations. To achieve a more thorough understanding of the business, data integration across these silos is required. For example, in telecom companies, revenue leakage occurs when calling services are provided, but these billable calls are not passed on to the billing system. Integrating network usage data, linked to devices with the billing systems, can uncover these unbilled calls.

Traditional systems use a process of **extraction, transformation, and loading** (ETL) to extract data from one or more source systems, integrate and transform the data, and load the resulting data into a target system. This transformation frequently includes performing aggregation or other functions to enable analysis. Where large data volumes are at play, the processing often more closely follows an ELT pattern where transformations occur in the target.

In IIoT systems, heterogeneous devices can have different syntax, semantics, and APIs. A transformation to a common semantic framework is often necessary for effective analysis. Domain transformation might be used for protocol conversions.

IIoT integration challenges can be addressed by taking the following steps:

- Address the APIs first to determine the integration requirements and if your existing integration capabilities are sufficient
- Identify the communication requirements for the devices and select the most appropriate technology, taking into consideration how the technology can handle the number and types of devices, while determining the network topology that best meets the requirements
- Leverage cloud-based deployment models to integrate IIoT platforms with business processes
- If the IIoT system data and applications are on-premises, or mostly on-premises, you might consider using traditional integration tools already in-house, but keep in mind that these tools might not be optimal for IIoT connectivity or cloud service integration
- Add an API management solution to your IIoT project, especially if the project has many APIs, or the APIs have large numbers of consumers or return restricted or sensitive data

Description and presence

Description and presence refers to awareness about devices, networking, software, and systems. This is required for effective management and the dynamic integration of new capabilities. Understanding data descriptions and availability is also a fundamental requirement.

Metadata provides the descriptive information. For example, when you select a movie to watch, you are probably interested in the movie name, movie genre, plot summary, movie length, the movie's star rating, release date, and digital format. This is the movie's metadata. It enables you to gain an understanding of the movie without having to watch it.

Metadata in IIoT describes the definitions and structure of the data. Description and presence enables discovery of information about the data structures and devices. Metadata analysis can reveal patterns, correlations, and trends without the need to examine the data itself.

Data framework

The data framework monitors the data exchange components and provides diagnostic data, such as the status and behavior of the components and information regarding data volumes and usage. As new data components are introduced to the framework, they are discoverable. The data framework can also be used to maintain a publish-subscribe data catalog so that users and components can discover updates to published data. The data can be exposed through dashboards and system consoles corresponding to the technologies and components.

The data framework tracks the following:

- Component presence discovery, identifying past and present framework participants and newly added components
- Component activity monitoring of data statistics such as update frequency, throughput, and system loads and memory usage
- Traffic monitoring of data flow statistics such as throughput, latency, and data volume

An IIoT-specific systems management console in the data framework enables testing and diagnostics.

Rights management

Rights management describes data ownership and rights and relies heavily on security functions to control data privileges to ensure privacy and to protect data from unauthorized manipulation. Data owners and managers maintain stewardship of the data under their purview. They can grant or revoke certain rights to all data or defined sets or subsets of raw data, aggregated data, or consolidated data.

Rights management is key to meeting regulatory and compliance requirements and to keep track of ownership when data-related functions are outsourced to cloud providers or other third parties. Rights can be associated with APIs for granting authority and accessing a device.

A graph database can be useful to manage the relationships between devices, users, location, networks, and permissions. Blockchain might provide a scalable mechanism for verifying and sharing access to data and assets in the IIoT system (see Chapter 11, *A Vision of the Future*).

Creating business value

Commercial industrial organizations, just like any business, must maintain and increase financial margins to stay in business and remain competitive. The industrial organization can achieve this, at least in part, by increasing production and reducing expenses and inventory costs. Industrial analytics can help the business stakeholders of your IIoT project identify bottlenecks and balance operational processes with demand, product, and inventory.

A focus on solving these business needs and success stories, where analytics enabled by IIoT projects, makes similar companies more competitive and often drives companies to move forward on these projects.

Analytics functionality

Industrial analytics footprints must provide certain features to deliver solutions to functional and non-functional requirements while addressing the complexity present in this multi-domain architecture. These features include the following:

- **Visualization**: Displays and manipulates data and analytic results using charts and graphs
- **Exploration**: Ad-hoc querying of stored data
- **Design**: Analytics automation for data quality, mining and machine learning, and business intelligence
- **Orchestration**: Distributes requests over clusters of computing resources to collect and aggregate data
- **Connection**: Exchange of data and work between components
- **Cleansing**: Removal of irrelevant and duplicated data and noise, and merging data from multiple sources
- **Computation**: Execution of statistical and machine learning calculations
- **Validation**: Governance ensuring analytic results are accurate
- **Application**: Analytic results used to improve or correct automation, or aid human decision making
- **Storage**: Historical archival of incoming data
- **Supervision and management**: Monitoring, updating, correcting, and optimizing the information model, metadata, data sources, processes, and computing resources

Industrial analytic activities depend on the availability and access to the data from industrial processes and assets. The distributed nature of IIoS, and the need for analytics to produce results in time to take meaningful actions, sometimes pushes the analytics to the edge or in middle tiers where data is streaming. Once the analytics are performed, the values might be archived via batch feeds to data management systems where further analysis is possible by data scientists and SMEs. There, they might interpret and validate readings or recommend additional filtering or sampling. If further analysis is not deemed necessary, the raw data can be discarded.

To enable the continuous processing of industrial data, an analytics workflow can be developed within the data framework and automated. The workflow automation orchestrates the transformation of raw data into analytic results and performs execution of the analytic prescriptions. Workflows and their content can be improved and fine-tuned to improve accuracy and produce better result as more is learned about the processes and should be versioned.

Finally, the analytic results should be communicated in an understandable format that improves human understanding and decision making. They will want to interact and visualize the data in diverse ways. Some might want to drill through aggregations to details via hierarchies and related items.

As the analytics are honed over time, increasingly meaningful patterns can be discovered. Anomalies might be detected and alerts can be sent to operators along with supporting data as required. The root cause of anomalies and faults can be diagnosed, and prescribed actions might be taken automatically or through human intervention. By applying analytics to optimize the operating parameters and operational efficiency, failures can be avoided. Failures caused by human error can be reduced or eliminated.

Applying analytics to improve operational efficiency can result in optimal operation of devices, equipment, and reduced human stress. However, the proper data must be provided at the proper time and appropriate analytical models and algorithms must be applied, guided by engineering and business domain knowledge.

Mapping analytics architecture to reference architecture

Industrial analytics can span the functional domains we previously described in `Chapter 4`, *Mapping Requirements to a Functional Viewpoint*. As a review, the domains in IIoT functional architecture include the following:

- **Control domain**: It provides functions for asset management, sensing, actuation, communication, entity abstraction, and modeling
- **Operations domain**: It enables provisioning, management, monitoring, diagnostics, and optimization of devices in the control domain
- **Information domain**: It consists of data ingestion, quality and cleansing, transformation, persistence, cataloging, analytics, and governance
- **Application domain**: It includes logic, rules, models and interfaces addressing business requirements
- **Business domain**: It includes enterprise resource planning, human resources, asset management, billing and payments, work planning and scheduling, and customer relationship applications

The following diagram illustrates these domains and where the analytics are primarily applied:

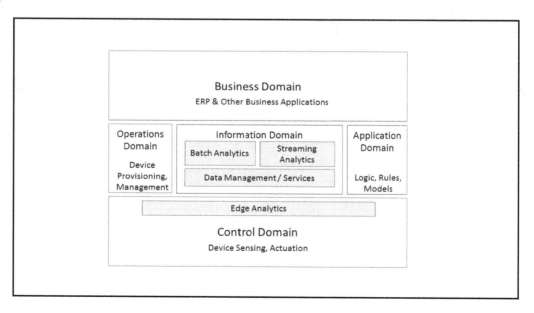

Analytics in the control domain consists of edge analytics that provides real-time insight into operations. Here, the device time horizon can be milliseconds or less. Analytics and resulting actuation that occurs in the control domain is usually automated.

Analytics applied in the application and operations domains requires responses measured in seconds, and these responses are also usually automated. Such responses based on results from streaming analytics might include automatic fault detection and diagnosis, or automated adjustments to improve efficiency.

Analytics relevant to the business domain can aid in business planning, improve processes, and enable intelligent business processes. These analytics are typically used for planning, and the required response time to make a business decision can be measured in days. Batch analytics is more typically applied here.

Advanced analytics

Advanced analytics involves applying mathematical functions to data to understand and forecast trends, define clusters using common features, and discover relationships. For example, in an industrial setting, advanced analytics can detect and predict potential faults.

Advanced analytics can be described in the following approaches:

- **Automated**: This performs continuous analysis and applies the results back into the system to improve optimization and performance.
- **Real-time**: Analysis occurs as data is received to provide immediate results and prescriptive actions
- **Streaming**: Analysis is performed on a data flow in memory or other transient location without loading the data into a full-fledged data-management system
- **Active**: Components share analytic results in real time to enable rapid response
- **Causal-oriented**: Physical and neural network deep learning are applied to identify causal relationships
- **Distributed**: Analysis is performed across domains and systems using shared processing

The unique characteristics of IIoT solutions often require additional robustness and speed and accuracy of the analytics, especially when the analyses impact viability of the business and safety.

Network latency and reliability are critical to taking real-time actions. Inadequate network bandwidth will inhibit the flow of data. If these limitations create timing constraints, analytics must be performed near both the data source and the target the analytic results are used to control.

In a control system where high-resolution time-series data is generated at high frequency, data volume constraints can overwhelm network bandwidth constraints. Real-time control can become impossible. In these systems, data needs to be dynamically bound to the analytic functions in the edge using dynamic composition and automated interoperability. High-volume data might then be transmitted periodically or on demand to analytic systems where it can be analyzed for patterns, anomalies, and causal relationships.

Now that we have provided the necessary background on data analytics requirements and capabilities, we will begin to explore the architecture in depth and then explore the components that are fundamental in the architecture.

The Lambda architecture and IIoT

Industrial Internet solutions gather data from smart devices "at the edge" in field locations that are often remote. These devices typically stream data that eventually ends up in cloud-based or on-premises data-management systems.

Many of you might be more familiar with traditional on-line transaction processing systems feeding data warehouses via batch data loads. Streaming data is data in motion, and that introduces the need for another analysis layer called the speed layer. This multi-layer approach is described by what is popularly called the Lambda architecture.

Traditional online transaction-processing systems feed the batch layer directly. Devices at the edge feed streaming data directly into a speed layer. The data usually then makes its way into the batch layer and is added to the data at rest.

The following diagram illustrates the main building blocks included in a Lambda architecture. The direction of most of the flow of data among these building blocks is indicated by the arrows:

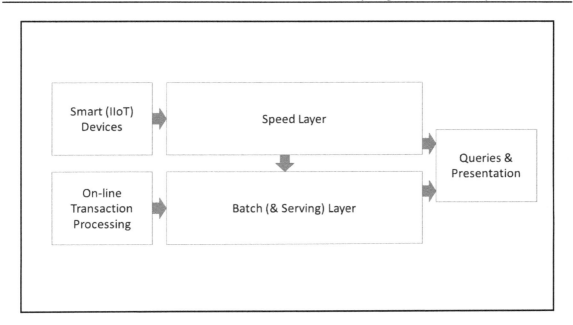

The following diagram shows the components we introduced in Chapter 4, *Mapping Requirements to a Functional Viewpoint*, and how they align to the Lambda architecture, including the presence of the speed layer for analysis of streaming data and the batch layer:

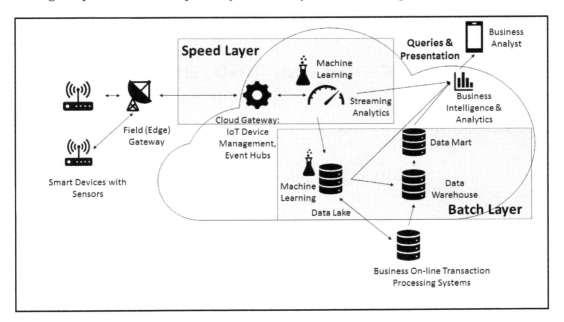

A serving layer is sometimes described to be part of the Lambda architecture. This layer provides indexing of views of data at rest for faster queries and is usually deployed as part of the data-management systems. The results of queries are presented in the business intelligence and analytics tools pictured in this diagram.

Business intelligence tools refer to a broad classification of tools used by the lines of business to retrieve, analyze, and transform data and report on business results. Interfaces typically include table and hierarchy definitions used to drill to detail. More modern tools often include native-language-like questioning and are beginning to leverage cognitive interfaces. We will describe how cognitive capabilities will play an increasingly important role in providing interfaces for humans using Industrial Internet solutions in the final chapter of this book.

The Lambda architecture works quite well for most organizations that have already built batch feeds to data warehouses and now are adding streaming data sources as part of their Industrial Internet project. In the supply chain optimization example introduced in earlier chapters, there is important data in legacy data warehouses that needs to be included in our analyses. So, we will design and deploy our solution as a Lambda architecture.

More recently, some organizations starting with an entirely new infrastructure have decided to eliminate batch feeds and process all incoming data as streaming data. This variation is called the **Kappa architecture**. The downstream data store only appends incoming data in this design, so a Hadoop cluster serving as a data lake is frequently chosen as the final landing spot for all data when this approach is taken.

Analytics, machine learning, and analyst tools

Analytics and machine learning applications are deployed in the speed layer, the batch layer, or are sometimes pushed to field gateways at the edge. Before exploring the architecture components of the speed and batch layers and where these applications are deployed, we'll have a look at how these applications are created and other tools that the business analyst might use.

A process for advanced analytics creation

Recognizing the coming deluge of huge data volumes, over 200 international organizations met to discuss and define an open standard for the analysis of these massive data sets at the beginning of this century. This consortium created what became known as the **Cross-Industry-Standard-Process for Data Mining (CRISP-DM)**.

Data mining versus machine learning

Data mining is an older term. It was originally differentiated from machine learning, in that, data mining referred to human-initiated modeling of data. Machine learning referred to computational engines doing the work. Today, these terms are often used interchangeably. Since machine learning is more in vogue, what were once called data mining tools (that enable data modeling by humans and produce code that is deployed to computers and devices) now often are called machine learning tools instead.

In Chapter 3, *Gathering Business Requirements*, we described gathering business requirements as an early step in our process. The CRISP-DM methodology begins similarly with the goal of gaining a business understanding. During the initial stage, we determine business objectives, assess the situation, including risks associated with a potential project, the skills required, and the potential costs. We also determine goals of our analytics efforts and produce a plan to deliver a solution.

We must then gather relevant data. We gain an understanding of the data we need and collect, describe, and explore it. We then assess its quality and prepare it for usage in our modeling tools by cleansing and formatting the data properly.

Modeling is the creation of a defined process for applying mathematical functions and algorithms to the data. Initially, the accuracy of the models is tested using a subset of the data with known results and then refining the models. In the next section, we will describe how using machine learning tools can speed this process.

Once we are confident with our models, we can then apply them to real-world situations and evaluate the results. This evaluation might cause us to see a need to reevaluate our business understanding or the models themselves. Alternatively, we might be ready to deploy and monitor the solution.

Some data scientists have questioned the agility of the CRISP-DM approach. However, the process we just described is not too different from the agile development methodology outlined in Chapter 4, *Mapping Requirements to a Functional Viewpoint*. Both approaches begin with a need to understand the business problems being faced rather than simply exploring data without a business context.

Machine learning tools

Machine learning tools provide a development environment for experimenting with mathematical modeling algorithm alternatives and then selecting the most appropriate model. Most often, experimentation initially occurs using a sample of the full data set.

Once the model is defined, many such tools also automate the process of building application code. Code generation into languages such as C#, Python, and R is typical. The code can then be deployed to the appropriate component in the architecture.

The tools usually come packaged with various statistical functions, machine learning algorithms, and text analytics functions and feature the ability to insert custom code. Statistical functions used to measure the variation in data often include linear correlation and probability distributions. Hypotheses testing, such as t-tests for two data sets, are also commonly provided.

Machine learning algorithms have various use cases. Clustering algorithms, such as K-Means, are used to model outcomes into various groups. Classification of data into various groups is possible using decision trees, decision forests, decision jungles, logistic regression, neural networks, Bayes, and two-class **Support Vector Machines** (**SVMs**). Anomaly detection, used to determine outliers or unusual events, might be solved using one-class SVM algorithms.

Modeling begins with the import of a data set. The data is examined for completeness and could require some transformation. Examples of data transformation that might be applied during the preparation phase include filtering, learning with counts, and manipulation by adding columns and rows, cleaning missing data, editing metadata, and joining data.

Next, the model must be trained. To do this, we use our machine learning tool to sample and split the data set or apply scaling and reducing (through normalization, grouping, or clipping). We can apply various algorithms to the data and measure the accuracy of each algorithm we apply in making predictions through scoring.

The following diagram, generated by Microsoft ML Studio, illustrates this process. We see a model that begins with raw data input. Then, data cleansing, splitting the data and applying a linear regression algorithm for training and scoring, and finally evaluating the model takes place:

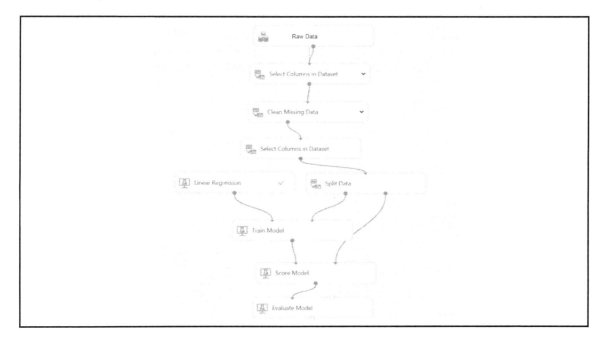

Once we are satisfied with the model, we can generate the code needed to deploy it in an application. The component in our architecture that we choose to deploy the code to is determined by the type and immediacy of action that is required.

Other analyst tools

Other analysts in your organization likely want to simply understand what happened or the outcomes of predictive analyses prior to making business decisions. If the organization has a data warehouse, many will already be familiar with ad-hoc query and analysis business intelligence tools and the reports such tools can produce, or are downloading the data from the warehouse to manipulate it in Excel spreadsheets for this purpose.

As noted earlier, in a Lambda architecture defined for IIoT solutions, NoSQL databases and Hadoop clusters (data lakes) often reside alongside the legacy data warehouses. Over the past decade, SQL support in these data-management systems has improved, and the same business intelligence tools are often used with these engines.

Organizations also sometimes see a need to observe the real-time updates of activity in streaming analytics engines in the speed layer. Many business intelligence tools are now capable of displaying such activity. The following is an example of how live activity might be viewed in a meter and historical chart of environmental readings rendered by Microsoft Power BI:

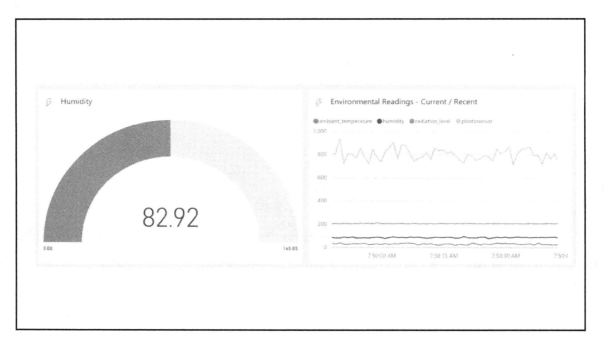

Finding the location of data in the multiple data-management systems in a Lambda architecture has sometimes been a challenge for business analysts and data scientists. As they access data using business intelligence and machine learning tools, great value can come from having access to a data catalog that uses previously extracted metadata from all of the data-management systems to provide guidance on what the data means and where it is found.

A data catalog can provide several important functions. It enables users of the catalog to register, enrich, discover, understand, and consume data sources. There are typically several classes of users. The most common business users can use the catalog to browse and search for data and better understand the context behind the data. Publishers can also register data sources and enrich or annotate the data. IT administrators apply policies to control access and track and monitor usage of the data catalog.

Data wrangling and information discovery tools

 A new class of tools emerged in the past decade to explore data residing in Hadoop clusters. Referred to as data wrangling or information-discovery tools, these tools can sample large data sets gathered from the huge volumes present in Hadoop and provide a business user interface to explore the relationships between entities defined in the data. They can also be used to generate new data sets and provide simple reporting and visualization of data.

Before we describe a possible role for field gateways in performing analytics and the components in the speed and batch layers, it is worth taking a look at how many earlier Industrial Internet applications were deployed, especially those in process manufacturing, and how that footprint is evolving.

Early Industrial Internet applications and historians

Early Industrial Internet applications often function in a standalone fashion within manufacturing sites. The devices produce what is commonly called time-series data. Time-series data arrives at its destination as a sequence of data points in a specific time order and typically at equally spaced points in time. So, the data has a natural temporal order to it.

Specialty applications and transient data stores, called historians, were developed to speed time series analysis and became popular in process manufacturing. Two of the more popular applications in these implementations are PI server (that processes the data and is often linked to relational databases to store retired data in archives) and GE Digital's Historian (that can now also be deployed to Hadoop). Sometimes, the archives are stored locally in the manufacturing plants, while at other times, they are stored in a central data store for further analysis, especially when a multi-plant view is needed. As we have seen previously, modern Lambda architectures define the latter as a model.

Historians are based on a time-series database structure optimized to store arrays of time-indexed data and are therefore designed for rapid uptake of operational data along with trending and discrete reporting of individual readings in a time-based manner. They include tools for performing analytics, issuing alerts and notifications, and auditing. Manufacturing operators, engineers, plant managers, and others typically use applications specifically designed to meet their data and operational needs.

The processing of such data has also been addressed using time-series functions in relational databases with varying degrees of success. While a relational database can be used to store time-series data, time-series analysis is complicated. To perform time-series analysis and time-zone conversions, relational joins across time spans become cumbersome. Time-series data might also be stored as **Binary Large Objects** (**BLOBs**) in relational databases where user-defined time-series functions can operate upon the BLOB (since the BLOB itself has no native awareness of the data stored within it).

As an alternative, NoSQL databases are sometimes used as time-series databases. They can provide efficient means to store time and other dimensional data, any associated logs, and sensor and other edge device data as key value pairs. NoSQL databases follow a schema-less paradigm. The sharding and indexing capabilities are advantageous for high throughput and associated high data volumes present in IIoT.

At the time of writing this book, the processing of this sort of data was also moving into the speed layer of the cloud. New public cloud analysis engines were being introduced for this purpose. So, time-series analysis might now occur in many locations in the architecture.

The speed layer and field gateways

Earlier in this chapter, we pictured a speed layer in our architecture consisting of an IoT hub and/or event hub(s) serving as a cloud gateway and a streaming analytics engine. A cloud gateway is paired with a field gateway at the edge, or the cloud gateway will sometimes communicate directly with the smart devices themselves.

Some organizations deploy the speed layer on-premises instead of in the cloud to be located close to their existing batch layer systems. If transmission of data occurs to a central on-premises location, the gateway architecture would be similar, except an on-premises gateway would be pictured in our earlier diagram instead of the cloud gateway. This is especially common in organizations that built Industrial Internet solutions prior to public clouds gaining in popularity and the functionality required for these types of solutions.

Field gateways gather event data at the edge from smart devices and sensors. They are usually sized based on the number of data streams that will occur, the data collection rate (events/second), and the data storage duration desired. These gateways might be custom developed or provided by vendors. OSIsoft and ThingWorx are two such popular vendors deployed as part of many custom-built solutions.

Field gateways ingest messages, filter data, provide identity mapping, and log messages (for auditing purposes) as well as provide linkage to cloud or on-premises gateways. A newer trend has emerged to also perform stream analytics and machine learning within the field gateways. The ability to push these applications to the edge is now provided by some of the public cloud vendors. In a sense, this extends the speed layer to the edge. When these capabilities are deployed at the edge, you will need to consider CPU and memory sizing implications when sizing the field gateway platforms.

Within the speed layer that is deployed in a central location, the packaging of components varies among vendors. Among various public cloud vendors focused on IIoT solutions, the following functionality can be found in their offerings and/or those of their partners:

- IoT hubs that enable **device to cloud (D2C)** via messaging protocols and **cloud to device (C2D)** communications contain information about the smart devices, support revocable access control for devices, enable operations modeling, and support message routing to event hubs or service buses
- Event hubs without the management capabilities of the IoT hub, but specifically designed for just handling rapid message ingress with data transfer rates of up to 1 MB/second typical in cloud deployment
- Streaming analytics engines providing a place to analyze data in motion with using machine learning algorithms or to view the current streaming data through business intelligence tools.

Since we are focused on data and analytics in this chapter, we will pay special attention to how quickly we can transmit data in the speed layer. The hubs can be scaled as needed. Our goal is not to create any bottlenecks.

Message volume and hubs

Most message volume comes from D2C transmissions of data from the devices. Of course, other volume is generated through file transmission, device identity management, job management, connectivity monitoring, and other tasks. Some of this data is transmitted C2D.

The hubs are not meant to be locations where data is stored for significant periods of time. Usually, a maximum of 24 hours of data records being stored is recommended, though it is possible to extend the length of time that data records are stored. The batch layer is the proper location for storing longer histories.

The streaming analytics engine enables real-time analysis of data that is being transmitted from the sensors and smart devices. Typical average data rates today are about 50 MB/second. As mentioned earlier, data can be directly queried from business intelligence tools. Data might also be queried using SQL, or machine learning scripts might be applied on an ongoing basis.

Data is typically then loaded into a batch layer data-management system (data lake, NoSQL database, or relational database). Immediate actions might be initiated after the analysis of incoming data, so scripts might be pushed upstream via event hubs or service bus queues.

In our supply chain optimization example introduced earlier, three critical success factors were identified:

- Operating factories at maximum capacity (24x7)
- Delivery of all needed components (parts) to factories just-in-time
- Maximized revenue from production by meeting product demand

The speed layer serves several purposes in this example. It provides the point of ingestion for data gathered from factories and transportation vehicles and transmitted by smart devices through field gateways at the edge. The streaming analytics engine analyzes the real-time flow of data and might initiate some of the following actions:

- Slow production rates if critical supplies are delayed
- Seek alternate delivery routes if supplies in transit are delayed
- Reroute transportation vehicles to alternate distribution centers if supplies are predicted to become critically low and the current distribution center is unable to fulfill demand for parts
- Initiate reordering of supplies if damage to components in transit is believed to be occurring (gathered by observing unusual temperature readings or vibration levels)
- Send alerts to supply chain and factory managers and finance if production disruption is likely due to supply chain issues

The batch layer

The batch layer is the location of data-management systems storing historical data in our architecture. Incoming data streams from the speed layer commonly land in a NoSQL database. Initially, a variety of NoSQL key-value pair databases were commonly used and scaled through a technique called sharding, the horizontal partitioning of a database across multiple database servers. Some organizations use this type of NoSQL database in PoCs for rapid deployment or as pre-processing engines in production solutions.

In the past few years, Hadoop clusters have gained in popularity as the landing spot and serve as a data lake in the Lambda architecture you saw in the diagram. They can support the large data volumes of historical data that are often present in IIoT projects and are an optimal location to run machine learning embedded solutions.

Relational databases continue to have a role in deployment strategies as the underpinning for data warehouses and data marts. These often provide the historic database of record for transactions in an organization and can provide important data needed to answer business questions.

The batch layer in the architecture is most often built in a public cloud today. Data volumes tend to grow tremendously over time and smaller data samples in separate engines must sometimes be spun up quickly. A public cloud provides the elasticity needed to meet these demands.

Data lakes and Hadoop

Hadoop was invented early in this century to enable analysis of data streams common in solving search engine problems. Given that Industrial Internet problems are also solved through analysis of streaming data, Hadoop became an important technology component deployed in many such projects.

Hadoop is supported as an endpoint from IoT and event hubs enabling loading from the speed layer into the batch layer. Events containing data can arrive continuously, and the data is simply appended providing the real-time loading needed for such data volumes.

Hadoop features a utility often used in loading streaming data called Kafka. Some organizations use Kafka to replace traditional message brokers. When Kafka is deployed, producers of messages write to topics and consumers read data in the topics. Consumers can be gathered into consumer groups when reading a topic. In Hadoop, topics are partitioned across the many nodes in the cluster. Kafka can handle messages storing objects in any format (string, JSON, and Avro are common). Keys can be attached to messages to direct them to specific partitions.

The streaming data from devices is often described as semi-structured. It has some identifiers or metadata and values embedded in the data stream that needs to be parsed. Hadoop has, as one of its earliest foundations, the ability to map data that arrived as streams and reduce it to the data of value through programming (hence, the MapReduce capability).

Though Hadoop was not initially noted for ease of use or speed of processing, much has changed in the past dozen years. Hive was introduced to provide SQL compatibility, and Spark in-memory processing now enables response times closer to those of relational database engines. Spark's in-memory processing engine runs on Apache Hadoop YARN (Yet Another Resource Negotiator) that is included in the major Hadoop distributions. Spark's APIs are used to enable fast execution of streaming, machine learning, and SQL workloads that often occur in frequent iterations.

Data entering the data lake arrives in its raw format and is typically not cleansed. This is often seen as desirable by data scientists who want to perform machine learning and advanced analytics on undisturbed data. In some organizations, data from transaction-processing systems or data warehouses also makes its way into the data lake if needed as part of the analysis.

Once the data lands, some organizations rationalize data in Hadoop, creating cleansed data sets. Some will also put structure around some of the data using HBase. As noted earlier, the tools of choice by data scientists and business analysts can include machine learning, data wrangling, and business intelligence tools in analyzing and manipulating this data.

The tremendous data volumes analyzed by search engine vendors (in the Exabytes and beyond) led to the introduction of next generation data-management engines separating compute from storage. Some popular next-generation engines leverage the Hadoop capabilities using YARN linked to more scalable backend data storage solutions (including BLOBs) that are now appearing in offerings from some public cloud vendors.

BLOBs and other data

Object data stores are also popular for managing other data in IIoT projects, such as captured images, engineering drawings, and other documents.

Compute nodes are sized based on processing demand (CPU type and speed) and in-memory Spark processing needs (memory size). The volume of data transmitted and retention requirements drive storage sizing. By default, data in Hadoop is triple replicated for performance and availability, so replication as well as compression must be considered when sizing storage.

Graph database

Graph or property graph databases feature a node, edge, and properties structure to represent data and the relationships inherent in the data. The graph structures are followed for semantic queries. Nodes represent entities such as people, places, or any trackable item. Edges represent the relationships between the nodes and are the key differentiators for a graph database, enabling the analysis of the connections and interconnections between the nodes, properties, and edges. Properties are additional attributes associated with the nodes.

Graph databases enable analysis of the relationships without the need for expensive join operations. Since IIoT solutions consist of many connected devices with many interaction points, graph databases can be used to understand dependency and perform impact analysis. Today, they might be deployed using highly distributed engines for scalability.

Data warehouses, data marts, and relational databases

Until this century, just about all analysis of data took place in relational databases or offshoots (such as multi-dimensional on-line analytical processing cubes, commonly referred to as MOLAP engines). These engines are the data-management systems under data warehouses and data marts. The data usually fits neatly into rows and columns when these data-management solutions are used.

Tables in relational databases are linked via foreign key relationships. A popular schema for data marts is the star schema consisting of a large fact table surrounded by multiple dimensions or look-up tables. This schema can contain multiple hierarchies and is relatively easy for business analysts to navigate using business intelligence tools. In MOLAP engines, the schema is similar, with tables pre-joined to speed query performance.

Previously, when data was being gathered that didn't align with the relational model, pre-processing of the data was executed to make the data fit into relational databases. In early Industrial Internet applications, this pre-processing often took place in the field on dedicated servers using historians or custom code. As we've just seen, there are now other data-management and analysis solutions for streaming data sources.

That said, there remain solid use cases for data warehouses and data marts and the relational database in a modern architecture. Because data is usually loaded in batch to data warehouses and marts, some latency in data arrival is expected. During this time, complex data transformations can occur between the source extraction and data warehouse loading process (ETL). As noted earlier, a more scalable manner gaining adoption where the data warehouse is also the transformation engine is referred to as ELT. The data transformations are used to rationalize and cleanse data enabling the data warehouse to serve as a historic database of record.

Each row of the data warehouse has a primary index to ensure uniqueness. This index is updated during the load process and can slow updates to the database when compared to the simple append used for Hadoop. However, it can also help speed query response times.

Many relational database engines now offer support for in-memory analysis to further speed queries. Typically, in-memory data is stored in a columnar format, while transactional updates remain row-by-row.

Querying data in a polyglot data management world

An architecture that includes multiple kinds of data-management systems is sometimes referred to as a polyglot infrastructure. Many vendors now offer solutions that query data from a mixture of relational databases, Hadoop clusters, and NoSQL databases. As you might expect, there can be a performance hit, but these tools can provide tremendous agility in analyzing diverse data without first relocating data into a single data-management system.

Most organizations have many relational databases and are familiar with the skills needed to tune and manage them. Skilled relational database individuals are relatively easy to find when compared to the number of people today that are skilled in deploying and managing non-relational engines. Because most organizations already have data warehouses containing data needed to solve problems and the data warehouses provide some unique capabilities, they are likely to continue to exist as key architecture components in IIoT solutions far into the future.

Sizing of relational database platforms can be complex. Among the factors taken into consideration in CPU and memory sizing are query concurrency, query complexity, data volumes retrieved, complexity of the data model, hardware and software assisted optimization present, and in-memory processing requirements. Most organizations fully mirror data, but also apply compression techniques, impacting the amount of storage required.

Supply chain optimization in the batch layer

As we described the speed layer in our supply chain optimization examples, we noted that we will have multiple types of streaming data being gathered. We wish to store this data for historical analysis, including machine learning. Hence, we will include a Hadoop cluster in our architecture, serving as a data lake.

In an earlier chapter, we noted the presence of data warehouse platforms. We will link our data warehouse(s) and data lake to enable queries across both engines and to load tables in our data warehouse after cleansing the raw data.

Business intelligence and machine learning tools will access all the engines in our architecture. We believe that our data scientists will develop predictive models using the data lake.

Summary

This chapter described data and analytics requirements and capabilities and then introduced the Lambda architecture. We then described analytics and machine learning, and various analyst tools that might be utilized.

Next, we revisited early Industrial Internet applications deployed into standalone manufacturing facilities and the role of historians. We also described how some of these capabilities are merging into the Lambda architecture.

Finally, we described the speed and batch layer components in this architecture. We took a deeper look at the components in the speed layer for real-time data processing and described newer trends to push analytics and machine learning to field gateways at the edge. We also described components in the batch layer, including Hadoop serving as a data lake and relational databases for data warehousing.

You now should better understand where each of these components fit and why you might include them in your architecture. In your mind, you are probably considering tradeoffs associated with the various architecture and deployment strategies that are possible. There is never a single right answer, and the choices you make will be driven by technical requirements, but also other considerations such as skills present and cost.

We are now ready to move on to considering what will happen during and after deployment. In the next section of the book, we'll describe deployment and management considerations for Industrial Internet architecture solutions. We will begin with Chapter 7, *Defining Technology Deployment Architecture*, that describes choices you have regarding deployment locations and how those choices will impact how the solution is managed. Then, we'll explore in Chapter 8, *Securing the Industrial Internet*, and complete the next section of the book with Chapter 9, *Governance and Assuring Compliance*, that covers the topic of governance and assuring industry compliance.

7
Defining a Deployment Architecture

You learned about the information domain components that govern the Industrial Internet architecture. We reviewed the data and analytics requirements of standalone manufacturing facilities and the emerging Lambda architecture in Chapter 6, *Defining the Data and Analytics Architecture*. We went over the speed and batch layers based on the business needs and use cases. We introduced Hadoop and the concept of the data lake for decision support.

In this chapter, we will look at the different considerations and trade-offs that are a result of the different deployment architecture and strategies. You will learn to fully appreciate that *architecture is the art of compromise* (https://www.world-architects.com/en/architecture-news/reviews/architecture-of-compromise). The current organization strategy and culture will play an inadvertent part in the deployment architecture for Industrial Internet applications. This chapter will focus on the design of this deployment strategy where the line of business and the CIO organizations may have a healthy friction. A savvy architect needs to understand how to facilitate such debate and discussions between the stakeholders.

Here we will deep-dive into the technology choices and the deployment architecture for Industrial Internet solutions. This chapter will show you the right place to deploy such applications all the way from the edge to the cloud and enterprise systems.

The chapter will covers the following topics:

- Past and current deployment architectures
- On-premises or cloud deployment
- Design for edge tier
- Networking considerations
- Device management
- Management and support infrastructure
- Consumption models

Current state of deployment architectures for IT systems

The architecture of IT systems has gone through several revolutions since early mainframe systems. *Mainframe* systems handled all data-management, computing, or business logic, and were housed in a very large cabinet. Early mainframes performed data processing in batches and could only be accessed by dumb terminal emulators with no intelligence, and dedicated printers. They had limited support for **graphical user interfaces** (**GUIs**) and couldn't access multiple databases from dispersed locations.

With the introduction of the **personal computer** (**PC**), small-to-medium-sized businesses could afford to shift their business functions and data to PCs, where the processing could be controlled by the user. The Early PCs were closed systems limited to a single PC and had limited memory and data storage capabilities, and a PC failure could result in a disastrous loss of data and business processing. Data and computing logic could only be shared via peer-to-peer networking or by making a physical copy of the data to transfer via external storage means, such as floppy disks.

Figure 7.1: Client-server architecture was enabled with the advent of networked PCs and modular programming approaches. With client servers, the database or file server resides in a centralized *server*, and the application logic is distributed to *client* workstations or desktops, while the data can be queried and presented using GUI tools such as **PowerBuilder** and **Forms**. With the business logic and presentation resources aburden on the client, it was often referred to as the *fat client* architecture in which each user of the system would interact using a client with the presentation tools and application logic installed locally. This could present challenges for upgrading software, as the upgrade needed to be coordinated among all the clients and server(s) in the system. Database engines added the ability to offset some of the computing capability with stored procedures, and functions were executed by the database engine, relieving some of the fat-client load.

The defining component of client-server architecture was the network. When the client application issues a query, the request is transmitted from the client to the server by the network. The server executes the request and returns the results or data back to the client via the network. Client-server architecture enabled distributed computing, and distributed databases led to more heterogeneity within a system and increased network and connectivity requirements. It also introduced challenges in managing transactions, especially in multi-user systems, and challenges in ownership (that is, *user* versus *central)* for hardware, network, support, data, applications, and configuration management:

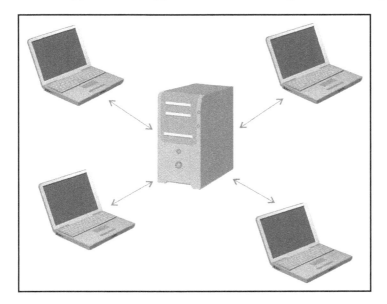

Figure 7.1: Client-server architecture

The internet provides the ability for systems to communicate across Internet-enabled servers and clients (*Figure 7.2: Internet computing*) and supports information flows and processes over the Internet. Rather than a fat client, the user only needs a Web browser to access data and business logic capabilities on an Internet-connected server and database. Middleware applications emerged to manage the communication between operating systems and applications in a distributed computing system in a network. Distributed computing middleware can provide services for human interaction (that is, web requests) and machine interaction, including embedded systems in some industries.

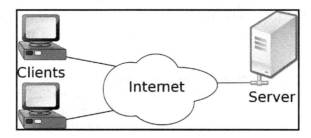

Figure 7.2: Internet Computing

Hosted systems and the cloud

Deploying an enterprise or industrial application can be an expensive endeavor in terms of hardware and software costs, infrastructure, time, hiring and training, and maintenance and risk. On-premise systems require significant investment in time and budget.

The Internet made it possible for users to interact with a system from any Internet-connected device. Hosting services enable all or part of a system to be hosted and accessed from a remote location. Most hosting centers deploy applications in virtual servers using VMware, Oracle VirtualBox, Microsoft Hyper-V, or containers, and can *spin-up* the desired application on-demand. Containers are frequently deployed in hosted systems to deliver the operating system and other services. Container capacity can be scaled automatically, and since containers do not have a hypervisor, they can deliver better performance than virtualization.

Hosted services

Hosted services began as **Application Service Providers** (**ASPs**), which provided business applications in a hosted, managed, and centralized computing model. In the ASP model, the host provided and maintained a separate instance for each organization.

SaaS represents the evolution of the ASP model to a multi-tenant architecture. SaaS licenses software on a subscription basis and is centrally hosted, and is commonly used to provide office applications, database, development software, ERP, CRM, and other software.

PaaS provides a platform for the subscriber to develop and run applications on a hosted platform. PaaS systems can include a database, servers, storage, middleware, network, and other services necessary for application development and deployment.

IaaS supplies infrastructure resources on-demand from a centralized data center managed by the provider. IaaS typically includes the operating system, storage, firewall, IP addresses, and virtual network.

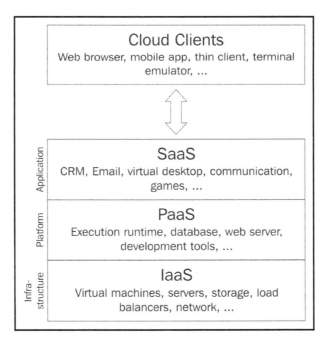

Figure 7.3: Cloud deployment options

Advantages of using hosted services are as follows:

- **Faster roll-out**: The hosting provider already has the infrastructure, servers, and skills in place
- **Low-entry costs**: No need to buy servers, additional network resources, and data center space; no need to hire specialized skills

Disadvantages of hosted services are as follows:

- **Cost**: Long-term costs may exceed on premises costs.
- **Dependence on Internet connections**: If the subscriber loses Internet connectivity or there is a disruption affecting Internet access to the host provider, the system becomes unavailable.
- **Bandwidth**: Depending on the application, a significant amount of bandwidth may be required.
- **Integration**: It can be difficult to integrate hosted software with local applications. Integration of hosted solutions requires that the hosting provider support the entire solution set. There is no integration between hosted services of one vendor to the hosted services of another vendor.
- **Regulatory concerns regarding privacy and data protection**: Many countries and other jurisdictions have strict, and sometimes unique, regulations for protecting privacy and securing data. Some jurisdictions require sensitive data to be stored locally (in the country) and not in a data center in another jurisdiction.

Single-tenant hosting

In single-tenant hosted systems, you buy the software and pay another party to host and maintain it in a hosting center.

Advantages of single-tenant hosting are as follows:

- **Ownership**: Once you purchase the software, you can choose to continue to pay for support, including regular upgrades. You can eventually stop paying for the maintenance, but continue to use your hosted environment with the existing version.
- **Data privacy**: Since there is only one user per instance, the risk of other businesses accessing your data is minimized.
- **Customization**: The system can be customized or the solution can be extended to fit your specific requirements.
- **Flexibility**: You have the option to transfer the application software to your own on-premises environment and discontinue the hosted service.
- **Security**: Application data is stored in a secure data center where the provider manages backups, multi-site redundancy, and infrastructure. You can access it from anywhere.
- **Response**: Your capacity and response time will not be impaired by other users' activities, and you can make full use of the system's resources for intensive jobs.

Disadvantages of single-tenant services are as follows:

- **Costs**: Single-tenant is usually more expensive than multi-tenant solutions

Multi-tenancy

Multi-tenant architecture consists of a single instance of software that is accessed by multiple tenants. Tenants are groups of users (from a subscribing organization) who share access rights and privileges to the software instance. In multi-tenancy, the business logic is shared by many subscribers, but the data privacy is preserved for each tenant. The hosting provider is responsible for ensuring their subscribers can only access their own data and not that of other subscribers.

Advantages of multi-tenancy are as follows:

- **Operational**: Like hosted systems, the provider maintains, updates, and backs up the applications and data
- **Cost savings**: Since many customers share the application logic and storage capacity, there is no need for dedicated servers for each customer

Disadvantages of multi-tenancy are as follows:

- **Scalability**: As many customers share the computing resources, resources may become overloaded.
- **Homogeneity and competitive advantage**: You're relying on the same code base as all the other tenants. Customization capabilities are very limited and confined to some general configuration parameters.
- **Reduced control**: Updates to software may be deployed to your system without authorization. Bug fixes, enhancements, patches, and upgrades by the provider are performed on their schedule and prioritized according to the hosting providers' largest customers.
- **Security**: While hosting providers make every effort to maintain data privacy and security, the sharing of computing and storage resources increases the risk of another user accidentally or purposefully accessing your data compared to single-tenant systems.

Cloud computing

The *cloud* is similar to hosted services, but the cloud uses virtualization for the deployment servers. Available cloud services range from IaaS, database cloud services, big data cloud services, analytic cloud services, IoT cloud service, SaaS, and so on). Analytic cloud services include data preparation, analytics, and visualization capabilities to enable an entire organization to explore and discover intelligence across the enterprise and devices.

Cloud computing's started with grid computing, which employed parallel processing for rapid processing of substantial amounts of data. Later, providers began to follow the utilities paradigm and offered computing resources on a metered basis, followed by subscription-based SaaS offerings. Modern cloud computing enables access to an array of IT resources as a service. Cloud services provide the capability to temporarily acquire or extend resources during periods of high demand and then release those resources when they are no longer needed. Cloud services are frequently used by large organizations for development and testing, while the deployment remains on-premises. The elastic nature of cloud usage billing makes it easy to use what you need and release resources when they are no longer needed.

Advantages of cloud computing are as follows:

- Low entry costs enable short-term development use and there is no need for heavy infrastructure, hardware, and software investment to get started
- Easy to transfer on-premises software to a cloud platform
- Security, redundancy, and scalability are provided by the provider
- Choice to buy or *rent* the software

Disadvantages of cloud computing are as follows:

- Long-term costs could exceed those of on-premises solutions.
- May be difficult to transfer cloud applications and data back to on-premises if needed.
- Integration with other cloud solutions or on-premises can be more difficult. Existing applications may need rework to enable integration.
- Fee structures mean you're paying for data units or the CPU. Usage is not per server on most on-premises software.

Public cloud

Public cloud systems make hosted service available to the public over the Internet and are generally self-service. Public cloud systems are generally not well suited for business and are not designed with privacy and security as high concerns. Photo and music storage services are typical public cloud services.

Private cloud

Private cloud services deliver similar advantages to hosting services and the public cloud, but a private cloud is dedicated to a single organization.

A private cloud machine can be deployed on-premises, within the organization's firewall, but can be managed and maintained by the hosting provider. This option is preferable where regulatory constraints and privacy and security concerns prevent the use of a public cloud, but resources and support to implement an in-house solution are limited.

Hybrid cloud

Hybrid cloud provides the best of both worlds. Hybrid cloud systems connect one or more cloud services to other cloud services or traditional on-premises systems. Hybrid cloud can combine private cloud service for sensitive data and processes and the public cloud for non-sensitive data and processes.

Hybrid cloud implementations have evolved along with cloud service availability:

- **Infrastructure**: Hybrid clouds can be used for connectivity and integration
- **Application**: Cloud services are integrated with traditional on-premises applications
- **API**: Integrates many clouds to on-premises applications
- **Data**: Integrates cloud applications to data-as-a-service cloud

Hybrid cloud provides an attractive option for IIoT systems. An IIoT organization can offload the more generic infrastructure and computing requirements as well as business systems to the cloud and integrate them with specialized on-premises systems. This enables the organization to focus resources towards creating business value and competitive advantage.

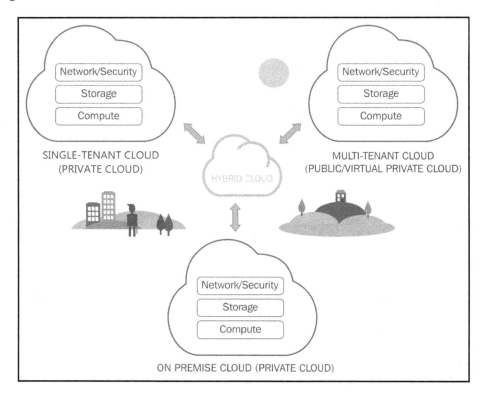

Figure 7.4: Hybrid cloud deployment

Billing

In hosted and cloud systems, the organization or user is billed on a subscription, pay-per-use, or license-fee basis. The provider assumes responsibility for the infrastructure, installations, patches, upgrades, and management of the system, reducing the burden on the subscribing company to provide resources for those functions.

Enterprise Resource Planning (ERP)

Enterprise Resource Planning (**ERP**) application systems manage, control, and plan for many core enterprise business functions, including accounting, finance, procurement, **supply chain management** (**SCM**) and risk management, and often include business intelligence and decision support analytics. Cloud ERP applications enable their subscribers to quickly get started with performing critical ERP functions and can easily be scaled up as their needs grow.

Deployment options for ERP systems have evolved as the available architectural topology evolved, from mainframe to client-server to Internet systems, and now to the cloud as SaaS.

On-premises ERP systems would struggle to consume and manage the copious amounts of data generated by IIoT systems, in which many industrial devices and sensors are generating large data volumes at high velocity. IIoT systems manage and control the production processes and collect data from sensor measurements. Cloud ERP provides a scalable and expandable option to consume IIoT data, such as inventory tracking, via RFID.

ERP data combined with IIoT data can help improve efficiencies in business and industrial processes and help breakdown information silos. IIoT technology can allow close integrating between production and ERP systems, for example, using RFID and other technologies to track supply inventory, optimize the supply chain, and automatically create purchase orders as the inventory is depleted. IIot systems are becoming an integration between ERP, CRM, SCM, and other enterprise applications, and sensor/actuators, and controls, providing a more holistic cross-functional view of the enterprise.

Considerations for SaaS cloud versus on-premises

Considering the following points for implementing the ERP on SaaS cloud versus on-premise:

- **Billing**: With on-premises ERP, you buy the software license and pay for ongoing support. SaaS providers follow a subscription, usually monthly or yearly, or the pricing is based on usage factors such as transaction count, the amount of data, number of users, or other factors.

- **Costs**: Traditional ERP systems entail significant costs upfront. Infrastructure, hardware, software, implementation time, and costs are needed, and personnel with specialized skills may need to be hired. IT staff and end users will need training in the new system.

    Once the system is implemented, the IT staff will still need to apply periodic updates and patches, perform backups, and make payments to the vendor for the ongoing support that needs to continue for as long as you use the software (or decide to forgo vendor support).

    Cloud or SaaS ERP eliminates most of the upfront costs and many of the ongoing costs, as the provider installs, manages, and updates the application and performs backup and recovery services. Long-term, ongoing cloud ERP subscription costs may eventually exceed the short-term savings.

- **Customization**: An organization can subscribe to and use the service, but with a SaaS solution, you sacrifice the ability to make customizations. Some level of customization may be possible, but is usually very limited in SaaS systems, particularly if they follow a multi-tenant architecture, in which the software is shared by multiple subscribers.

- **Maintenance**: No ERP application is static. Bug fixes and periodic updates need to be applied to ensure ongoing reliability, accuracy, relevance, and compliance. Cloud systems are generally updated more frequently than on-premises. Updates can impact customization, which are more likely in an on-premises deployment.

- **Integration**: On-premises ERP systems typically need to have some level of integration with other systems, and in the case of best-of-breed implementations, integration between the components is necessary and will need to be developed by the implementer if the integration or API is not packaged with the application. Cloud ERP systems generally use APIs to facilitate information exchange. Care should be taken that the selected cloud ERP system provides capabilities to integrate with your other systems.

- **Security**: Security is an essential requirement for an ERP system, due to the sensitivity of the data being stored (that is, HR details, customer accounts, and corporate earnings). Most cloud vendors employ encryption to protect the data from breaches and against illicit access by their own employees who have access to the backend database. On-premises ERP has similar concerns that need to be managed by the implementer and IT.

- **Reliability**: As an ERP system plays a critical role in the management and operations of an enterprise, downtime can result in significant losses. In on-premises systems, the network, hardware, and software rely on the in-house or contracted IT staff to ensure the system is always available. Cloud ERP also depends on Internet access to use the application; therefore, businesses in remote locations or with unreliable networks need to carefully consider the impact.
- **Mobile access**: Mobile devices make it possible for users to interact with the ERP system from remote locations to view status, receive alerts and notifications, and submit approvals. Providing mobile access can be problematic for on-premises deployments. As cloud ERP systems are web-based, they usually provide native mobile access.

Customer Relationship Management (CRM)

CRM systems automate and manage the relationship between the organization and its product or service offerings, and current and potential customers.

CRM compiles data from multiple communication channels with the goal of enhancing knowledge about their customers and how to meet their needs and fulfil them. CRM can be characterized into the following components:

- Sales force automation and optimization
- Marketing automation
- Service automation

CRM systems also provide analytic capabilities against customer behavior data and prescribe appropriate marketing responses. Another objective of CRM is the incorporation of external data from suppliers, vendors, and carriers to collect data for technical support and share customer information across the organization.

CRM use in IIoT includes proactive customer care--analyzing sensor and usage data to analyze how customers are using equipment, and when a service or upgrade is needed and proactively offer maintenance. Other applications include digital marketing, customer care, customer loyalty, improving customer and partner engagement, and managing the life cycle of products for the customer.

Advantages of CRM are as follows:

- Improve customer targeting
- Provide integration across sales and marketing channels
- Optimize pricing
- Customize products and services
- Improve customer satisfaction

Disadvantages of CRM are as follows:

- May lead to customer favoritism (CRM paradox)

As in ERP systems, hosted SaaS and cloud-based CRM systems provide similar benefits and risks in terms of low entry costs and off-loading the infrastructure, maintenance, upgradeability, and scalability.

Human Resource Management Systems

A **human resource management systems** (**HRMS**) is an integrated combination of information systems that enable the optimal management of an enterprise's employees and related data. Human resource software consists of storing and managing employee - and workforce - related data:

- Employee self-service
- Payroll processing
- Benefits administration
- Recruitment and hiring
- Attendance
- Performance evaluations
- Skills and talent, training, and certification tracking
- Safety and security

HRMS systems are widely available as SaaS and cloud offerings. Integration with IIoT systems can enable the system to automatically dispatch an engineer with the necessary skills to proactively perform maintenance or repair defects before a failure occurs.

Data warehousing and big data

Relational databases were developed to ensure data integrity, reduce duplication of data and redundant storage, and minimize the disk space requirements for data storage. Most enterprise systems follow **Third Normal Form** (**3NF**) design rules to organize the data into schemas. Normalization is the process of organizing data to eliminate redundancy (data is stored in one place), and define logical data dependencies (storing related data items together).

As relational database-based applications were designed for efficient transaction processing and enforcement of data integrity, performance options such as indices are geared towards supporting high-cardinality queries to retrieve a few specific records or rows. A typical query would return the current accounts receivable for customer A. In a 3NF-based application, optimizational features favor retrieving the status for a single known entity, customer A. Here, the query starts with the customer member, retrieves the unique identifier for customer A, and then searches accounts receivable for the current state of the account.

3NF structures were not efficient for reporting and for analytical requirements across substantial amounts of data, in which the query is more likely to be *Which customers purchased over $1000 in high-end widgets between January 2016 and March 2016, and are included in customer segment early adopters, and have an affinity to the web channel and CNet?* In this query, the transactions must be aggregated, and customers must already be segmented to fulfil the query filters. The preliminary query results of the transactions between January 2016 and March 2016 need to be aggregated to determine which customers spent over $1000 for high-end widgets. Next, the customers are further filtered by the segment *early adopters* and how often they watch CNet compared to other customers.

These analytic requirements required a different type of data structure for efficient performance; these are answered to some extent by data warehousing.

Data warehouse and decision support

Decision Support Systems (**DSS**) and data warehouse technologies were developed to address the reporting and analysis shortcomings of the 3NF schemas employed by enterprise applications. A data warehouse is a subject-oriented integrated copy of data in one or more applications or operational systems. A data warehouse is made up of an ecosystem of several functions with the end goal of maintaining an operational history, and enabling and performing analytics to support decision making. As many enterprises have grown through acquisitions, they may have multiple systems performing the same function at various locations from different vendors. As they are from different vendors, there is no integration between them.

Characteristics of data warehouses are as follows:

- **Data integration**: Data from many sources is integrated
- **Subject oriented**: Data is limited to one or more related subjects and organized accordingly
- **Time variant**: Data warehouses include past historical and current data
- **Nonvolatile**: Data is added, but not altered once stored in the data warehouse

Many data warehouses are used to store only aggregated data (that is, sales by region), but not the raw data, and enable time-series analysis of trends and analysis of correlations between disparate data sets. An operational data store is a type of data warehouse used to store data from an application. This data may be maintained for a short-term analysis, usually a few months, and then purged to make room for newer data, while the KPIs, analytic results, and aggregate data are preserved long term.

Functions of a data warehouse are as follows:

- Integrate, organize, and standardize data for analysis and reporting
- Preserve data and maintain data history
- Analyze and query substantial amounts of data
- Enable decision support

The following figure illustrates the data warehouse architecture:

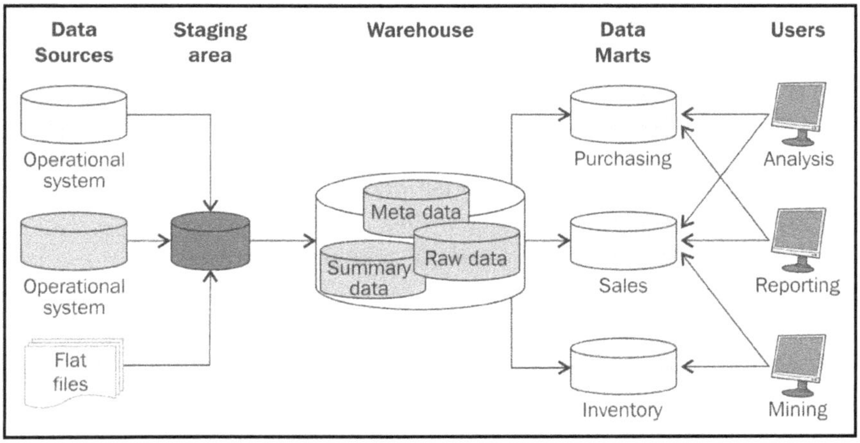

Figure 7.5: Data warehouse architecture

Management considerations for data warehouse

Since a data warehouse is a historical copy of data, the storage requirements will increase over time. In the case of an upgrade of the source system, the data warehouse may need to be updated accordingly.

Some application vendors provide a corresponding integrated data warehouse, but this is not typical. Most data warehouse systems are custom-built.

Advantages of data warehouses are as follows:

- Integrate data from heterogenous sources
- Perform historical analysis over large amounts of data without impacting operational systems
- Enable cross-functional analysis
- Improved data quality
- Converge disparate systems to a common semantic

Disadvantages of data warehouses are as follows:

- Usually require large IT investment to develop and maintain.
- Lag time in loading data from source systems.
- Data ownership, security, and access are important features. Data warehousing integrates data from multiple systems and locations. Many users access the data warehouse to perform analysis. Access rights to the data need to be carefully managed at the row level, and consideration needs to be given to who can access the aggregate data.
- Can require large, and growing, data storage requirements.
- Queries from business intelligence tools are usually ad hoc, which may result in a slow response if the system tuning is not optimal for the query.
- Assumptions must be made as to what data has value for inclusion in the warehouse.
- Data must be transformed to a common, inelastic schema.

Big data

Relational databases generally expect data to conform to defined structures; therefore, unstructured and semi-structured data must be transformed to a predefined schema structure in a relational database or stored as a blob object. High-velocity and high-volume data present additional challenges in mapping each record or packet to its proper place in the database within a short-term time horizon. Queries are also difficult to perform without the benefit of structure and data normalization.

Hadoop file systems

As Internet search engines were emerging, the requirement to provide search capabilities on unstructured, variable, and high-volume data increased dramatically. Unlike enterprise systems, there is little need to enforce referential integrity and perform deduplication or other data management functions on text data, photographs, social networks, and time-series measurements. The **Hadoop file system** (**HDFS**) provides inexpensive storage and search capabilities for highly variable, high-volume, high-velocity, and high-variety data, or the 4 Vs of big data, and provides inexpensive storage for very large volumes of data.

As described in `Chapter 6`, *Defining the Data and Analytics Architecture*, the Hadoop storage platform distributes data across many inexpensive servers, enabling massive data sets to be analyzed in parallel and with a rapid response time. The file system maps data to its location on a cluster, and the data processing occurs on the server near the data, rather than in a centralized server. Hadoop also supports storage of unstructured data and data sets with variable schemas.

Advantages of Hadoop are as follows:

- **Scalability**: Additional nodes are easily added as the system grows.
- **Low cost**: Hadoop can operate on commodity hardware and provide enormous value through analytics.
- **Flexibility**: Hadoop does not require a schema, and enables a wide variety of data types and data sources.
- **Speed**: Query data is mapped, processed (reduced), and then transmitted. Hadoop can quickly process terabytes of data in minutes.
- **Resilience**: Data is duplicated across nodes. A failure in one node does not result in loss of data.

Disadvantages of Hadoop are as follows:

- **Interactive analytics**: Hadoop's design makes highly interactive analytics difficult.
- **Security**: The nature of the Hadoop file system makes securing sensitive data difficult.
- **Risky functions**: Hadoop is built on Java and is vulnerable to exploitation by hackers.
- **Big data only**: Hadoop doesn't perform well on small data sets.
- **No optimization and inefficient execution**: Since there is no cost-based execution plan, Hadoop clusters tend to be larger than a normal database.
- **Limited SQL support**: Basic SQL functions such as *group by* and subqueries are not supported.
- **Expertise**: Hadoop requires specialized expertise, and savvy developers command very high salaries.
- **Open source**: Hadoop is open source software, with inherent problems in quality and security. There are several vendors working to extend and improve on Hadoop's shortcomings in their own versions of Hadoop.
- **Not designed for updates**: HDFS can insert all kinds of data, but there is no update function once it is stored.

Data lakes

A data lake is a repository of data in its natural format and can consist of data of all types, schema, structured, and semi-structured. Its purpose is to serve as a repository for all analyzable data, including raw and transformed structured data from applications and relational systems, semi-structured data such as document collections (for example, email), logs, clickstreams, devices, geolocation trails, social media, and weather using HDFS. Unstructured data such as images, video, and audio can also be included in a data lake. Data can simply be dumped in the data lake with no consideration for integration and transformation.

Data stored in its native format can later be parsed for analysis. It can serve as a staging area for a data warehouse or can be accessed by data scientists to *discover* correlations, connections, or classifications and other intelligence.

The data lake provides a way to explore and analyze data without moving or duplicating it. A data lake makes data collection more efficient for industries, where data of high or unknown value is generated at high velocity.

Data lakes do not enforce a rigid metadata schema as in relational databases or data warehouses. Instead, data is bound to a dynamic schema created during query execution in which users build a custom schema into the query. This technique is called late binding or schema on read, and shifts the schema design from the data warehouse architect, who may not be familiar with the data or its use, to the data scientist or analyst.

Management considerations for data lakes

It's easy to dump data into a data lake without a clear idea of what it will be used for or with the intention of using it later. Without some level of control, you can easily end up with a data swamp in which its difficult to manage or find relevant data, or worse, a data graveyard where data is stored but never used. A data lake needs a centralized index to keep track of data and information, and any different versions of it, and where it came from. It can also be useful to score the information as to how useful or accurate it is, and for which uses and applications and it's suitable how long it will be relevant or useful, with data governance to enforce retention and disposition policies.

Security and access rights also need to be considered, especially once it is aggregated and ownership becomes murky. As underlying Hadoop systems generally have minimal security, an analyst or data scientist with access to one cluster could easily access all the data. Depending on the level of data sensitivity or criticality, a corresponding governance process should be put in place to control authorization, access, and audit.

Some data refinery technologies are available to provide automated transformation to make a governed big data set available on demand for the business analyst.

Advantages of data lakes are as follows:

- Data is stored in its raw form, no integration or transformation or predetermined schema is required, and there is no need to classify data. Any data format and type can be stored and analyzed.
- Silos of data as in application databases and most data warehouses can be avoided. Data can be analyzed across the enterprise by different disciplines in different contexts for a variety of purposes.
- Maintains data provenance, lineage, and ownership.
- No need to make assumptions as to which data has value.
- Data integration requires fewer steps.
- Since the data lake resides on the HDFS, huge volumes of raw data can be stored for future reference.

Disadvantages of data lakes are as follows:

- Risk becoming a data graveyard in which data is dumped but never used
- Data silos and empty sandboxes are still possible without data-management discipline
- Data management techniques need to be employed to keep track of data

Big data analytics and data science

A well-managed and governed data lake can provide new opportunities for analysis and critical decision making. Analytics insights that were not possible or scalable in standard data warehousing or relational systems can be achieved against an integrated data lake using mining, big data analytics, and data science tools. Over time, the analysts and organization's knowledge of the data will improve, enabling even greater insights to be achieved.

Converged infrastructure and engineered systems

Converged infrastructure brings the operating system, server, storage, and network together in a single system. Converged infrastructure can provide a platform to get started in an IIoT project, but you still need to integrate applications and databases into the infrastructure.

Engineered systems offer another opportunity to offload routine and generic system-management tasks. Engineered systems include hardware and software, and provide integrated, tested, and optimized platforms and systems. Engineered systems are available for enterprise and mid-range organizations and include database machines, cloud machines, middleware machines, intelligent storage systems, and big data appliance. Engineered systems can help shorten deployment time and reduce risks, as the arduous work of installation, integration, optimization, and security is provided by the vendor. Integration performance is enhanced with high-speed connections.

Database machines provide a hardware platform with intelligent storage that is integrated with a database to provide extreme performance. Big data appliance or machines provide integrated, optimized big data capabilities.

Engineered cloud systems provide cloud platform servers for on-premises deployment and deliver the flexibility and advantages of cloud services within your data center, but managed by the vendor. Engineered cloud options include databases, big data, and public or private cloud services.

Engineered cluster machines provide database and application platforms along with a secure cloud infrastructure.

Engineered analytics provide hardware and software engineered to support business intelligence and decision making, and advanced visualization.

Advantages of engineered systems are as follows:

- Unify computing strategies across the cloud and data center
- Simplify the IT environment
- Standardized, secure, and scalable platform
- Single-vendor accountability

Deployment considerations

IIoT system architectures need to provide capabilities to connect, store, analyze, automate, visualize, and secure the components and data throughout the system. The connectivity framework provides communications between a myriad of devices and systems. Deployment of the initial system starts with a limited POC and advances incrementally. IIoT system deployment architectures vary according to the system's objectives and topology.

IIoT constraints

IIoT systems encompass a variety of platforms from small devices to enterprise machines, with an even greater variety in terms of environments, memory footprints, CPUs, and programming language across the components and systems, which must be supported by the connectivity framework. Each platform has its own unique constraints for memory, processing, and storage capacity.

Incremental upgrades

In most IIoT systems, components, software, protocols, and so on will need to be upgraded incrementally as newer versions are released and older ones become obsolete. The connectivity framework needs to provide backward and forward compatibility for communications protocols and data structures to enable incremental upgrades.

Sustaining engineering requires the prototyping and testing of upgrades and enhancements. Prototypes and testing need development and test platforms where ongoing patching and upgrades can be developed and tested before deployment. These environments typically need to be included and supported within the connectivity framework and network. The tested component can be provided to the system via the provisioning network. As new components are added to the system, the provisioning framework manages the chain of trust and delivers certificates for authentication.

Virtualized or cloud environments make upgrades easier, as the entire upgraded component can be dropped in rather than installing and configuring upgrades.

Edge devices, network systems, analytics, and other components may necessarily be added, upgraded, or replaced over time. New devices go through an enrollment processes to configure and authenticate themselves to the network. As new components are added to the system, the provisioning framework manages the chain of trust and delivers certificates for authentication

On-premises versus cloud

Connectivity is paramount in IIoT systems for both OT systems and IT systems. The critical nature of IIoT systems also requires reliability and availability. Availability is a key feature or a reliable system.

Hosted or cloud services offer flexibility and can provide temporary or long-term capacity for IT resources. Cloud computing enables PoC development without requiring a large capital and services investment, and without requiring specialized skills to deploy and maintain the service and regardless of how the components are physically connected. Computing platforms, databases, analytic capabilities, business systems, and IOT platforms are available as cloud solutions.

When evaluating and planning an IIoT system, the following criteria should be considered to determine the usefulness of a cloud solution:

- **Scalability and elasticity**: As IIoT architecture can involve many sensors, each generating a potentially substantial number of messages, the solution must be able to accommodate both the initial capacity requirements and the anticipated growth, and be able to scale back when the capacity is no longer required. Cloud solutions provide the elasticity to provision and de-provision resources or capacity as needed. While public clouds tend to have larger capacity, it may not be an option due to regulatory or privacy concerns. Private clouds can provide dedicated resources that can scale as needed.
- **Data bandwidth**: With the large data sets that are generated by the devices in IIoT systems and corresponding rapid response requirements, bandwidth limitations often instruct that the processing be moved to the data rather than data moved to the processing. Cloud systems can abstract the physical location of the data and processing, with continuous, just-in-time optimization.
- **Data sovereignty**: Regulatory requirements may vary from country to country, or governing body. Some jurisdictions, such as the European Union (EU), have stringent privacy regulations, and many countries require that sensitive data must be stored in-country, making the location of the cloud's data center a concern, and the customer must retain control over where the data storage and processing occur.
- **Resilience**: Resilience and fault tolerance are key features of IIoT systems. Critical systems must be fault-tolerant and not reliant on any single component or single point of failure, and must be made resilient. Cloud systems can provide data replication and redundancy.

Networks in IIoT also require resilience and availability. Connectivity must ensure resilience on critical networks.

- **CPU and computation**: Public, private, and hybrid cloud services are highly scalable in terms of computing capacity as well as storage. Big data computing, either on-premises or in cloud, can provide massively parallel processing. Cloud applications can leverage powerful processors to enable real-time in-motion analysis.

- **Data volume**: IIoT data volumes can quickly exceed the capacity of traditional IT systems and analytic capabilities, and traditional systems may not scale to meet performance requirements. Older data that has lost relevance and has already been processed and analyzed can be discarded. Cloud systems provide flexibility to add and remove storage resources as required.

- **Security**: Sensitive data about people, financial data, and operational intelligence requires additional protection and data governance. Private cloud or on-premises data hubs can act as assembly and distribution points. Cloud systems frequently employ tools to monitor and control data access. Hybrid cloud systems allow centralized data maintenance in-house to meet regulatory compliance. Once confidential data has been obfuscated through aggregation and analytics, the summarized data may be distributed to cloud storage.

- **Provisioning**: Cloud systems provide flexible computing and storage capacity, enabling optimized provisioning based on usage criteria. Cloud delivers the elasticity and ability to provision and deprovision resources, computing capacity, and storage on demand.

Consumption models

The most common and simplest pricing model is subscription-based pricing, in which the customer pays for access on a periodic basis or based on the subscription time frame. Most hosted and cloud services provide elastic and scalable provisioning and de-provisioning of capacity used in computing, storage, network, and so on, on an as-needed basis. Billing for cloud services follows similar flexible options, letting the subscriber pay for what they use or consume, thus allowing them to quickly adjust to changing demands for production due to changing customer demands.

Subscription models offer predictability, but it can be difficult to expand their capacity. Consumption pricing makes it easier to expand or contract the digital footprint. These pricing structures are based on what the customer uses or reserves, not what they could have used.

Billing and metering can be computed on the following:

- Compute/CPU usage
- Storage
- Memory
- Bandwidth usage

Chargeback, billing considerations (business operations)

Business units in an IIoT-enabled enterprise are billed internally for their respective cloud usage. This makes each business unit accountable for usage; however, departments rarely see the bill.

Outcome-based pricing models or technology resources-based models

Outcome-based pricing places more constraints on the parties to define in a contract and provide oversight. Outcome-based pricing is based on a negotiated business outcome.

Analytics capacity considerations

One of the benefits of IIoT is being able to benefit from the combined wisdom of IT and OT. Due to the separate nature of these systems, they each need a different approach. IT relies on elasticity to grow or shrink capacity as needed; OT relies on predetermined capacity.

Elasticity is a fundamental feature of cloud computing where the system capacity can adjust to the current workload by provisioning or de-provisioning resources, in much the same way retailers increase staffing during holiday seasons and release them when no longer needed; however, the cloud changes capacity automatically.

Determinism involves a pre-determined capacity to support known or predictable computation and message transmission between devices and corresponding responses. Operational systems are designed for continual processing, regardless of demand or operational status of the surrounding plant and systems. Determinism presupposes that analytics will be performed and transmitted at predetermined time periods and a response will occur within a predetermined time frame for each request.

These approaches to capacity are complementary in many ways. It is appropriate for dedicated resources to provide predictable capacity in an operational system, while just-in-time capacity is more appropriate to cloud computing to adjust to variable capacity requirements and changing service levels. There are signs that manufacturing systems will move towards an on-demand model for services using shared assets to deliver just-in-time parts or products.

Analytics considerations

Most analytics have traditionally been performed in a data warehouse or data mart where data has been consolidated from multiple applications and sources; however, there is a growing trend toward embedding analytics in applications themselves. The primary question in architecture analytics boils down to where the analysis needs to be performed: do they need to be performed at the edge, in a data warehouse, or in a data lake, or somewhere in between? IIoT imposes unique constraints that may impact the architectural requirements for analytics.

Key constraints in analytics architecture design

The following are the key constraints in designing the analytics architecture:

- **Scope**: The scope is defined by the business viewpoint and in turn defines the requirements and constraints for the system. The location of the analytics depends on the business use case and value proposition as determined in the business viewpoint and becomes a question as to where and how the derived analytic results need to be acted upon.

    If the goal is local machine optimization, the analytics should be performed and acted upon locally. They could potentially be performed anywhere else in the system if the derived data and prescriptive results can be supplied to the actuator within the required time horizon. If the analytics are not performed locally, network availability and latency become critical factors. If the goal is to optimize a supply chain across a manufacturing and distribution network, then data from many sources needs to be collected and analyzed. The derived data and any prescribed actions should be published at a higher architectural tier to be consumed by subscribers across the system.

- **Response time and reliability**: If time and reliability are critical to the response, then the analytics must be performed locally. If there is a more generous time horizon, the analytics can be performed after the data collection.

- **Bandwidth**: When large numbers of sensors are generating large amounts of data, it places a burden upon the network and other components to transmit and integrate data. Infrastructure costs need to be balanced against the value of the analytic insights that can be achieved.

- **Capacity**: Although it may be optimal to perform analysis at a particular tier, the tier's capacity constraints, including latency, bandwidth, and computational capacity, may force the selection of another tier to perform the analysis.

- **Security**: The value of collecting and moving raw data should be balanced against the risks of securing the data as it is stored and transmitted. By performing analytics locally within the domain, summary, redacted, and anonymized data can be shared with other domains, while either discarding the raw data or storing it in a hardened database.

- **Volume**: Data generated by an IIoT system needs to be stored for analytics and processing, and possibly longer. The IIoT system must have sufficient capacity for storing the data. Collecting large amounts of high-volume, high-velocity raw data requires a large and expandable storage capacity. Storage costs can be reduced by storing only the derived data and discarding the raw data; archiving older data to cheaper but slower devices can alleviate some costs. Using cloud storage can provide additional costs savings.

- **Velocity**: Industrial systems typically collect measurement in real-time and cyclically. Data-processing speeds need to be able to keep up with high-frequency data collection, such as vibrations in an engine or machine. In the case of transient events data collection, accurate timings and the order of occurrence of the measurements are needed to determine the causality. When there are low-latency requirements on high-velocity data, it is best to perform analytics close to the source of the measurement.

- **Variety**: In some IIoT systems, the problem may not be so much velocity or volume, but variety. This can occur when there are many types of equipment for similar functions, with different interfaces, controls, and data measurements. This situation can occur as equipment is purchased over time or in the event of acquisitions. Reliable analytics depends on the ability to interpret the format (syntax) and the content (semantics).

- **Analytics maturity**: The ability to benefit from analytics results should not be limited to where the analytics are performed. Measurements, information, and results can provide additional value when aligned with data from the broader system, outside events, and business and operational functions.

- **Temporal correlation**: When the analytics requirements involve the correlation of data from multiple devices, sensors, and control states; the correlation is better performed at the lower tier near the data-collection points, rather than trying to perform correlations for analytics in a higher tier.

- **Provenance**: It is often desirable or required to maintain the lineage of data from the source. Once measures are combined in computations in higher architecture layers, it is difficult to maintain the lineage. Performing analytics at or close to the source makes it easier to maintain the data's lineage.

- **Compliance**: Government regulations may impose restrictions that will impact architectural decisions. Regulations pertaining to security, privacy, and so on can prevent large-scale analytics from being performed at a higher architectural tier and in the cloud.

These combined characteristics determine where the analytic capabilities should be deployed. Most systems take a hybrid approach, with both local and centralized analytics. The main factors in determining the location of the analytic capacity include the maximum acceptable network latency and jitter for events, the analytics' criticality to the operation, and the cost of transmitting large amounts of data.

The following table (*industrial analytics location*) lists the considerations for analytics deployment between plant, enterprise (on-premises), and the cloud (hosted):

Criteria	Plant	Enterprise	Cloud
Analysis scope			
Single-site optimization	x	x	x
Multi-site comparison		x	x
Multi-customer bench-marking			x
Results response time			
Control loop	x		
Human decision	x	x	
Planning horizon	x	x	
Connectivity reliability			
Site	x		
Organization	x	x	
Global	x	x	x
Connectivity bandwidth			
Raw data	x		
Processed results	x	x	
Summarized results	x	x	x
Storage and compute capacity			

Server	x	x	x
Multiple servers		x	x
Data center			x
Data security			
Secret	x	x	
Proprietary	x	x	
Shared	x	x	x
Data characteristics			
Volume			x
Velocity	x		
Variety	x	x	x
Analytics maturity			
Descriptive	x	x	x
Predictive	x	x	x
Prescriptive	x	x	x
Event correlation			
Sub-seconds	x		
Seconds	x	x	
Tens of seconds	x	x	x
Data provenance			
Sensor	x		
Assent	x	x	
Site	x	x	x
Regulatory compliance			
Asset	x	x	x
Process		x	x
Industry			x

Design for the edge tier

The edge tier contains intelligent devices and special and general-purpose computers. Sensors that connect to edge computing resources in a network gateway can also be included in the edge tier. Edge computing enables some data management and analysis functions to be performed in the edge tier, in small datasets, using data, applications, and services contained in the edge. By performing small-scale pre-processing and analytics in the edge, where fast decision making is paramount, larger-scale or big data processing in higher tiers becomes easier to manage.

In the case of requirements for real-time and near real-time processing, edge computing comes to our rescue. A simple analogy for edge computing is the fire protection sprinkler oven used in residential and commercial buildings. Let's see how it works.

The actuating assembly is a hermetically sealed frangible glass container with specific amount of fluid. In the event of fire, the heat expands the fluid and breaks the glass at a predetermined temperature. This leads to the actuation of the sprinkler to discharge the water over the fire. This is a good low-tech example of the local or edge processing. However, in addition, the fire-detection system may notify the central monitoring service or the city fire department, the analogous to cloud processing:

Figure 7.6: A fire protection sprinkler

Networking considerations

IIoT systems rely on data-sharing mechanisms between the things, the Internet, and industrial systems, and can encompass a multitude of connectivity technologies and standards. These technologies are often optimized for domain-specific use cases; however. IT networks were intended to support business applications, and to connect client or middleware to server (or server to server to) support business processes spanning organizational units. Networks do not generally embed technologies that generate data for the enterprise. OT networks were largely self-contained environments designed for factory and process automation. Prior to the IoT, the two networks were completely segregated. The challenge in IIoT is to develop a connectivity framework that enables data and communications sharing across the system to connect IT and OT, and realize the potential of IIoT.

IIoT systems require data to be exchanged among many endpoints in the system, with a growing trend toward including IT decision making in the industrial process. Big data analytics against large volumes of data collected across end points would be impractical to perform across the network and drive the requirement to perform analytics first against smaller datasets to reduce load on the network.

A connectivity function is needed to share data within and across functional domains within the system, and it provides interoperable communications among endpoints to enable component integration. It fulfils the functional requirements within each domain and cross-cutting function, and ensures that an endpoint can communicate with other endpoints via a gateway. Trade-offs need to be made between system, data, performance, scalability, availability, deployment, and operational considerations.

The IIoT connectivity stack model consists of the layers and protocols involved in connecting the physical model, or endpoints, to the information layer via a network layer and connectivity layer in which connectivity is a defined as a cross-cutting function.

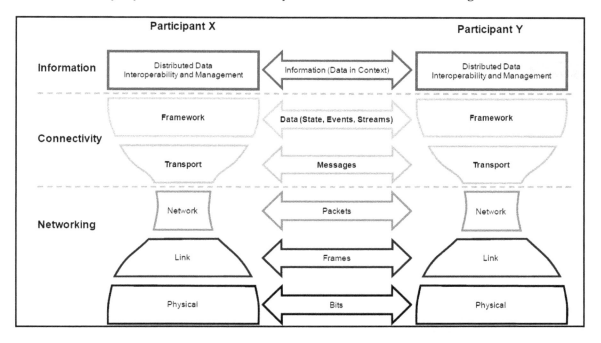

Figure 7.7: Industrial Internet connectivity stack model

Connectivity transport layer

The connectivity transport layer provides *technical interoperability* among the endpoints via a logical transport network. The connectivity transport layer delivers the key functions of endpoint addressing, modes of communication, network topology, connectedness, prioritization, timing and synchronization, and message security:

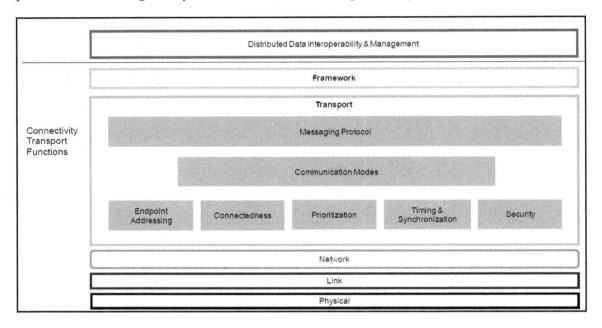

Figure 7.8: Connectivity transport layer

Network layer consideration

As described in Chapter 2, *Architectural Approaches for Success*, IIoT systems generally follow established architectural patterns:

- Three-tier architecture
- Gateway-mediated edge connectivity
- Layered databus

Networks enable data flows between tiers and gateways. The devices in the edge tier are connected by a proximity network. An access network connects the edge to the platform tier. A service network connects the enterprise tier to the platform tier, and potentially to the edge tier via the access network.

Topology

Local network topologies in IIoT systems include the following:

- **Point-to-point**: The network connects only two hosts, or devices, or network nodes, and communication only takes place between the two nodes, or devices, such as a Bluetooth link to a wireless device.
- **Hub-and-spoke**: An edge gateway provides a hub to connect clusters of edge nodes to each other and to the wide area network. This topology can quickly run out of capacity. Upgrading requires shutting down the hub, which in turn brings down the spoke sites.
- **Meshed (peer-to-peer)**: This is like hub-and-spoke, but some edge nodes have routing capability and must capture or transmit data, and serve as relays for other nodes. This topology is well suited for the broad area coverage of low-power, low data rate applications on resource-constrained and geographically distributed devices. Meshed networks are more complex than point-to-point or hub-and-spoke, and have higher network latency.

Advantages of meshed network topology are as follows:

- **Parallel communications**: Data can be transmitted simultaneously from different devices, enabling high-traffic communications
- **Reliability**: Other components are available in the event a component fails
- **Scalability and flexibility**: Changes and additions to the topology can be done without disrupting other nodes

Multiple networks and topologies can by bridged using connectivity gateways. The transport may require or exclude a network topology, but should not restrict it.

Edge connectivity

The following figure explains the different communication technologies that can be used for the edge tier. The X axis is the distance over which the devices need to connect with each other. It could be the sensor or a collection of sensors connecting to the gateway device, such as several temperature sensors in the factory environment connecting to the gateway device. The possible options here are as follows:

- **Wired**: Use of RS-232, commonly called the **serial port**, is one option to connect the sensor pack to the gateway device via a wired connection. This is good for distances in the range of 15 m or 50 ft. To extend this range up to 300 m or 1,000 ft, low-capacitance cables could be used in some cases. RS-485 can be used for distances up to 1,200 m or higher data rates over shorter distances.

- **Wireless**: The sensors could communicate wirelessly to the gateway device using Bluetooth or Wi-Fi. Depending on the power level or class, Bluetooth could be used in the 1-100 m range. Wi-Fi, using protocols such as 802.11a, 802.11b, 802.11g, or 802.11n, would operate typically in the 2.4 GHz to 5 GHz range. The coverage is in the range 50 to 100 m, but provides higher data rates over Bluetooth. Image or video sensing may need higher data rates compared to temperature or pressure sensing:

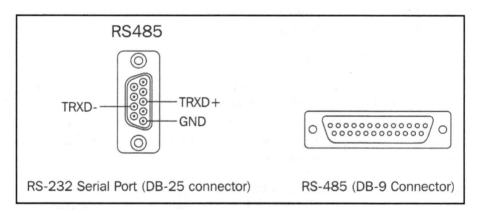

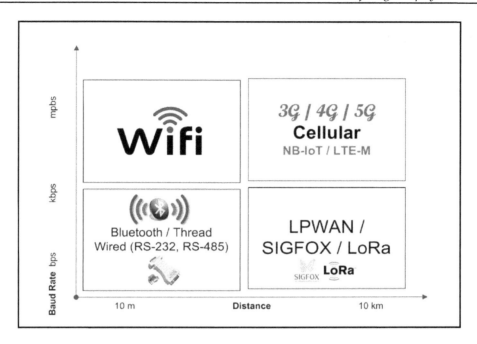

Figure 7.9: Edge communication and connectivity

For Industrial Internet scenarios where the asset is mobile, connectivity technologies from the two boxes on the right are useful, as explained here:

- **Cellular**: Cellular technologies such as 3G and 4G are commonly used, and 5G is being introduced. These services are provided by telecom companies such as AT&T, Verizon, or Vodafone. Typically, the SIM (Subscriber Identity Module) card can be used in the device to provide the connectivity to the cloud, for IoT data. NB-IoT is a low-power technology for Wide Area Network (WAN) and enables a wide range of IoT devices to be connected using cellular telecommunications bands. This is meant for lower cost and for relatively lower bandwidth needs compared to the 4G or 5G technology. Likewise, LTE-M can be a lower-cost, lower-power (longer battery life), and lower-data-rate (about 100 kbits/s) option for connectivity.
- **LPWAN / LoRa / SIGFOX**: These are some of the technologies best suited for longer battery life and connectivity at lower cost but for distances much larger than typically covered by wired or wireless (Wi-Fi or Bluetooth). Some of these standards are still evolving, but greenfield Industrial Internet solutions should look at these technologies for connectivity.

Management and support infrastructure

IIoT systems require life cycle management at all stages of development and deployment. IIoT connectivity and analytics can give rise to new operational efficiency and disruptive business, and in turn, new skill requirements and new complexities. Industrial analytics need a forward-thinking, flexible architectural approach to meet current and future operational and business requirements, and to accommodate emerging technologies and usage changes.

Governance systems manage data and component deployments and versions. Automated provisioning allows the system to grow and shrink on demand. A provisioning framework controls the deployment of new components and ensures they meet the security criteria.

Summary

In this chapter, we discussed deployment location trade-offs and management considerations, and the deployment architectures leading us to the Industrial Internet. We also covered how various cloud services available for use in IIoT systems can be incorporated into the system to provide flexibility, scalability, and resilience, and the billing options available for them. Finally, management of the edge tier and IIoT systems was discussed.

8
Securing the Industrial Internet

One aspect of architecture planning for an IIoT implementation that requires special attention is defining a secure Industrial Internet solution. This topic seems to spring to mind whenever reports of hacking these solutions are prevalent. The downside to not considering protective and proactive security measures and their impact upon the architecture is the potential failure of the entire infrastructure at critical times. The resulting implications can include negative impact to the business, danger to safety, and exposure to ransomware.

The IIC defines IIoT security as simply protecting the Industrial Internet solution from unintended or unauthorized access, change, or destruction. Data and infrastructure confidentiality, integrity, and availability must be maintained to assure trustworthiness of the solution. Proper security can be measured in the reliability, resilience, privacy, and safety provided by the solution.

Designing a secure solution requires taking an holistic view of the devices provided by various manufacturers, device interconnects and networks, and backend infrastructure component providers. Architects, systems integrators, deployment specialists, and solutions operators all play a part in securing the implementation.

Most dangerous tactics meant to compromise the security of Industrial Internet solutions rely on ways of getting around authentication and authorization measures that are put in place and linked to roles. Authentication is the process of proving the validity of a party. Authorization is the permission granted to a party to perform a specific task.

The IIC defines a role as a set of capacities assumed by an entity to participate in the execution of tasks or functions in an IIoT implementation. Roles are assumed by parties that could be humans or automated agents.

One technique sometimes used to bypass authentication is spoofing. Spoofing can trick devices or systems by hiding or faking the identity of a party that would not otherwise be granted access. The bypassing of authorization limits for devices or users to obtain higher privileges can take place through rogue privilege escalation techniques.

Trustworthiness of the solution can also be destroyed in other ways. Data tampering, including its altering, destruction, or removal, can occur when access to devices and systems is gained without proper authorization. This is sometimes accomplished through unauthorized privilege escalation of authenticated users or agents. Unauthorized information disclosure might occur if non-repudiation capabilities are not in place to assure proper authentication of devices and users.

The entire infrastructure can become unavailable because of **Denial of Service (DoS)** attacks. These attacks prevent authorized processes and users from accessing devices and systems by flooding networks with data and/or overloading servers. In a variation called **Distributed Denial of Service (DDoS)** attacks, multiple devices are compromised such that they then work together to flood the networks and overload other components with data.

Understanding potential threats and where they might occur is critical to defining a secure architecture. One must evaluate the devices and sensors, gateways, the data stores, data flows, and external entry points. Proper operational techniques must also be implemented. Taking proactive steps to avoid and mitigate risk is just the first step.

Many security experts now believe that security breaches and compromises are inevitable. So, there is some acceptance of risk. To counter these eventualities, fast detection of threats, including identification of their nature with appropriate responses and recovery, are necessary. Rapid threat detection and response is a focus of public cloud vendors, as we will note later in this chapter.

We will begin the chapter by reviewing fundamental security concepts. Since this book focuses on architecture, we will then explore potential security issues and ways to protect against them from the edge (devices and sensors) to the data center in the next two sections of this chapter. Then, we'll introduce the scope of risk assessments and best practices used to assure security and apply what you have learned to the supply chain example.

In this chapter, we will cover the following topics:

- Examples of cybersecurity attacks
- IIoT security core building blocks
- NIST cybersecurity frameworks
- IIoT security guidelines
- Securing devices and the edge to the cloud gateway

- Securing backend services
- Risk assessments and best security practices
- Planning for security in the supply chain example

When you complete this chapter, you should be able to understand the potential vulnerabilities in the various IIoT architecture components and steps you can take to secure these components and counter the threats that will exist.

Examples of cybersecurity attacks

The introduction of sensors and control systems on factory floors and in other Industrial Internet settings and their networking enabled the collection and analysis of big data, revolutionizing automation techniques and making manufacturing processes smarter. However, the growing frequency of cybersecurity attacks has now led to a growing focus on counter measures.

Today, most studies rank security concerns as a priority in IIoT implementations. This has been true for many years. A Gartner study from this year listed security concerns as the top *Barriers to IoT Success*. In a Morgan Stanley Automation World Survey in 2015, over 40 percent of the manufacturers rated cybersecurity as their top concern in IIoT adoption, outranking the lack of standardization, challenges presented by their legacy installed base, the need for significant upfront investments, lack of skilled workers, data integrity challenges, internal system barriers, liability of current technologies, and social and political concerns.

Given this focus, architects designing IIoT solutions must often deal with questions such as:

- What risk might be introduced by Industrial Internet solutions to the existing systems?
- How can sensitive data be protected during the information technology and operational technology integrations across multiple systems?
- How is data separated across the multiple tenants in public cloud solutions?

For example, in a manufacturing setting, IIoT attackers often try to intrude into SCADA systems. They tend to exploit the software vulnerabilities prevalent in **Human Machine Interfaces** (**HMIs**). Often, a human operator controls a SCADA system through the HMI installed in a network-enabled location. Ideally, the HMI should only be installed on an air-gapped system or isolated on an industrial-grade trusted network. However, in early real-world experience, this was rarely the case.

What is an HMI?

 An HMI enables the human operator and displays data from machines. It accepts commands from a human operator to machines. Via HMI, an operator monitors and responds to the system information. Modern generation HMI may also display the current state of the industrial control using advanced graphics-based visualizations.

The following diagram illustrates a typical HMI for controlling filter operations and showing the status relevant to managing liquid stored in a tank (`http://www.pcmag.com/encyclopedia/term/44300/hmi`):

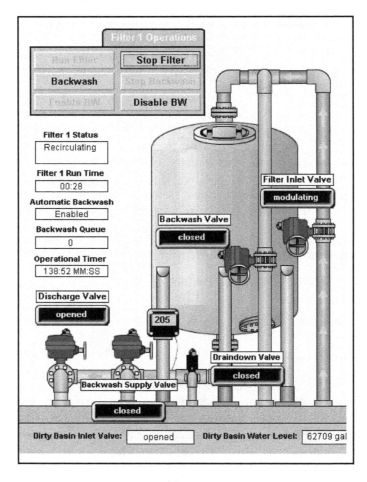

Figure 8.1: HMI for Industrial Operations

To analyze the vulnerabilities of the industrial control systems, we will break down the industrial controls landscape into the following zones:

- **Zone** 0: Sensors and actuators
- **Zone 1: Programmable Logic Controllers (PLCs) and Remote Terminal Unit (RTU)**
- **Zone 2**: SCADA
- **Zone 3: Demilitarized zone (DMZ)**
- **Zone 4**: Corporate network

The internet or intranet are also frequently looked at for vulnerabilities.

Data obtained from the period of February 2013 to April 2016 indicates that 465 of 801 vulnerability disclosures impacted Zone 2. The devices in Zone 2, such as the HMI and engineering workstations, directly control the industrial processes. For example, in the attacks in the Ivano-Frankivsk region of the Western Ukraine on December 23, 2014 inside the Prykarpattyaoblenergo power plant, the attackers used the **BlackEnergy** malware propagated to the Zone 2 HMI to gain access to open and close the switches and actuators. This left about 230,000 residents in dark. The Ukrainian power grid attack impacted business operations and the public.

Computer malware has also been used to target other industrial control systems used in water-treatment facilities, gas pipelines, and related infrastructure facilities. In factory automation, SCADA and PLCs have been targeted.

Stuxnet is a typical form of malware that was first identified in 2010. It consists of three modules:

- **Worm**: This is used to execute the routines related to the main attack payload
- **Link file**: This is used to execute the propagated copies of the worm automatically
- **Rootkit**: This is a component responsible for hiding all malicious files and processes, which makes detecting the presence of Stuxnet harder

Zero-day vulnerabilities are security holes in software that the vendor is unaware of. Stuxnet has exploited such security holes in zero-day attacks before fixes were available or could be applied. It was first identified after being spread via the Microsoft Windows operating system and targeted Siemens industrial control systems. In one spectacular example, Stuxnet was used in an attack on an Iranian uranium-enrichment plant where the PLCs were compromised. Damage to the fast-spinning centrifuges led to them tearing themselves apart.

Malware was behind a DDoS attack in 2016, targeting servers that belonged to a company named Dyn, a provider of **Domain Name System (DNS)** services. The attack created a disruption of legitimate internet and e-commerce activities in the United States, including IIoT transmissions. The attackers targeted the DNS servers to create the disruption. Devices with **Mirai** malware directed massive spurious traffic at the targeted servers. The attackers exploited many internet-connected digital devices, such as surveillance cameras and home routers, to create a botnet. Even though each individual device was not very powerful in compute capacity, together they generated massive amounts of traffic enabling the DDoS attack to succeed.

What is a botnet?

Botnets are networks of connected devices, each running one or more bots. Botnets can be used to orchestrate DDoS attacks or distribute spam and might be controlled by one or many outside sources. Control of the device is typically achieved by infecting it with malware, giving the attacker access. The device might seem to be operating normally even though it is part of a botnet being directed by the attacker.

The **United States Computer Emergency Readiness Team (US CERT)** provided the following recommendations where it was believed that Mirai malware could be present in devices:

- Disconnect the device from the network or internet and reboot. While disconnected from the network and internet, perform a reboot. Since the Mirai malware resides in dynamic memory, the reboot clears the malware from the device.
- Change the default password to a strong password.
- Create a plan to periodically change the password (such as on dates when daylight saving comes into effect).
- Reconnect the device only after a reboot and change of password to prevent reinfection with the Mirai malware.

Obviously, it is better to proactively plan defenses against possible malware infection. The following measures, recommended by US CERT (`https://www.us-cert.gov/ncas/alerts/TA16-288A`) should influence architecture design and policies:

- During installation, replace the default password with a strong password since default usernames and password for common devices can be easily found on the internet via sites such as `http://www.shodan.io`

- IoT devices should be updated with security patches as soon as they are made available
- **Universal Plug and Play** (**UPnP**) features on the routers should be disabled when not needed
- Buy IoT devices from credible manufacturers who have a proven record of secure devices
- Operate Wi-Fi-enabled devices with a secured Wi-Fi router only
- Medical devices that transmit data or can be operated remotely are also at a risk of being infected by malware with possible dangerous outcomes, so best practices from the device manufacturer should be closely followed to secure these devices
- **Internet Protocol** (**IP**) port 2323/TCP and port 23/TCP should be diligently monitored since these are often used for attempts to gain unauthorized control using the Telnet protocol over the IoT devices
- Infected IoT devices often try to spread malware using port 48101, so this port should be monitored for any suspicious traffic

As noted earlier, connected medical devices require special consideration. As early as 2007, when the United States vice president Dick Cheney had his implanted defibrillator replaced, there was debate about whether the wireless feature should be disabled. In the end, the doctor ordered the manufacturer to disable the wireless feature so that an attacker could not possibly send a signal to the defibrillator and shock him into cardiac arrest.

So, how do we create an architecture that can help protect our IIoT solution from attacks? We will begin exploring the core building blocks needed to ensure a secure IIoT architecture and solution in the next section.

IIoT security core building blocks

The IIC has defined a security framework that consists of several overlapping building blocks, including endpoint (edge to cloud) protection, communications and connectivity protection, security monitoring and analysis, and security configuration and management. These are surrounded by a data protection layer that is, in turn, surrounded by a security model and policy layer, as shown in the following diagram:

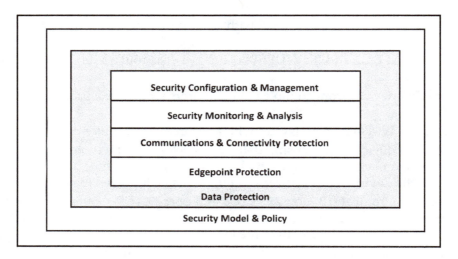

Figure 8.2: Building blocks of security

Protecting your IIoT infrastructure relies on taking the proper steps needed to protect physical components, related software components, and data.

The four core building blocks are defined as follows:

- Endpoint (edge-to-cloud components) protection, including defensive capabilities such as physical security, cyber security, and authoritative security
- Communications and connectivity protection based on authorizations linked to identities required to access components from the edge to the cloud over networks and the authentication and authorization of related data traffic
- Security monitoring and analysis used in capturing data from endpoints and in motion between endpoints, detecting possible security violations or threats and then responding appropriately
- Security configuration and management capabilities used to define system functionality and security changes

Physical component security focuses on providing limited physical access to the devices and the data center (in the cloud or on-premises). These security measures include defined procedures for gaining access and limiting available physical connections to devices and systems.

Endpoint protection and communications and connectivity protection rely heavily on proper authentication. Authentication is the first step in gaining access to a platform.

Endpoints

The IIC uses *endpoints* to describe any smart device, gateway, or computational engine in the IIoT architecture. Each should be secured, including cloud-based or on-premises backend systems.

You are likely very familiar with authentication as a concept as you, no doubt, provide a password when you log into platforms today. Your username and password combination proves that you are who you say you are and should therefore gain access. In a world in which these combinations are sometimes compromised, it is becoming increasingly common for multi-factor authentication to be required. This is usually accomplished by having you verify that you are attempting to log in by acknowledging it through a PIN or other recognition of you from your personal device. The same concepts are applied in IIoT infrastructures, albeit in a bit more complicated model.

Authentication of devices and gateways often relies on the presence of an X.509 certificate issued by a certificate authority. The certificate contains a private key that is matched to a public key shared between devices or gateways. When matches are made, data transmissions are allowed. Given the real-time nature of these transmissions, **pre-shared keys** (**PSKs**) are typically used.

Authentication in the backend services often relies on the presence of a directory of users that is also a source of user access rights and credentials. Commonly used directories include the **Lightweight Directory Access Protocol** (**LDAP**) and Active Directory. Authentication might also rely on more complex schemes such as those offered by **Kerberos**, an authentication method that relies on a service ticket issued by a key distribution center to validate credentials.

Proper authorization is also needed to prevent compromises at endpoints and over communications channels and connectivity locations. Access rights to data-management servers are typically defined for specific roles by data lake and database administrators managing those engines. **Access Control Lists** (**ACLs**) can provide a granular way to manage authorization across the infrastructure.

Data is the lifeblood of the IIoT ecosystem. Data must be protected while it is at rest, in use, and in motion. Methods to protect data include confidentiality controls, integrity controls, access controls, isolation, and replication. Protection of data often includes encoding it to hide its content from unauthorized devices and people. Encryption algorithms are most commonly applied to data prior to its transmission (data in motion) and when it is at rest (in storage). When data is read by valid users and devices, it is unencrypted into plain text.

During architecture design, it is not too early to think about the current security models and policies in place in the organization or mandated by regulatory compliance requirements. The policy defines the security objectives of the architecture. The model provides a formal representation as to how the policies can be enforced. Security policies that need to be addressed include the following:

- Configuration and management policy
- Monitoring and analysis policy
- Communications and connectivity policy
- Endpoint security policy
- Data protection security policy

While the IIC security framework is a suitable place to start, there are other cybersecurity frameworks that also deserve our attention.

NIST cybersecurity frameworks

Understanding the concepts from a variety of cybersecurity frameworks is important for architects since many security and risk-management leaders in IIoT projects embrace them as a means of streamlining their efforts. The President of the United States issued an Executive Order 13636, on February 12, 2013 for *improving critical infrastructure cybersecurity*. Subsequently, the **National Institute of Standards and Technology** (**NIST**) drafted a **Cybersecurity Framework** (https://www.nist.gov/sites/default/files/documents////draft-cybersecurity-framework-v1.11.pdf). The Framework was created via public-private collaboration and is a follow-on to the **Risk Management Framework** (NIST special publication 800-53) that we will describe in Chapter 9, *Governance and Assuring Compliance*. At the time of writing, the new framework is still in draft form.

The goal is to help businesses address and manage cybersecurity risks in a cost-effective way. The Framework has three parts:

- **Framework core**: A set of cybersecurity processes, outcomes, and informative references shared across critical infrastructure sectors to provide detailed guidance for developing individual organizational profiles
- **Framework profile**: Profiles enabling organizations to align cybersecurity activities with specific business requirements, risk tolerances, and resources
- **Framework implementation tiers**: A way for organizations to view and understand the characteristics of their approach to managing cybersecurity risk

The Cybersecurity Framework provides a common taxonomy for organizations to do the following:

- Describe the current state of cybersecurity
- Describe the desired target state for cybersecurity
- Identify and prioritize areas for improvement to develop continuous and repeatable processes around cybersecurity
- Assess progress and maturity toward the target state
- Create a common mode of communication among various internal and external stakeholders about cybersecurity risks

In the next chapter, we will look further at **governance, risk, and compliance (GRC)** and explore maturity models and standards and those that should be embraced. A maturity model can be defined as a set of characteristics, attributes, indicators, or patterns that represent the current capability and progression in a specific field. Models are often used to highlight best practices and reference or incorporate standards in the related field. These models can be used for self-evaluation and descriptive guidance.

IIoT security guidelines

Protecting the IoT, including IIoT deployment, is often seen as being in the national interests of a country. This has led to many of the standards from around the world, which we will describe in the next chapter.

In the United States, the US **Department of Homeland Security (DHS)** (`https://www.dhs.gov/securingtheIoT`) stepped in to also provide guidelines regarding securing the IoT. The DHS defined the seven strategic principles for securing the IoT:

- Incorporate security at the design phase
- Promote security updates and vulnerability management
- Build on recognized security practices
- Prioritize security measures according to potential impact
- Promote transparency across IoT
- Connect carefully and deliberately

The strategic principles from the DHS are targeted toward several roles among security stakeholders. Architects and developers should consider security implications when defining, designing, and developing devices, sensors, services, or any other component of the solution. Device manufacturers should focus on improving the security of their devices. Service providers should adopt secure operating procedures and select secure devices and infrastructure for enabling their services. Finally, the Industrial Internet users in organizations deploying these solutions have a critical role in maintaining security.

The DHS is also actively promoting public-private partnerships to improve security. The DHS Science and Technology Directorate runs a **Silicon Valley Innovation Program** (**SVIP**) and funds companies to promote work involving IoT security (https://www.dhs.gov/science-and-technology/news/2017/02/21/news-release-st-awards-nearly-1m-five-start-ups-phase-2-rd). Innovative technology solutions to security issues are sought as part of this effort.

For example, in early 2017, the DHS funded five different companies, each to address a different area of innovation:

- Improved authentication of devices and data integrity through blockchain
- A distributed data-protection model to solve authentication, detection, and confidentiality challenges of devices
- Creation of a deployable open source and lightweight version of the SPECK cryptographic protocol to be run on devices
- Improved visibility and detection as components connect and disconnect from networks
- A secure wireless gateway for IoT devices conforming to IEEE 802.11 standards

SPECK

SPECK is a software-based lightweight block cipher that is designed to run on small form factor IoT devices with about 256 K or more memory. It is based on publicly released work by **National Security** (**NSA**) in June 2013. SPECK offers performance characteristics that are half the size and yield twice the performance of the comparable AES encryption. The **Machine-to-Machine Intelligence Corporation** (**M2Mi**) was tasked with building the open source version of DHS as this book was being published.

The DHS also hopes to improve situational awareness and security measures for protecting IoT domains related to critical infrastructure (such as airports) through these partnerships. Situational awareness addresses the following three capabilities:

- **DETECT**: This is the ability to know what IoT devices and components are connected to a given network or system
- **AUTHENTICATE**: This is the ability to verify the provenance of IoT components and prevent and detect spoofing
- **UPDATE**: This is the ability to securely maintain and upgrade components

In Germany, a similar partnership has formed between the government and various companies and organizations through formation of Industrie 4.0. It published a point of view on Industrial Internet security (`https://www.plattform-i40.de/I40/Redaktion/EN/Downloads/Publikation/it-security-in-i40.pdf?__blob=publicationFilev=5`) titled *IT Security in Industrie 4.0*. Industrie 4.0 also created a working group on the security of networked systems with a goal of helping resolve *the outstanding issues concerning secure communication and secure identities of value chain partners* (`http://www.plattform-i40.de/I40/Redaktion/EN/Standardartikel/plattform.html;jsessionid=EFC5334B6C9902B04CF6A24303BC01C0#sicher`). In addition, the work group is addressing detection of cyber attacks on industrial production processes and evaluating their business implications. Finally, the work group is looking at the cultural transformation needed for employees in such companies, including additional knowledge and experience required to respond to security issues.

We'll now focus in the next two sections of this chapter on two specific regions of the IIoT architecture that align well with two centers of security expertise found in many organizations today: devices and connectivity from the edge to the cloud gateway and the backend services.

Securing devices and the edge to the cloud gateway

Devices on the edge are typically located some distance from the backend data center and require unique physical, software-related, and data-security precautions. The data the devices gather is sometimes transmitted to other devices or is transmitted directly to cloud gateways or via field gateways onto the cloud.

In the following diagram, the shaded area indicates the components and networks that we will discuss securing in this section of the chapter:

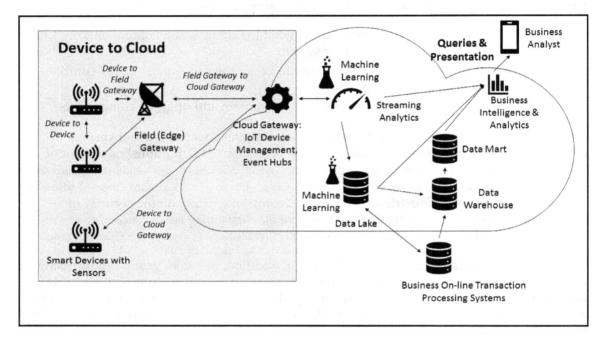

Figure 8.3: Device to cloud security

Connections and routes are established when peering occurs between the devices and the gateways. Secure devices never accept unsolicited network connections. They might be peered directly with cloud gateways or first with field gateways that are then peered with cloud gateways. Transmissions are secured at the transport and application-level protocol layers and authenticated to the services or gateways that they are connected to.

Device considerations

When customized devices and sensors must be considered to provide the necessary metrics, the design phase assumes even more importance in minimizing the possibility of future security breaches. The hardware should be scoped to minimum requirements at access points such as I/O ports and should be made tamper proof. Secure software upgrade procedures for firmware and applications must also be planned.

In many situations, you will be faced with defining security measures around predefined devices that lack the features needed to put into place adequate security measures. In these situations, much of the focus often turns to securing field gateways at the edge to control unauthorized access from the outside world.

Many of the sensors and devices encountered in an Industrial Internet deployment are designed to function with minimal power requirements. These devices are typically networked using the IEEE 802.15.4e specification (instead of 802.3 Ethernet or 802.11 wireless). The IPSO Alliance has defined a protocol stack for these devices, as shown in the following figure:

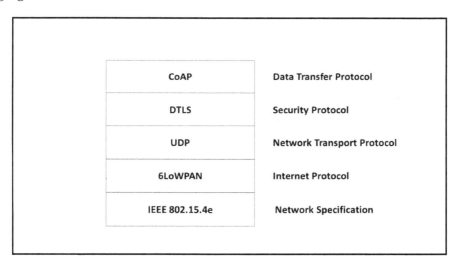

Figure 8.4: IIoT Protocol Stack

In the Industrial Internet, such devices will often use the **Constrained Application Protocol** (**CoAP**) for data transfer, a variation of the HTTP protocol that was defined by the **Internet Engineering Taskforce** (**IETF**). CoAP is promoted as a standard by the **Open Mobile Alliance** (**OMA**) and is intended for usage when resources are constrained, such as for low power transmissions over a **Wireless Sensor Network** (**WSN**). The protocol is designed to easily bridge to standard HTTP-based networks such as the internet and connect to nodes located there.

To assure proper authentication, data integrity, and confidentiality (such as for preventing eavesdropping of messages), the **Datagram Transport Layer Security** (**DTLS**) protocol is used with CoAP and deployed over UDP-based networks and upon low-power wireless personal networks (6LowPAN). The 6LowPAN networks feature a typical range of up to 20 meters in a WSN.

Alternatively, proper authentication, data integrity, and confidentiality can be assured via the IPSec protocols, an IETF standard for deployment over IP networks. IPsec can be deployed over IPv6 upon a 6LowPAN network.

Because of its limited 20 meters range, an alternative to 6LowPAN is sometimes sought for WSNs. The **Bluetooth Low Energy** (**BLE**) protocol can be used by enabling connections with a range of up to 100 meters. BLE is packaged with its own passkey authentication for the pairing of devices and encryption capabilities.

It is sometimes desirable to use a mobile phone to directly access a device to manage it or check its status. While BLE provides one option for doing this, a second option is to use **Near Field Communications** (**NFC**) protocols. NFC protocols enable the mobile phone or mobile device to establish communications only when it is within a few centimeters of the second device, so strong pairing is enforced by distance limitations.

When power is not an obstacle, the traditional internet protocol stack is deployed. This well-known stack is illustrated here:

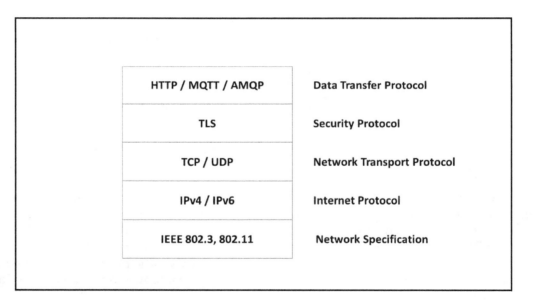

Figure 8.5: IP Stack

Transport Layer Security (**TLS**), the more recent replacement for SSL, enables proper authentication, data integrity, and confidentiality to be maintained. For example, DoS attacks instigated against device-to-device communications networks are typically prevented by implementing TLS using PSKs.

A **trusted platform module** (**TPM**) is recommended for storing keys in on-chip circuitry where possible so that keys can't be disclosed to unauthorized parties. When hardware-based security is not present in the device, a **Hardware Security Module** (**HSM**) might be added, usually as a plug-in USB device or SD card inserted into the device.

IPsec might also be deployed here as an alternative to TLS. Generally, IPsec is preferred to meet site-to-site communications security needs since it can provide full access to a local network.

Data storage provided in the devices can be susceptible to tampering and information disclosure. Data encryption can be applied to prevent this when devices support cryptography. Digital signatures and **access control lists** (**ACLs**) are used for control access and encryption and de-encryption of data. The operating system images are sometimes signed to prevent someone from tampering with them.

Device to gateway connections

Devices might be paired with field gateways at the edge or directly to cloud gateways. Authorization and authentication of devices requires recognition of their identities. Device identities are typically stored behind cloud gateways in IoT hub databases. Indexes of these devices enabling rapid look-up are sometimes maintained in separate locations for enhanced security.

To fight spoofing, device identification and authentication typically uses TLS or IPSec. PSKs are used when devices do not support cryptography. Other directory services might be leveraged for authentication (such as Active Directory). IP filtering can be used to accept or reject specific IP addresses.

Devices commonly use their own pre-existing X.509 certificate to authenticate with gateways. Periodically, a certification authority generates new certificates for the devices and gateways to use. Obviously, keeping authentication keys safe is important in maintaining secure connections.

Careful control of granted authorizations is required to fight unwanted privilege escalation. These are often managed using access control lists associated with the devices.

Application payload data in transit is usually secured separately. The data is transmitted in encrypted form (encoded with Avro or some other means). Transmissions might use secure messaging protocols, referred to as AMQPS, MQTTS, and HTTPS, that are deployed with TLS. The secure messaging protocol implementations protect transmissions with a combination of encryption and security certificates.

Field gateways are sometimes subject to spoofing attempts that falsely represent the gateways as devices. Similar authentication methods to those previously mentioned should be used between the field and cloud gateways and a TPM is suggested for storing certificates. Memory in the device might be encrypted to protect data residing there.

Management of devices is through agents that are installed in the field gateways or on the devices themselves. These often follow standards such as the **OMA lightweight management standard for devices (OMA LW2M2M)** and are intended to work over power-constrained communication wireless networks. Based on a REST approach, OMA LW2M2M defines a resource and data model that is extensible and builds upon CoAP for secure data transfer.

Gateways can also be subject to unauthorized privilege escalation attempts, and the data stored in them and transmitted over networks can be subject to attempts at data eavesdropping and disruption. Access control lists are also used here to eliminate attempts to escalate privileges. Data at rest and in motion and gateway operating systems are often encrypted to maintain security.

Throttling limits in the cloud gateway

 Cloud gateway throttling limits are imposed to help ensure that DoS attacks do not cause critical connections to become unavailable. Typically, limits can be put on identity registry operations, device connections, device-to-cloud sends, cloud-to-device sends, cloud-to-device receives (for devices using HTTP), file upload notifications, device twin reads and updates, job operations, and other parameters in certain IoT hubs.

Architects will sometimes specify that IP-capable devices communicate over the internet directly to cloud gateways, provided they can establish secure communications. Transmission might occur using secure messaging protocols and/or a **virtual private network (VPN)**. The VPN capabilities are sometimes provided by gateways or firewall devices paired in the field with those in the cloud-based or on-premises data center.

Communications might also occur over a private dedicated network between the edge and the data center that many often view as a safer and more secure alternative to transmitting over the internet.

Securing the backend

We will now turn our attention to strategies for securing the backend components. The following diagram indicates the components we will consider, as shown in the shaded area:

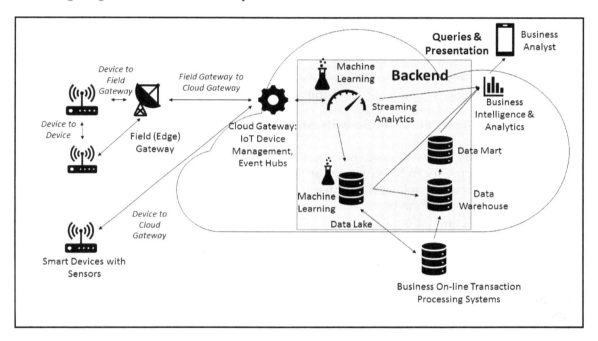

Figure 8.6: Backend Security

The streaming analytics engines provide a location to deploy applications, such as those that apply machine learning algorithms, on transient data. The security mechanisms for streaming analytics engines are less sophisticated today when compared to the data-management systems (such as the data lake, data warehouse, and data mart that are pictured). This is due, in part, to the limited requirements for administrative capabilities, but also due to streaming analytics engines being relatively new.

The primary means for assuring secure streaming analytics is through authentication using methods that can include using Kerberos, LDAP, or Active Directory. Authorization is generally tied to authorized logins for initiating applications. Once the credentials are verified and jobs are initiated on the streaming analytics engine, the credentials for the job typically can't be changed.

For the batch data-management systems, administrators usually manage security. The administrators can have many roles with privileges that must be well-protected, including the following:

- Installation and configuration of the data-management system
- Management of users, groups, and privileges
- Management, monitoring, and securing of data files (including backup and recovery and encryption policies)
- Monitoring of security and auditing
- Performance monitoring and tuning

The ISO/IEC 27001 Security Standard

Though we will describe various certifications and standards related to governance in the next chapter, introducing this standard here is particularly relevant as it mandates how information must be secured under strict management control. The standard describes the implementation, monitoring, and maintenance requirements as well as best practices in documentation, responsibilities, availability, access control, security, auditing, and corrective and preventive measures that should be taken.

Administrators and security specialists must focus on many possible undesirable exposures of the backend infrastructure. Among the areas they typically focus on and monitor are the following:

- Unauthorized SQL injections
- Broken authentication and session management
- Unsecure direct references
- Redirects and forwards that are not validated
- Security misconfiguration
- Sensitive data exposure
- Missing ACLs
- Components with known vulnerabilities

We will now take a deeper look at security considerations for the data-management systems.

Data lake security

The most common platform deployed as a data lake is Hadoop. Early management techniques for the **Hadoop Distributed File System** (**HDFS**) relied on POSIX style access control permissions for file owners, groups, and users. ACLs granted read, write, and execute rights, and these were managed by the operating system (Linux) super user.

Authentication and authorization of users and administrators was greatly improved with the introduction of Kerberos. The client authenticates to an Authentication Server and receives a timestamped **Ticket-Granting Ticket** (**TGT**). Authorization occurs when the client submits the TGT to a **Ticket Granting Server** (**TGS**) and receives a service ticket, enabling access to the server. The authentication server and TGS form what is known as the **Key Distribution Center** in Kerberos. More recently, authentication incorporating LDAP and Active Directory has become possible for some Hadoop distributions and in some deployment models.

As security has matured, so have the management tools that are available in the distributions and in cloud offerings. For example, administrators that use Apache Ambari or similar tools in other distributions and cloud-based offerings can create users, delete users or set them as inactive, change user passwords, and edit user settings. They can control certain privileges for users defined locally in Hadoop or LDAP, including giving others administrative privileges and changing group memberships.

Numerous audit logs are maintained in Hadoop that can be explored to help determine who or what service took specific actions on objects. Logs that might be explored include those created by HDFS, MapReduce, Hive, HBase, Sentry, and Impala.

Administrative users and roles and Hadoop

In addition to a user management role (such as through Ambari), Hadoop requires other administrative users for specific roles. Virtual machines are provisioned by an administrator with root privileges through access to SSH. Domain users can join VMs to a domain and can create service principals and sync Active Directory users. Policies can be set up by Apache Ranger users, and they can delegate administrative tasks to other users. Active Directory users can be privileged (with access to all cluster endpoints) or regular users (with access only to Ranger-managed endpoints).

Cloud-based deployment strategies often rely on disk encryption to encrypt data and the operating system and use DM-Crypt present in Linux. Many distributions also support data encryption managed through the tools that they provide.

Securing other NoSQL databases

As noted in `Chapter 6`, *Defining the Data and Analytics Architecture*, NoSQL databases other than Hadoop are sometimes deployed in an IIoT architecture. For example, the time series data from sensors often resides in NoSQL databases on edge devices and field servers.

Many NoSQL databases are open source and are rapidly changing, so the attack vectors for NoSQL databases are not well mapped out. New attack vectors continue to emerge and can put the NoSQL data stores at risk.

 An attack vector is the route that a hacker uses to get access to a computing resource or sensitive data to orchestrate a malicious outcome. Attack vectors become a means for hackers to exploit both human and technology components vulnerabilities.

Often, NoSQL product vendors recommend use of their products in a "trusted environment" without defining a need for authentication or additional security. An assumption that only trusted devices will have access to NoSQL database TCP ports makes them vulnerable, especially in a highly networked world.

A search using Shodan (`http://www.shodan.io`), the **Sentient Hyper-Optimized Data Access Network (Shodan)** search engine for IoT devices, identifies over 50,000 MongoDB NoSQL databases. Such visibility makes them more susceptible to attack. In January 2017, ransomware attacks caused about 27,000 MongoDB servers to be compromised. The NIST Computer Security Resource Center revealed (`https://nvd.nist.gov/vuln/detail/CVE-2016-3104`) that `mongod` execution files in MongoDB 2.6 were vulnerable when using 2.4-style users. MongoDB 2.4 enabled remote attackers to cause a DoS using the memory consumption and process termination by exploiting an in-memory database representation when authenticating against a non-existent database. Another similar vulnerability was exploited causing a DoS when local users bypassed authentication when using MongoDB on Red Hat Satellite 6 by logging in with an empty password and then deleting the information.

Cassandra is another commonly used NoSQL database considered to be open source. Using the default configuration in Apache Cassandra on Version 1.2, 2.0 and 2.1, remote attackers could execute arbitrary Java code via a **Remote Interface (RMI)** request. This was possible since Apache Cassandra allowed binding of the unauthenticated **Java Management Extensions (JMX)** /RMI interface to all network interfaces.

Although we have noted these two databases, almost any NoSQL database is prone to various kinds of attacks due to their rapid adoption of new features and openness. Frequent and timely application of patches will especially be relevant.

There are dozens of NoSQL databases in addition to Cassandra and MongoDB. Apache HBase appears in Hadoop distributions from vendors such as Cloudera, Hortonworks, and MapR. Other NoSQL vendors that are fairly well known include Amazon DynamoDB, Couchbase, DataStax, MarkLogic, Microsoft Cosmos DB, Neo4j, and Oracle NoSQL Database.

Where Kerberos authentication modules are available for use with NoSQL databases, they should be leveraged. The vendors sometimes offer an Enterprise grade product with higher levels of security. For example, the commercial version of MongoDB, called Enterprise Server, comes with advanced security features that deliver improved security through Kerberos and LDAP authentication and can achieve Red Hat Identity Management Certification. However, proper policies and management are also required, as with any data-management solution, to fully gain the necessary levels of security.

Data warehouse security

Data warehouses and data marts have been deployed on relational database-management systems for decades. They feature extremely mature capabilities for assuring secure access and security of data in the architecture.

Relational databases are provisioned by users with operating system administrative roles. Once provisioned, relational databases are managed through the administrative tools they feature that are accessible to users that who defined administrator roles. Administrators can assign usernames, tie users to groups and roles, and define user privileges. Basic user authentication is through a combination of usernames and passwords with identification management typically through LDAP or Active Directory. Many relational databases also support Kerberos for additional authentication.

Relational databases typically feature audit logs where data containing usernames, session identifiers, physical user device information, schema objects accessed, operations performed or attempted, and data and time of operations are collected. During auditing activities, this data can be used to report privileged user access, data access, account management activities, and failed login attempts.

Administrative users and roles and relational databases

While most relational databases have an all-powerful administrator user and role, in large-scale deployment, various administrative roles might be divided among a team of users to balance their workload but also to enforce security policies in the organization.

Advanced database features can include support for virtual private databases, label security, and data redaction. A virtual private database implementation uses fine-grained access control, and appropriate rows of data are accessible to a user based on their role in an organization (for example, they might have access to details about the customers that they manage, but they will lack such access to other customers). Label security matches appropriate roles to security levels granted (such as top secret, secret, and public). Data redaction obscures certain predefined data items (such as credit card numbers) that are returned in response to a query.

Many relational databases provide **transparent data encryption** (**TDE**) for data in the database and traversing network connections. Some cloud providers also provide encryption of data managed by these engines and the operating system on disk storage via **BitLocker** in Windows and the **DM-Crypt** feature in Linux.

Risk assessments and best security practices

A secure IIoT deployment strategy begins with architecture planning. As a design comes together, an evaluation of the proposed components' capabilities for supporting authentication and authorization capabilities, encryption of data, and configurability of software and firmware should begin. Proposed interfaces, such as those to be provided by the network, edge devices, and gateways, as well as user access, are also evaluated.

As the design nears completion, many choose to perform a risk assessment, identifying potential threats to the planned IIoT implementation and their consequences. Threats can come in many ways including through physical attacks, network attacks, attacks on software, attacks on operators, and attacks on the IIoT supply chain itself. The assessment is used to understand both classic information system risks and the physical consequences of errors and attacks.

The Center for Internet Security, a non-profit organization consisting of over 180 members, defined 20 areas that can provide the foundation of a risk assessment of an IIoT architecture and deployment of the solution. During the architecture definition, the ability of the proposed architecture to provide these capabilities should be evaluated:

- Inventory of authorized and unauthorized devices
- Inventory of authorized and unauthorized software

- Secure configurations for hardware and software on devices, laptops, workstations, and servers
- Continuous vulnerability assessment and remediation
- Malware defenses
- Application software security
- Wireless access control
- Data recovery capability
- Security skills assessment and appropriate training to fill gaps
- Secure configurations for network devices such as firewalls, routers, and switches
- Limitation and control of network ports, protocols, and services
- Controlled use of administrative privileges
- Boundary defense
- Maintenance monitoring and analysis of audit logs
- Controlled access based on the need to know
- Account monitoring and control
- Data protection
- Incident response and management
- Secure network engineering
- Penetration tests and red team exercises

Choosing trusted component builders and providers and trusted systems implementers is essential. Some risks can be mitigated by defining security perimeters around devices and deploying networks and information systems using best practices (or relying on cloud providers to do so). Once IIoT solutions are deployed, trusted systems owners and operators will help assure that security is maintained.

Understanding the best practices that should be put into place after deployment is recommended at an early stage as these can influence the architecture and selection of components. Foundational controls should be placed on hardware and software configurations that are defined.

Once the solution is deployed, vulnerabilities must be assessed continuously and remediated. Certainly, monitoring of audit logs in data-management systems is required. Ensuring software and firmware upgrades are secure while keeping software up-to-date as security patches are released is fundamental. However, as much data is also processed in real time, detection and response to real-time threats is also required.

Detection often focuses on targeting specific signals and monitoring behavior. When problems are detected, automated responses might include blocking and a quarantine of suspicious devices, elevation of access requirements based on identity risks, revoking access to data, blocking risky applications, and wiping untrustworthy device data. Public cloud-based solutions are sometimes chosen for backend deployment because of the advanced machine learning these cloud vendors put in place to detect threats and respond immediately by taking actions such as these.

Once IIoT solutions are implemented, security methods should be tested via simulations to determine where vulnerabilities exist. Some organizations create teams of people who try to defeat the security measures to test the robustness of the solution. Architects and operations planners will sometimes specify that some duplicate devices, networking, and backend components be placed in a development lab and be utilized for testing security vulnerabilities and procedures.

Planning for security in the supply chain example

You will recall from the generic supply chain example and the CEMENTruck Inc. example that data is captured from sensors on equipment in the plants and from vehicles in transit. This data is transmitted to cloud-based backend systems for real-time streaming analytics processing and for batch processing in a data lake and data warehouse infrastructure.

The following diagram represents such a scenario:

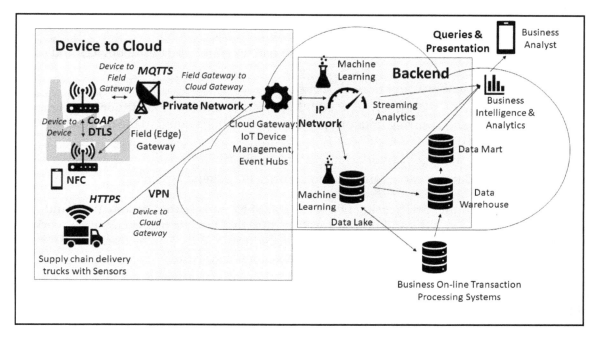

Figure 8.7: IIoT End-to-End Security

To ensure a secure infrastructure, we will need to put in place many of the security measures that we previously discussed in this chapter in the devices and vehicles, across the networks, and in the backend engines. We'll also need to be able to assess the ability of our infrastructure to prevent compromised security proactively and detect and respond to security threats on an ongoing basis.

In the preceding diagram, we noted that device-to-device communications use CoAP and DTLS for secure WSN transmissions. Devices can be monitored by our operations personnel using mobile phones connected via NFC. At our field gateway in the plants, we are converting the protocol for transmission to MQTTS and using a private network to connect to the cloud for data transmissions. From the vehicles, we are transmitting using HTTPS over a VPN connection into the cloud to its virtual networks there.

In completing the design and planning for securing our IIoT architecture in the supply chain example, we would also focus on the following:

- Minimize any device and sensor vulnerability and data loss
- Perform secure firmware and software patching and updates to devices and sensors
- Manage gateway and firewall security
- Assure network resiliency (in addition to authenticating and authorizing data transfer and assuring data privacy through methods noted in the preceding diagram)
- Securely manage network changes and traffic
- Ensure data privacy, validity, and security in backend systems

For example, we might specify using OMA LW2M2M to manage the devices. We could specify larger gateway sizes and procedures to ensure that no data loss occurs if network connections are lost. We could begin to define procedures and tools to be used in the administration of the pictured backend data-management systems.

Summary

The broad footprint of IIoT solutions can make securing these solutions challenging. Security considerations must extend from devices in the field at the edge to the data center and include the networking that ties them together.

In this chapter, we explored cybersecurity, including methods of attack, core building blocks, frameworks and guidelines, securing devices and the edge-to-the-cloud gateways, and securing backend services, and considered the scope that is covered in risk assessments and best security practices. We applied some of these techniques to the supply chain example.

You should now have gained an understanding as to where potential vulnerabilities might occur. You should also better understand how the components that are part of your architecture design can be secured.

Various compliance standards exist around the world that the IIoT architecture must comply with. A proper implementation of solid government practices is important in assuring a secure infrastructure. So, in the next chapter, we will explore a cybersecurity maturity model, governance, and the various compliance standards that might apply to your IIoT solution.

9
Governance and Assuring Compliance

Governance can be broadly defined as putting into place the organizational structures and processes needed to ensure that business and technical strategies and objectives can be achieved. In the previous chapter, we described how to secure the IIoT architecture to mitigate risk associated with cybersecurity threats. Here, we'll describe how architectural planning for governance and risk avoidance in Industrial Internet projects can lead to compliance with worldwide, domestic, and industry regulations. The assessing of governance, risk, and compliance is sometimes referred to as GRC.

We will take a broader view of GRC here beyond standards and certifications. In addition to securing the infrastructure and data, we will also touch on data governance that will help assure data validity and maintain the integrity of the project's goals.

We will begin the chapter by discussing the fundamentals of GRC. We'll then consider some of the international certifications that should be understood. Then, we'll describe data sovereignty considerations and some of the government and public institution compliance regulations. Finally, we'll look at compliance certifications that are unique to specific industries and some of the complexities in determining which guidelines might apply. Then, we'll explore GRC in our supply chain optimization example.

The chapter is divided into the following major sections:

- Assessing governance, risk, and compliance
- International compliance certifications
- International consortia and emerging standards

- Government and public institution compliance
- Industry compliance certifications
- Which guidelines apply
- GRC in the supply chain optimization example

When you complete this chapter, you should understand the fundamentals of GRC. You should also gain an understanding of the scope of compliance requirements that could be relevant for your project.

Assessing governance, risk, and compliance

Governance begins with the establishment of data and security policies in an organization. Many of these policies are likely pre-existing in the organization you are defining a solution for. So, your first step is to understand these policies, as the architecture that you define should provide some consistency in its ability to support the policies already in place.

IIoT projects can also introduce extensions to the architecture that were not previously deployed in the organization (such as those caused by the introduction of new devices and extended networking). These extensions will take a look at the additional standards and policies that will need to be put into place.

What is an SDO?

Standards Development Organizations (SDOs) are organizations whose primary activities are to develop, coordinate, interpret, revise, amend, or otherwise produce technical or operating standards, with the goal of addressing the needs of a group of affected adopters.

SDOs are increasingly playing big roles in the Industrial Internet landscape, building on years of experience. The **American National Standards Institute** (**ANSI**) was founded in 1918 and oversees the creation, announcement, and utilization of thousands of practices and guidelines for many diverse business sectors, including construction equipment, engineering and materials design standards, energy generation and distribution, and agriculture.

While ANSI is based in the United States and formed by American interests, it influences international standards. It is one of several SDOs active in the US. ANSI provides a portal listing many SDOs (`https://www.standardsportal.org/usa_en/resources/sdo.aspx`). In similar fashion, the **International Organization for Standardization** (**ISO**) was created in 1947 to promote industrial and commercial standards worldwide.

Key data governance and cybersecurity roles and responsibilities must be defined, coordinated, and aligned as the project is executed. Most organizations implement their first IIoT project by assessing their current governance capabilities and then develop a strategy for dealing with any anticipated shortcomings. As you plan the architecture, you should be aware of possible impact on the organization and its culture. Ultimately, project success could depend on this. Later in this chapter, you will learn about other industry consortiums that are related to IoT and Industrial Internet.

Data governance

Individuals involved in data governance roles will be responsible for data security, data access control, data rights management, and data resilience. A mixture of a line of business operations and IT specialists is needed to fulfill these roles. The value of data, risk to the project success if no further governance steps are taken, and potential tools for improving data quality are considered.

We previously introduced how ETL / ELT tools and machine learning tools can be used to transform data and improve its quality in `Chapter 6`, *Defining the Data and Analytics Architecture*. An agreed-upon definition as to what data means might be accomplished by populating data catalogs and using enterprise metadata management tools or through **master data management** (**MDM**) solutions that might be defined as part of the project.

Various individuals take part in data governance projects. Data consumers and analysts in the lines of business use data to make decisions and are usually best suited to judge its quality. Because they understand what the data means, some IT organizations push data stewardship, the management of content and metadata, to the consumers and analysts (and they maintain the data catalogs). IT organizations more often take on some data stewardship roles in building ETL / ELT scripts to cleanse data arriving from data producers, defining data management system structure and driving MDM projects. In organizations where data governance is a best practice, everyone who touches data on an ongoing basis becomes a data owner accountable for its quality.

Assessing risk and trustworthiness

Governance activities that secure edge, backend, and networking components and data at rest and in motion are usually the domain of security specialists in IT. Relevant legal and regulatory requirements regarding cybersecurity, including privacy and civil liberties, must be understood, so IT will often partner with company lawyers having a background in securing data in an organization. Many begin by researching standards, such as those published by the **International Society of Automation (ISA)**, **Information Systems Audit and Control Association (ISACA)**'s **Control Objectives for Information and Related Technologies (COBIT)**, the **International Organization for Standardization** and **International Electrotechnical Commission (ISO / IEC)**, and the **National Institute of Standards (NIST)**. As we'll soon see, this is just the beginning. You will likely quickly discover additional compliance requirements that are defined by a host of other standard bodies in your country and/or industry. Your solution should be designed to conform with these standards to mitigate potential risks and meet business objectives.

At this point, you will begin to assess risks to the project. You might find some external legal and regulatory requirements to be quite challenging and compliance difficult to achieve. Your response to these risks will likely depend on the perceived gravity of the risks, the cost associated with eliminating the risks, your ability to transfer risks to a third party, and the potential danger to your data and business. These criteria can help you prioritize the need to mitigate potential risks and initiate corrective action and design changes in your architecture.

NIST Special Publication 800-53 identifies security and privacy controls for United States federal information systems and organizations. By targeting government agencies, NIST guidance and nomenclature often finds its way into other standards, so it serves as a useful place to start our discussion. Much of the content in this NIST publication eventually made its way into ISA standards used in establishing an industrial automation and control system security program (ISA 99.02.01).

NIST suggests a three-tiered approach to risk management, targeting the organization, mission and business processes, and information systems, as pictured in the following diagram:

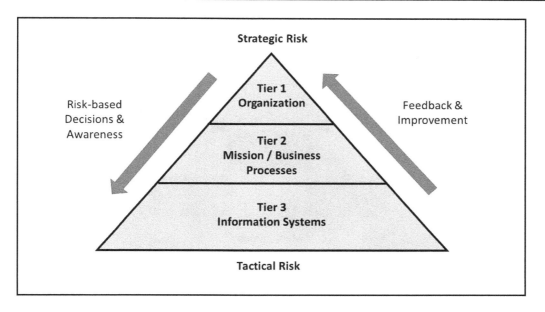

Some of the fundamental tasks and policies recommended to overcome risk include the following:

- Clearly documented security requirements and specifications
- Well-designed and current hardware, firmware, and software
- Sound systems and security principles and practices for integration of components
- Well-documented security practices and training that becomes part of daily routines
- Continuous monitoring of the organization and infrastructure to determine effectiveness of security controls and changes in systems, operations, and compliance
- Ongoing data and infrastructure security planning and life cycle management

NIST defines a **Risk Management Framework (RMF)** that describes the security life cycle in six major steps. We've adapted some of the nomenclature to fit broader Industrial Internet solutions as pictured in the following diagram:

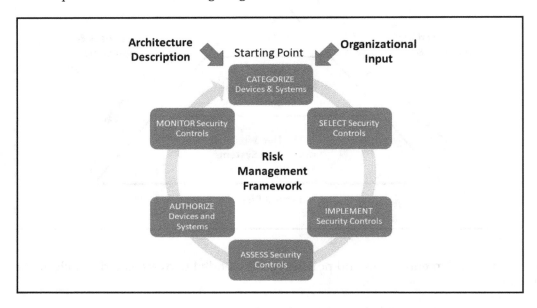

RMF begins with an architecture description and input from the organization regarding potential security risks and considerations. Devices and systems (endpoints) as well as the networking between them are categorized. Security controls are selected for each, implemented, and then assessed for effectiveness. Devices and systems are authorized, and then, the security controls are monitored. As new components are introduced, the process repeats itself.

ISA 99.01.01 provides definitions for **security assurance levels (SALs)** that are relevant to steps along the life cycle. Assurance is an ongoing process and the basis for trusting that policies are implemented. Multiple kinds of SALs are defined. Target SALs are the desired levels of security. Capability SALs are the security levels that can be provided when components are properly configured. Design SALs are planned levels of security. Achieved SALs are the actual level of security provided.

SALs are based on foundational requirements defined in the standard. The following foundational requirements are evaluated for each kind of SAL:

- Access control through identification and authentication
- Use control through specified privileges

- Data integrity (data protected against unauthorized manipulation)
- Data confidentiality (data protected against eavesdropping or exposure)
- Restricted data flow (flow eliminated beyond acceptable zones or conduits)
- Timely response to an event (including real-time response to attacks)
- Resource availability, preventing DoS attacks

SALs are evaluated for each zone of the IIoT architecture solution. Zones are defined in ISA documents as the industrial network (consisting of edge devices in field locations such as plants and local networks), the industrial/enterprise DMZ (the edge to backend network), and the enterprise network (backend systems and networking residing in a data center in the cloud or on-premises).

SALs help us determine the trustworthiness of the IIoT solution. The degree by which the solution is deemed trustworthy is determined by the confidence in preserving the confidentiality, integrity, and availability of data that is being processed, stored, or transmitted by the systems and devices when facing a range of threats. A trustworthy solution can operate within defined risk tolerances and deliver desired business solutions despite the environmental disruptions, human errors, structural failures, and attacks that might be expected.

Next, we'll explore standards and compliance requirements. We will begin by describing international compliance certifications that many of these solutions must meet.

International compliance certifications

ISA standards often eventually become part of the IEC standards and extend interpretations of existing IEC standards. For example, the previously mentioned ISA 99.0.1 standards became IEC 62443 for industrial network and system security. This standard's pedigree includes earlier defined ISO / IEC 27000 series standards.

IEC 62443 addresses securing external network communications paths into device networks, including the control network interconnect, interactive remote access to the control network, inter-control center access to the shared control net, standalone embedded devices, portable engineering computers and devices, and portable storage medium. It also addresses securing internal network communications paths within device networks for inter-area communications, control center networks within a single control area, and field control networks within a single control area. Finally, it addresses securing devices within their networks, including the control network host and field device.

It joins a host of other standards created by ISO/IEC, including ISO 27001, 27002, 27003, 27017, 27018, and 22301 that we'll describe here. Each has applicability in an IIoT architecture.

ISO 27001 defines the requirements for *establishing, implementing, maintaining, and continuously improving an Information Security Management System (ISMS)*. Adherence to the standard requires that an organization systematically examines security risks, including threats, vulnerabilities, and impacts. Architecture design and implementation must include a suite of information security controls or handle risk in other ways (such as a documented means of risk transfer or avoidance). The controls must be managed on an ongoing basis to ensure security.

The standard focuses on the controls in the following areas:

- Information security policies
- Organization of information security
- Human resource security
- Asset management
- Access control
- Cryptography
- Physical and environmental security
- Operations security
- Communications security
- System acquisition, development, and maintenance
- Supplier relationships
- Information security incident management
- Information security aspects of business continuity management
- Compliance with internal requirements (policies) and external requirements (laws)

The standard evolved over time, initially focusing primarily on planning and execution with later focus on measuring and evaluating how well the ISMS is performing. This guidance further evolved to address the impact of cloud computing. As noted in earlier chapters, the cloud is commonly used today in deployment of IIoT backend components.

ISO / IEC 27002 is an advisory standard that aligns to the same controls covered in ISO / IEC 27001 and describes the best practices for each. ISO/IEC 27003 provides additional guidance for these same controls with the goal of making the management systems consistent in structure and form, especially for ISMS certification purposes.

ISO/IEC 27017 provides further guidelines for information security services in cloud deployment related to provisioning and usage. ISO/IEC 27018 focuses on protection of **Personally Identifiable Information** (**PII**) in the cloud.

ISO/IEC 22301 provides standards for assuring business continuity so that the IIoT solution will continue to operate in some form and/or return to normal as quickly as possible when a disruptive incident occurs. This standard defines the role of a **Business Continuity Management System** (**BCMS**). Business continuity goals can be achieved by the following:

- Defining scope based on the organization's needs
- Gaining proper leadership and resources
- Identifying risks and setting clear objectives and criteria for success
- Ensuring that individuals with proper skills and communications channels are available when incidents occur
- Performing business impact analyses and risk assessments to take a balanced approach to proper planning and performing exercises and tests to prove objectives can be met
- Evaluating and auditing performance
- Defining actions to improve BCMS

As we've just seen, many of these standards form a basis for performing detailed assessments. The Cloud Security Alliance, a coalition of companies and stakeholders, teamed with the British Standards Institution in 2013 to create a Security, Trust & Assurance Registry, known as CSA STAR. CSA STAR is used in publishing these GRC self-assessments. It includes a **Cloud Controls Matrix** (**CCM**), a framework covering security principles in 16 domains, and a **Consensus Assessments Initiative Questionnaire** (**CAIQ**) used to assess compliance with GRC best practices. The 16 domains covered are as follows:

- Application and interface security
- Audit assurance and compliance
- Business continuity management and operational resilience
- Change control and configuration management
- Data security and information life cycle management
- Data center security
- Encryption and key management
- Governance and risk management
- Human resources
- Identity and access management
- Infrastructure and virtualization security

- Interoperability and portability virtualization
- Mobile security
- Security incident management
- Information security across the information supply chain (third party)
- Threat and vulnerability management

Many Industrial Internet solutions can impact the financial results of an organization once they are deployed. You will recall that we discussed financial justification for a project in the supply chain optimization example covered in the earlier chapters of this book. The **System and Organization Controls** (**SOC**) provides a suite of services that CPAs can use to audit these deployments and determine their service level controls.

SOC 1 is based on the **Statement on Standards for Attestation Engagements** (**SSAE 16**) and the **International Standards for Assurance Engagements** number 3402 (**ISAE 3402**). These provide the basis for performing audits of **cloud service providers'** (**CSPs'**) internal controls affecting financial reporting.

SOC 2 audits determine how well the CSP follows the AICPA Trust Service Principles and Criteria (AT Section 101). SOC 3 is an abbreviated version of SOC 2.

Finally, a broader standard mandated in many organizations is ISO 9001. The certification can apply to many aspects of the business, including the deployment and management of IIoT solutions. This standard is based on quality management principles, including a strong customer focus, leadership by top management establishing unity of purpose, a process approach to optimizing performance and managing risk, and continual improvement.

International consortia and emerging standards

As you saw in the previous chapter, there are multiple consortia defining many aspects of IIoT today, especially in newer areas such as how IIoT devices communicate and are discovered. At the time of writing, there were still consortia being formed or realigning and/or changing names.

For example, the **Open Interconnect Consortium** (**OIC**) had become the **Open Connectivity Foundation** (**OCF**) and grown to over 300 members. OCF members were developing a specification, an open reference implementation (IoTivity), and a certification program.

The **Object Management Group** (**OMG**) efforts extended to several areas relevant for IIoT projects. Standards were proposed for the **Data Distribution Service** (**DDS**), Threat Modeling, a **Structured Assurance Case Metamodel** (**SACM**), a **Unified Component Model** (**UCM**) for distributed real-time and embedded systems, automated quality characteristic measures, and the **Interactive Flow Modeling Language** (**IFML**).

We introduced the IIC earlier in this book and referenced its documentation in many places. The IIC has liaison agreements with several SDOs and government organizations such as Industrie 4.0, NIST and other non-profit organizations establishing standards and guidelines from various countries. Among the documents are the following ones:

- **Industrial Internet Reference Architecture** (**IIRA**)
- **Industrial Internet Security Framework** (**IISF**)
- **Industrial Internet Connectivity Framework** (**IICF**)
- **Business Strategy and Innovation Framework** (**BSIF**)
- **Industrial Internet Vocabulary Technical Report** (**IIVTR**)

These publications provide common terminology or vocabulary, best practices, and frameworks in multiple areas, including governance. IIC's IICF document describes the requirements of core connectivity technology for IIoT to be an open standard with strong independent, international governance from bodies such as IEEE, IETF, OASIS, OMG, or W3C. The BSIF document states that governance of elements from both the IT and OT sides of the enterprise should support the following:

- Optimization of operational objectives and data
- Overall business strategy and market objectives and data
- Specific objectives for **lines of businesses** (**LOBs**) within the company
- Existing and developing standards for OT, IT, and IIoT within the company
- IIoT strategy and objectives
- Any internal program development

Such an integrated approach to governance requires a unified view of the enterprise to ensure that data and insight are used to benefit the entire enterprise end to end. This implies that governance efforts should include representatives from the LOB and both the IT and OT sides. Being able to use a common vocabulary is required in such initiatives. This is where the IIVTR comes in handy.

One of the challenges of defining an IIoT architecture is selecting among still maturing standards that begin to show momentum through wide adoption. The ISO/IEC formed a working group (ISO/IEC/JTC 1/WG 10) to create an **Internet of Things Reference Architecture** (**IoT RA**). The working group was working with other ISO/IEC working groups and consortia (when this book was published) that will eventually establish a new international standard and set of guidelines, ISO/IEC 30141. Among the proposed standard's goals are the following ones:

- Describing the characteristics and aspects of IoT systems
- Defining IoT domains
- Describing the IoT RA
- Describing interoperability of IoT entities

Government and public institution compliance

Data sovereignty means data that is gathered, transmitted, and stored in edge, networks, and backend components is subject to the laws of the country in which it is located. Many countries have established specific compliance standards and certification processes, especially relevant for government agencies and for the backend components present in their IIoT architecture. These standards also make their way into the private sector in these countries. Many of these requirements are based on the international standards we just described.

There is no single United Nations resolution, European Union mandate, or international trade agreement to dictate one blanket set of data sovereignty requirements for all stakeholders and nations to follow (The EU's General Data Protection Regulation, GDPR, focuses on protecting personal data). So, laws covering data privacy and data hosting often differ by country and states. As companies adopt more cloud-based services for IIoT solutions, the location where the data *lives* is significant.

Germany and China require that nationals of those countries run the data centers. International **cloud service providers** (**CSPs**), such as AWS and Microsoft Azure, have local companies managing those data centers. In other countries, certain kinds of data can't be hosted out of the country. For example, Canada has strict rules regarding financial information.

In addition to specific requirements in many countries outside of the United States, the US. government has established an extensive set of standards within specific agencies. These are often replicated worldwide in other similar government agencies. We will describe a representative list of many of these standards and requirements in this section of the chapter.

As with international standards, these standards and certifications are periodically updated, and new standards continue to be introduced. So, you should use these lists to familiarize yourself with some of the concepts, but explore the details of applicable standards and certifications required in your country and your organization at the time you begin your project.

Non-U.S. government standards and certifications

Here are some of the standards and certifications that have been adopted outside of the United States in various countries around the world:

- **Argentina**: The **Argentina Personal Data Protection Act** (**APDA**) was put in place to protect personal data to ensure privacy of individuals and provide them with a right of access to their data that has been gathered.
- **Australia**: The **Australian Signals Directorate** (**ASD**) identifies cloud services that have successfully been certified in the **Information Security Registered Assessors Program** (**IRAP**) and provides a **Certified Cloud Services List** (**CCSL**) primarily used by government agencies in Australia and New Zealand. The scope of the certification includes communications and information systems.
- **Canada**: Canadian privacy laws cover the safeguarding of personal data gathered and the rights of citizens to access the data. Relevant laws include the Privacy Act, **Personal Information Protection and Electronic Documents Act** (**PIPEDA**), Alberta **Personal Information Protection Act** (**PIPA**), and **British Columbia Freedom of Information and Protection of Privacy Act** (**BC FIPPA**).
- **China**: The **Trusted Cloud Service Certification** (**TRUCS**) is a cloud service quality-evaluation system organized by the Trusted Cloud Service working group of the **Data Center Alliance** (**DCA**) under the guidance of the **Ministry of Industry and Information Technology** (**MIIT**). The **Ministry of Public Security** (**MPS**) authorizes organizations to evaluate cloud services for information system classified security protection (known as DJCP) according to classification guides (GBT 22240-2008, GBT 22239-2008).

- **European Union**: EU Model Clauses are contractual clauses that cloud providers must offer that are consistent with personal data-protection laws regarding the transfer of data outside of the EU.

- **Germany**: The Federal Office for Information Security (BSI) mandates usage of the IT-Grundschutz methodology (BSI Standards 100-1 and 100-2 consistent with ISO 27001), a risk analysis method (BSI Standard 100-3), and the IT-Grundschutz Catalogs that describe threats and safeguards.

- **India**: The Government of India **Ministry of Electronics and Information Technology (MeitY)** defines accreditation for IT-related policies and guidelines, including cloud services. These guidelines must be followed by government agencies and are often adopted in the private sector in India.

- **Japan**: The **Cloud Security Mark (CS Mark)** is accredited by the **Japan Information Security Audit Association (JAS)** and is based on ISO/IEC 27107 and ISO/IEC 27002 for cloud services. An audit is performed on over 1500 controls, including data and physical facility security, human resources, business continuity, disaster recovery, and incident management.

- **Netherlands**: Agencies operating in the government sector must comply with the **Baseline Informatiebeveiliging Rijksdienst (BIR)** 2012 standard. The standard is based on ISO / IEC 27001 and 27002 and includes definition of a **Privacy Impact Assessment (PIA)**.

- **New Zealand**: The office of the New Zealand **Government Chief Information Officer (GCIO)** created a Cloud Computing and Risk Assurance Framework and Requirements for Cloud Computing document used by government agencies. The *Cloud Computing: Information Security and Privacy Considerations* document includes a questionnaire focused on data sovereignty, privacy, security, governance, confidentiality, data integrity, availability, and incident response and management.

- **Singapore**: The **Information Technology Standards Committee (ITSC)** of Singapore's **Infocomm Development Authority (IDA)** directed preparation of the **Multi-Tier Cloud Security (MTCS)** Standard. Based on ISO/IEC 27001 and other standards, MTCS includes 535 controls used in audits to evaluate basic security (Level 1), more stringent governance and tenancy controls (Level 2), and reliability and resiliency (Level 3).

- **Spain**: The **Esquema Nacional de Seguridad (ENS)** High Level Security Measures were designed to ensure access, integrity, availability, authenticity, confidentiality, traceability, and preservation of data and services as governed by Royal Decree. Government agencies (and their technology providers) must achieve accreditation through audits that utilize the ENS framework.

- **United Kingdom**: The G-Cloud is intended for utilization in UK government technology initiatives and is based on a series of framework agreements with cloud service providers. Self-attestation of compliance by the CSPs to 14 CSPs is typically followed by verification performed by the **Government Digital Service** (**GDS**). Three levels of security can be classified from attaining compliance: OFFICIAL, SECRET, and TOP SECRET.

U.S. government standards

The following are some of the standards that have been adopted by U.S. government agencies:

- **Criminal Justice Information Services** (**CJIS**): The CJIS Security Policy defined by the **Federal Bureau of Investigation** (**FBI**) defines 13 areas that private contractors, such as cloud service providers, must evaluate to determine consistency with CJIS requirements. They correspond closely to NIST 800-53, which is also the basis of FedRAMP.

- **Department of Defense** (**DoD**): The **Defense Information Systems Agency** (**DISA**) provides information infrastructure and communications support in a secure and resilient manner for organizations playing a role in the defense of the United States. DISA developed the DoD cloud computing **Security Requirements Guide** (**SRG**) that defines baseline requirements for CSPs and the DoD's usage of cloud services. It maps to the DoD Risk Management Framework and NIST 800-37/53.

- **Federal Risk and Authorization Management Program** (**FedRAMP**): The **Office of Management and Budget** (**OMB**) requires all executive federal agencies to validate the security of cloud services using FedRAMP. Other agencies have adopted it as well. FedRAMP provides a standardized approach for assessing, monitoring, and authorizing cloud computing services and their compliance with NIST 800-53 under the **Federal Information Security Act** (**FISMA**). Cloud service providers can earn a **Provisional Authority to Operate** (**P-ATO**) from the **Joint Authorization Board** (**JAB**), receive an **Authority to Operate** (**ATO**) from a federal agency, or develop a package that meets program requirements. A technical review by the FedRAMP **Program Management Office** (**PMO**) and an assessment by an independent third-party organization that is accredited by the program is required.

- **Family Educational Rights and Privacy Act (FERPA)**: FERPA is a federal law that protects the privacy of the education records of students, including personally identifiable and directory information, against unauthorized disclosures. It applies to any institution receiving funding from the U.S. Department of Education.

- **Federal Information Processing Standard (FIPS)**: The FIPS Publication 140-2 is a U.S. government standard that defines minimum security requirements for cryptographic modules in products and systems used in federal agencies. Testing against the standard is achieved through the Cryptographic Module Validation Program, a joint effort between NIST and the Communications Security Establishment of Canada. Cryptographic modules must each have their own precise specifications of the security rules they will operate under and employ approved cryptographic algorithms, cryptographic key management, and authentication techniques.

- **Internal Revenue Service (IRS)**: IRS 1075 is a publication that provides guidance to government agencies that access **Federal Tax Information (FTI)** to ensure the confidentiality of that information. IRS 1075 describes security and privacy controls required for applications, platforms, and datacenter services.

- **International Traffic in Arms (ITAR)**: The **Directorate for Defense Trade Controls (DDTC)** manages entities governed under this program (and other U.S. Department of State programs related to the temporary import of defense articles, including technical data). Cloud service providers design services to meet ITAR requirements and obligations.

- **National Institute of Standards (NIST)**: As we've just observed, NIST SP 800-53 provides a baseline standard for many of the other U.S. government compliance requirements. We described it in the first section of this chapter. In addition, NIST SP 800-171 describes protecting controlled unclassified information in non-federal information systems and organizations and addresses access control, awareness and training, audit and accountability, configuration management, identification and authentication, incident response, maintenance, media protection, personnel security, physical protection, risk assessment, security assessment, system and communication protection, and system and information integrity.

- **Voluntary Product Accessibility Template (VPAT)**: Government agencies must consider the accessibility of IT to disabled employees and the public when they purchase or deploy it. VPAT is a standardized form developed by the Information Technology Industry Council (ITIC) that is used to document whether the technology meets Section 508 regulations.

CSPs and Unique Government Requirements

CSPs often face unique requirements when working with government agencies as illustrated by these special standards. While CSPs such as Amazon Web Services, Microsoft Azure, and others have created fenced-off areas within commercially available data centers to deal with some of these standards, dedicated government data centers were required for some federal clients, and unique cloud regions were created to service these needs by AWS and Microsoft.

Industry compliance certifications

In addition to the standards and compliance types we have outlined previously, some industry-oriented standards and certifications exist. In this section, we will focus on biomedical and healthcare rules and certifications along with those present in the financial community.

Biomedical devices are frequently deployed as part of IIoT footprints. Device makers that seek certification from the US **Food and Drug Administration** (**FDA**) must demonstrate adherence to FDA standards. The **Code of Federal Regulations** (**CFR**) Title 21, part 11 sets the rules for technology systems that manage data used by organizations under FDA oversight, including the devices and systems that govern **GxP** processes such as the following ones:

- **Good Laboratory Practices** (**GLP**)
- **Good Clinical Practices** (**GCP**)
- **Good Manufacturing Practices** (**GMP**)

The best practices defined in this CFR include the following:

- Standard operating procedures and controls that support electronic records and signatures
- Computer system security, data audit trails, and signature authentication
- Documentation that demonstrates validation that the device works as designed (or redesigned) and that any anomalies can be detected

The gathering of **personal health information (PHI)** data, such as data gathered from devices and accessible by doctors, hospitals, and health insurers, falls under the **Health Insurance Portability and Accountability Act (HIPAA)** in the United States. This law covers the following:

- Data privacy
- Data security (physical access and access via technology)
- Data identifiers indicating whether research data can be released
- Codes for electronic transmission of data

Enactment of the **Health Information Technology for Economic and Clinical Health (HITECH)** Act extended HIPAA and covers the following:

- The rights of individuals to keep their PHI data private
- Administrative, technical, and physical security
- Notification of individuals and the government if a breach involving PHI data occurs

Many other countries have similar laws and regulations covering personal health information. For example, in England, the **National Health Service (NHS)** commissioned the **Health and Social Care Information Centre (HSCIC)** to create and maintain the **Information Governance Toolkit (IG Toolkit)** to assess patient data privacy and security. Organizations that process PHI data in the Netherlands are subject to the NEN 7510 standard.

You might consider an ATM deployed by a bank to be an IIoT device. Financial service companies that gather credit cardholder data or store, process, and or transmit payments as part of their IIoT solution are subject to **Payment Card Industry (PCI) - Data Security Standards (DSS)**. This global standard is designed to prevent financial fraud.

The Japanese Ministry of Finance established the Center for **Financial Industry Information Systems (FISC)** in 1984. Technical and operational guidelines have been established for information systems security, including basic auditing of computer systems controls, contingency planning, and security policies and standards.

Which guidelines apply

In many Industrial Internet solutions, the guidelines that might apply for GRC are not as simply determined as one might think. Data might be captured from devices in multiple countries, transmitted over networks between countries, and reside in data centers in yet other countries.

The passenger airline industry provides a useful and extremely complicated scenario. As you no doubt realize, aircraft and aircraft components, such as engines, are very expensive. The aircraft are often leased. Efficient routing of planes and crew and scheduling of maintenance is critical to on-time performance. Passenger satisfaction is determined by their experience in airport and airline interactions.

It is a common scenario where the following activities take place:

- The aircraft is manufactured by Boeing, Airbus, or a regional jet manufacturer
- The engines are manufactured by GE, Pratt and Whitney, or Rolls Royce
- A jet lessor, such as GE's Gecas, owns the aircraft fleet
- An airline leases the aircraft and is the operator of the asset(s)
- The airline buys a long-term service contract with the aircraft manufacturer and the engineer manufacturer
- The aircraft depart from and land at many different airports, using the associated ground services
- Ground services, including baggage handling, fuel, catering, and tugs are provided by many different companies
- The airport is owned by the city/country or a private company
- Most airline passengers are not affiliated with any of the above-mentioned companies or entities
- Taxi, ride share, rail, and car rental companies facilitate transportation of the passengers
- Retail stores in the airport are owned and operated by different companies
- The security gates are staffed by government security specialists or private companies
- Immigration is staffed by government agencies

Gathering and analyzing IIoT data to make smarter decisions is often seen as key to optimizing the airline performance and passenger satisfaction and drove many early Industrial Internet projects. The following data can be relevant in this solution:

- Airline flight schedule
- Air crew scheduling data
- Air cargo scheduling
- Aircraft engine performance and maintenance data
- Aircraft parts locations
- Repair crew expertise and locations
- Weather data
- Airline passenger itinerary information
- Passenger movement from curbside, to terminals and then boarding
- Checked passenger baggage
- Security line passenger interaction and carry-on bags
- Purchases and interaction at the terminal, including duty-free stores

There are many parties who could be interested in this data. The airline, manufacturers of aircraft and aircraft components, the leasing company, airline services providers, and government agencies could all be interested in the performance and repair of planes and their ability to meet schedules. Passengers are probably interested in the outcome (especially whether the airline is on time), but not the same level of detail. However, passengers and the government might be concerned about who has access to *personal identifiable information* about their travels.

Ownership of such data is often not clear cut today given the many entities that might find the data useful and the many regulations that might or might not apply. That said, GRC rules usually must be applied to locations where data is being gathered and where it is stored and analyzed. Data must be protected during transmissions between sites along the way.

You might think that if a CSP meets the certifications and guidelines we outlined, you can be less concerned about the backend of your IIoT architecture. However, it is up to you to assure that the necessary controls are put in place. This is critical to prove the compliance if audited.

Industrial Internet architects must closely work with the security and compliance specialists and operational managers of the infrastructure to carefully review the applicable local laws, cloud-provider contracts, and management processes. The architect and security experts must also schedule conversations with all applicable LOB to gain an understanding of any GRC concerns they have and plan accordingly. Such due diligence is required to prevent surprises later.

IIoT Center of Excellence

 Centers of Excellence (CoE) are often formed around new and complex initiatives to share knowledge and lessons learned. An IIoT CoE might be formed to address GRC, as well as address other complexities such as identifying and applying best practices and change management, rethinking business models, managing human resources, and assessing maturity.

GRC in the supply chain optimization example

In the previous chapter, we described securing the supply chain optimization example through secure networking and alluded to the other approaches we would need to take to secure the rest of the infrastructure. To ensure that our solution will remain available and avoid security compromises, we should make sure that our architecture follows appropriate guidelines and standards and that a GRC strategy can be put into place.

We begin with an assessment of governance and certifications requirements already in place at the organization that must be followed. We then assess any additional standards that we must comply with.

In the CEMENTruck Inc. example, a relevant industry group is the **National Ready Mixed Concrete Association** (**NRMCA**). Such industry groups sometimes self-regulate, determine best practices, educate members regarding relevant industry regulations, and lobby for favorable terms. The **Federal Motor Carrier Safety Administration** (**FMCSA**) governs the hours of service for drivers in this industry. The relevant guidelines come from 49 CFR Part 395 (https://www.law.cornell.edu/cfr/text/49/part-395). Increasingly, IoT is being used for compliance-related activities. Use of **Electronic Logging Devices** (**ELDs**) (https://www.fmcsa.dot.gov/sites/fmcsa.dot.gov/files/docs/FMCSA-ELD-Final-Rule_12-10-2015.pdf) is governed by Section 395.24. This section lists the cementing truck driver's responsibilities as follows:

- A truck driver must correctly provide the information that the ELD requires as prompted by the system and required by the motor carrier
- A driver must input the driver's duty status by selecting among the following categories available on the ELD:
    1. Off Duty, OFF or 1
    2. Sleeper Berth, SB or 2 when sleeper berth is used
    3. Driving or D or 3
    4. On-duty but not driving or ON or 4

- A driver must also provide the following:
    1. Manual entry of this information in the ELD:
        - Annotations when applicable
        - Driver's location description when prompted by the ELD (https://goo.gl/CrtPes)
        - Output file comment when directed by an authorized safety officer
    2. Manual input or verify the following information on the ELD:
        - Commercial motor vehicle power unit number
        - Trailer number(s) if applicable
        - Shipping document number if applicable
    3. An authorized safety official can request that a driver produce and transfer from an ELD the driver's hours-of-service records in accordance with the instruction sheet provided by the motor carrier:

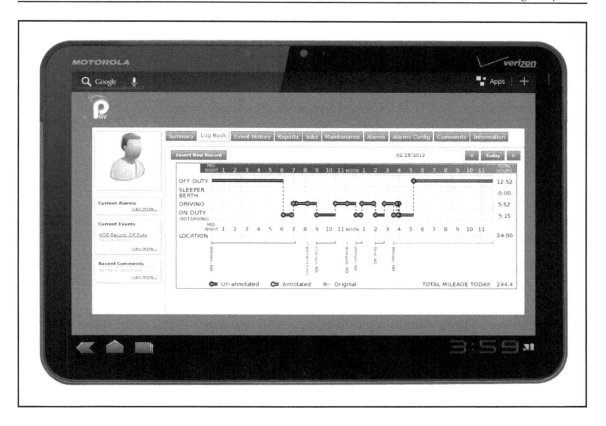

The ELD for Hours of Service in Trucking Industry (`https://calhountrucklines.com/wp-content/uploads/2014/11/electronic-logging-device.jpg`) illustrates industry-specific compliance and provides the Industrial Internet architect with more than simply best practices. In this case, we can see the metadata needed for system design (from the pick list for drop-down options in the user interface) and the supporting data structures underneath.

The architect must understand such regulatory landscapes to do the following:

- Properly design the Industrial Internet solution so that country- or region-specific compliance can be handled (using appropriate cloud regions and availability zones)
- Propose how IIoT solutions can be used to help the management comply with GRC (such as how wearables can self-report the different states of the driver automatically and remove any human data entry errors)

Many companies involved in Industrial Internet projects, such as the company in our example, place importance on the ISO 9001 standard and certification. The IIoT architecture developed should support processes for optimizing performance, managing risk, and continual improvement. The design should also include components useful in assuring data quality so that fact-based business decisions can be made.

The proposed design in our example includes the networking of devices over a private network and public networks (with VPN deployed there). This part of our design will be evaluated using the IEC 62443 guidelines.

When choosing a public cloud service provider, we'll first check their certifications for compliance with relevant international, domestic, and industry standards. In our example and our organization, several ISO /IEC standards as well as NIST standards are relevant.

Though CSPs certify the footprint they provide can meet these standards, it is up to us to implement an architecture that fully complies with the standards. As we create our architecture, we will also create a preliminary GRC plan to assure that standards will be met throughout the life of the project and the solution.

Summary

You should now have gained an understanding of the scope of GRC and its possible implications when defining an IIoT architecture. In this chapter, we described some of the fundamental concepts in GRC and some of the many relevant international, domestic, and industry standards and certifications that might be considered as you define your architecture. We then briefly described how we would consider GRC in defining our supply chain optimization architecture used as an example in this book.

Existing standards and certifications continue to change over time. Many new standards for IIoT are under consideration, and industry consortia continue to be formed and converge upon new standards. This is particularly true, as the book was being published, in the areas of device discovery and management (and is part of the ongoing work defining the ISO / IEC 30141 standard for the IoT).

Our goal was to introduce this topic to you in this chapter. You should further explore these topics, researching on the relevant standards documentation that exist as you start your project, including the standards that your organization currently embraces and additional standards that would apply. Proper planning at this stage can help assure that you do not introduce incompatible solutions that will require expensive rework later.

Throughout the early chapters of this book, we focused on defining a supply chain optimization solution and the CEMENTruck Inc. example. The Industrial Internet consists of a wide variety of solutions and use cases today. In the next chapter, we will introduce several more examples and describe those in detail.

10
Industrial Internet Use Cases in Various Industries

The previous two chapters covered security and the GRC landscape of the Industrial Internet. `Chapter 9`, *Governance and assuring Industry Compliance* mainly covered regulatory compliance in an industry-agnostic manner across various verticals and scenarios. The case studies and the use cases covered in this chapter will demonstrate some security and industry-specific regulations in practice. Where applicable, we will reference and further describe industry vertical resolutions and recommended practices.

We will begin this chapter by differentiating between use cases and customer case studies. We will then look at common use cases in the following industries: agribusiness, alternative energy and environmental control, construction, logistics and transportation, manufacturing and **consumer packaged goods** (**CPGs**), oil and gas, pharmaceuticals, medical equipment and healthcare, and utility companies. Following that section, we'll look further at the IIoT architecture and examples associated with manufacturing, including a manufacturing test bed, factory operations, visibility and intelligence, and omnichannel initiatives.

Next, we'll describe use cases that cross many of these industries. We'll explore predictive maintenance, asset tracking and handling, and environmental impact and abatement IIoT initiatives.

So, the chapter is divided into the following major sections:

- Use cases versus case studies
- Use cases within industry vertical
- Manufacturing IIoT architectures and examples
- Predictive maintenance
- Asset tracking and handling
- Environmental impact and abatement

When you complete this chapter, you should understand some of the common IIoT use cases, problems addressed, and architecture solutions. This level of comprehension will be useful to you as you consider your own projects.

Use cases versus case studies

Often, use cases and case studies are interchangeably used to describe how users interact with the system to achieve a specific business outcome. This is an incorrect use of these terms.

What is a use case?

 A use case describes a scenario where a specific problem can be solved by a combination of products and services to reach a defined goal. Use cases often explain exactly how a solution is applied to obtain the desired outcome.

In an emerging area, a use case can help one understand and visualize how technology and related solutions can be applied to solve real-world problems. Technical descriptions, including features and functions, are often too abstract and do not explain how the technology is useful. Too often, technical architects and developers tend to gravitate toward the technology because they think it would be intellectually fun to use. Applied in this vacuum, one might develop a use case through a proof of technology but might not be able to develop a case study.

What is a case study?

 A case study describes an application of a solution consisting of products and or services to solve a business problem and achieve a desired outcome, typically with measurable business benefits. The end customer and solution and the business outcomes are described in a case study, except in the case of a blind-case study.

Case studies often help extend the analogy of where the "rubber meets the road." In the context of this chapter, a use case is often a theoretical exercise in understanding a horizontal or industry vertical problem and how to solve it using the available technological solutions in the Industrial Internet realm. Sometimes, use cases may involve a **proof of technology (PoT)**.

While use cases are good starting points, whenever possible Industrial Internet architects should ask for case studies as proof points when evaluating the available solutions. Case studies and the ability to talk to customers enables a vetting process. Lessons learned from the PoC and prior implementations provide valuable input to the architect. In the following sections, we will look at use cases and case studies from across multiple industry segments.

Use cases within industry vertical

Before investigating use cases in some detail that include manufacturing or that cross several industries, let's have a quick look at use cases within industry verticals commonly associated with Industrial Internet applications. We'll look at use cases in agribusiness, alternative energy and environmental control, construction, logistics and transportation, manufacturing and CPGs, oil and gas, pharmaceuticals, medical equipment and healthcare, and utility companies.

Many of these are deployed using cloud-based solutions as backends. Architectures deployed within these use cases will be like the architecture outlined earlier in the book, using reference architectures from the major CSPs or Industrial Internet solutions providers, combined with custom development and the deployment of edge devices and sensors.

Use cases in agribusiness

Agribusiness includes farming and the companies that provide fertilizers, seeds, equipment, and transportation and facilitate farming. Farmers increasingly rely on IIoT solutions to manage planting and harvesting and analyze crops and conditions in the field using sensors and through images of fields captured from the air.

Benefits from IIoT solutions in agribusiness most frequently appear in the following areas:

- Farm production: Improved quality and yield through analysis of field conditions and optimized planting, fertilization, and harvesting through "smart" farm equipment, and intelligence gathered and shared by farm suppliers and producers of consumer products that contract with farmers
- Supply chain optimization: Improved demand forecasting through better understanding of market conditions, crop conditions, and yields as well as just-in-time availability of the necessary resources
- Product development: Improved seeds and fertilization matched to weather conditions and field conditions through genome and other research
- Transportation and logistics: Delivery of right seeds and fertilizers to right locations at the right time; optimal pickup of harvested crops to food processors

Much of the initial focus on IIoT in farming was on highly-valued crops yielding a large revenue per acre (such as vineyards). Today, IIoT in farming is becoming common in many developed countries where large-scale farm production occurs. Companies such as Land O' Lakes and Monsanto have long had initiatives in this area, working closely with their farming communities and deploying IIoT solutions.

Use cases in alternative energy and environmental control

Early consumer IoT items appearing in homes often included thermostats from companies such as Nest (Alphabet), Emerson, Honeywell, Johnson Controls, and others. Environmental controls remain a major IIoT development area as these companies embed sensors and smart devices into heating and cooling units, refrigeration, and other products that have large energy needs.

Alternative energy suppliers, including solar and wind providers, rely heavily on IIoT to monitor the energy being gathered and optimize the gathering of energy. Wind providers determine when excessive wind is present near their equipment and shut it down automatically to avoid damage.

In summary, some of the main use cases include the following:

- **Energy generation**: Determine sub-optimal energy generation and steps needed to match supply to demand
- **Environmental controls**: Optimize energy utilization and determine optimal use of scarce resources, including recycling where possible
- **Predictive maintenance**: Perform maintenance on under-performing equipment or replace it as necessary or economically justifiable

For example, Schneider Electric builds dashboards that provide a consolidated view of solar generation infrastructure health. Such dashboards can be used to show when firmware needs updating, batteries are overheating, or when solar panels are not operating at peak efficiency. Many companies producing energy controls we have worked with often see an opportunity to develop energy-monitoring offerings that extend beyond their products, enabling them to consider entering new businesses.

Use cases in construction

At the time of writing this book, many construction companies were just beginning to realize the benefits possible from IIoT. Some of the major use cases envisioned included the following areas:

- **Construction operations**: Match nearest crews, equipment, and tools to tasks
- **Optimal tools performance**: Automatically adjust tools (for example, speed and torque) to the task at hand
- **Safety**: Determine potential problems remotely, including the time that crew are on-duty (beyond normal working hours) and crew locations

Manufacturers of building tools are enabling high-end tools to be tracked and linked to individual usage. For example, Milwaukee Tools' One Key enables tracking of tool performance levels and location. The tools' performance can be customized for power, speed, and consistency.

Use cases in logistics and transportation

This category includes companies building transportation vehicles (automobiles, locomotives, and airplanes) and those managing transportation networks (freight and overnight delivery, airlines, railroads, rapid transit, highway traffic, and others). Some of the major focus areas and benefits obtained from IIoT projects include the following:

- **Distribution center and warehouse management**: Increased inventory turnover and decreased write-downs, reduced stock transfers among centers
- **Network resource planning**: Improved demand forecasting, optimal fleet utilization, optimal driver/crew scheduling and availability, improved safety
- **Route optimization**: Predictable time to delivery, optimal fuel utilization
- Self-driving vehicles and automated controls: Safer and more predictable operation of vehicles
- Transportation maintenance: Reduced downtime, improved service levels, minimized liability

Much of the news in this area is focused on the development of self-driving vehicles. The proliferation of sensors in automobiles and continued refinement in algorithms and technology needed is driving continued IIoT development efforts. In the United States, mandated **Positive Train Control** (**PTC**) standards also led to IIoT projects needed to ensure that locomotives operate at safe distances from other trains.

Management of mass and public transportation networks has long required sophisticated network resource planning and route optimization. Today, such operators are investing in IIoT projects to understand equipment degradation by monitoring for unusual temperatures and vibrations and performing predictive maintenance before failure occurs and there is an impact on service.

The San Diego project

 As part of an outdoor lighting upgrade, the City of San Diego is investing $30 million in deploying the world's largest smart city IoT sensor platform. The solution will include 3,200 intelligent sensor nodes to help optimize traffic and parking. Data gathered from the project will also be used to enhance public safety and environmental awareness.

We'll focus on preventive maintenance in one transportation industry, the aviation industry, in a subsequent section of this chapter.

Use cases in manufacturing and CPGs

As the manufacturing and production of CPGs company products becomes more automated, IIoT becomes fundamental to running production lines. Many of these companies are also embracing IIoT initiatives to gather information about the utilization of their products by the ultimate customer (the consumer) and link that data to data that indicates customer sentiment and buying patterns.

Use cases and their potential benefits include the following:

- **Manufacturing production**: Improved product quality and yield, optimal utilization of plant equipment
- **Product development**: Agile adjustment of product offerings based on demand and utilization
- **Sales**: Fast understanding of success of promotions, advertising, and sales initiatives
- **Supply chain**: Improved demand forecasting, enhanced negotiation capabilities
- **Support and warranties**: Proactive support and problem resolution, reduced support costs, new service opportunities

Manufacturers of heavy equipment are using IIoT to gather data about the equipment they build and sell. For example, Sandvik Coromant, a Swedish company that produces metal cutting tools, gathers data from their sensor-equipped tools that helps their customers minimize idle time during manufacturing by 50%. They can make instant recommendations on proper feeds and speeds and when a new or different tool should be ordered or used.

We'll take a further look at manufacturing use cases and an IIC testbed initiative in the next major section of this chapter.

Use cases in oil and gas

As we described in `Chapter 1`, *The Industrial Internet Revolution*, the oil and gas industry was an early proponent of using analytics at the edge, even before IIoT was a concept. Today's IIoT initiatives rely on sensors and smart devices in remote locations and in both downstream and upstream oil and gas production. Some of the projects currently focus on these areas and provide these benefits:

- **Drilling and production**: Predictive maintenance of equipment, improved energy and water utilization.

- **Exploration**: Improved geologic analysis.
- **Supply chain and logistics**: Predictable time to delivery of equipment and personnel.

A significant portion of Rockwell Automation's business today focuses on building pumps, monitoring energy, and providing other equipment used in the production, transportation, and delivery of oil. Rockwell Automation built IIoT solutions for monitoring submersible pumps on drilling equipment, tracking the movement of oil through pipelines in real-time, and monitoring performance and inventory at the gas pump. They are an example of a company that has evolved from a traditional manufacturer of equipment to also become a provider of information needed to run the business.

Use cases in pharmaceuticals, medical equipment, and healthcare

Pharmaceutical and medical equipment companies face several challenges, including highly competitive landscapes for the introduction of new drugs and equipment, the need to analyze patient data that is not always easily integrated, and stringent data privacy requirements. Much of this data has tended to remain in silos. Many of today's IIoT initiatives are focused on making this data more accessible in real time, driving the following use cases with these potential benefits:

- Clinical trial innovation: More completed tests and improved time to market
- Distribution: Matched distribution to local needs and minimized waste
- Outcomes: Understand adherence to prescriptions, utilization of equipment, and success of drugs and equipment

Healthcare providers have progressed in reporting patient status through the adoption of **Electronic Medical Records (EMRs)** and data exchange standards. That said, the automation of patient information reporting from equipment directly into EMRs is still a work in progress for many providers. Meanwhile, IIoT initiatives are also being pursued in non-patient data areas such as supply chain management.

At the time this book was published, there was much speculation about how IIoT devices and their integration could automate and improve healthcare in the future. Government requirements and regulations and bold innovations by non-traditional players will likely be driving forces behind some of the increased IIoT adoption that we'll see.

Use cases in utility companies

IIoT initiatives in many countries have centered on the proliferation of smart meters installed by electrical power companies and water utilities. The devices are largely used as part of automated billing solutions. However, there are other initiatives underway that some forward-thinking utility companies are pursuing, including the following:

- **Energy demand response**: Match supply and demand, target lowered energy utilization programs during peak utilization, and mitigate the need for construction of new peak demand plants
- **Operations and outage response**: Match nearest crews and equipment to problems and reduce cost of response
- **Preventive maintenance**: Dispatch crew where problems are suspected due to unusual readings before they are reported by the customer
- **Safety**: Determine problems remotely and model problems locally using digital twins

Some utility companies are now sharing customer energy utilization data in near real time with their customers, enabling them to better manage their own utilization.

The application of IIoT in water utilities is sometimes overlooked. However, a growing water shortage is now regarded as the top global challenge affecting both developing and developed nations according to the World Economic Forum (The Global Risks Report 2015). An estimated 40 to 50 percent of the water produced in developing countries is lost. About 16 percent of the water produced in the United States is lost.

Water is lost due to a variety of reasons. Some of them are as follows:

- Leaks in pipes and other infrastructure
- Leaks typically go undetected or are responded to after the event
- Water lost due to excessive irrigation (70 percent of all water used is consumed by agriculture)

Deployment of sensors and IIoT solutions can reduce the amount of water lost through these activities:

- More timely detection of leaks
- Preemptive detection of potential leaks
- Precision irrigation of watered areas

Now that we've briefly assessed some of the use cases for IIoT across a wide breadth of industries, let's take an in-depth look at one of these industries: manufacturing.

Manufacturing IIoT architectures and examples

When many think of the Industrial Internet, they only think of manufacturing. As you've just seen, our definition is wider in this book. However, manufacturing requires a closer look, and we'll provide that in this section. We'll begin with an IIC testbed initiative and then provide some more examples of IIoT deployment in manufacturing.

A manufacturing test bed

The **Industrial Digital Thread** (**IDT**) is a manufacturing-related testbed under the IIC. The IDT aims to drive efficiency, speed, and flexibility through digitization and automation of manufacturing processes and procedures.

Manufacturing processes should rely on feedback from customers and the field operations staff to help improve the product family over time. Field engineers and service teams also need data and digital insights to assess, troubleshoot, and determine work scope for large industrial assets when performing corrective and preventative maintenance activities.

Quality Assurance (**QA**) engineers often need to understand why a specific problem in a specific part frequently occurs and why parts from certain suppliers do not stack up well in the assemblies of the complex industrial assets. The root cause is usually hidden in design, manufacturing processes, supply chain logistics, or production planning. This testbed is designed to solve the problem of collecting the right data and associated insights that are otherwise hard to obtain.

The IDT tackles the scenario where a service engineer observes an incoming part component that is wearing out and degrading at an unexpected rate. Leveraging this testbed, the service engineer can identify the correlation between that specific part's field performance data and its associated manufacturing machine, operations, and quality validation data from when it was produced. The data can come from sources that include sensors on the assembly line, the **Manufacturing Execution System** (**MES**), the Enterprise Asset Management System, and ERP supply chain modules. Through this insight, the service engineer identifies the cause, selects a work scope to repair the part, and then informs the supplier about the finding to prevent future occurrences.

The following visual from GE, pictures the *Digital Thread* of a complex physical asset, illustrating the flow of data in a manufacturing environment:

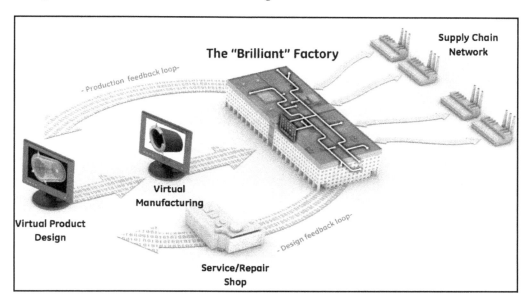

Source: http://dsg.files.app.content.prod.s3.amazonaws.com/gereports/wp-content/uploads/2016/02/03201500/Screen-Shot-2016-02-03-at-3.19.47-PM.jpg

The Digital Thread helps link the product design, shop floor manufacturing, field operations and repair, and the supply chain network.Problems in manufacturing are often not revealed by the traditional quality tests in the factory. Some problems show up while the product is in use by the customer. Digital Threads are used to highlight how to solve this problem.

The seamless digital integration of design systems into manufacturing that is pictured enables a model-based enterprise and virtual manufacturing before even one physical part is created. Sensor-enabled automation, manufacturing processes, procedures, and machine data enable optimization in operations and the supply chain. Once the manufacturing process is complete, a *digital birth certificate* (an as-built signature) can be compared to the as-designed engineering intent. This provides an opportunity to apply analytics to provide service teams and field engineers with better awareness, insights, and practical actions to improve the servicing and maintenance of critical assets.

The following visual shows a typical high-level architecture based on the GE's Predix platform, which complies with the IIC's IIRA:

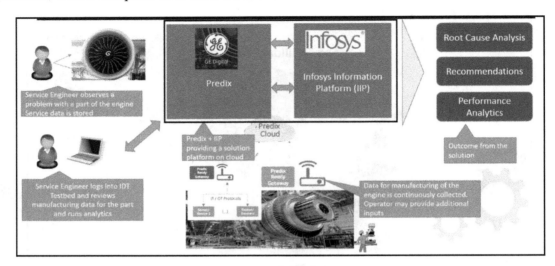

Factory operation visibility and intelligence

Visualizing factory operations data is a challenge for many manufacturers today. One of the IIoT initiatives some manufacturers are pursuing today is providing real-time visibility in factory operations and the health of machines. The goal is to improve manufacturing efficiency. The challenge is in combining and correlating diverse data sources that greatly vary in nature, origin, and life cycle.

Fujitsu has conceptualized a **Factory Operations Visibility and Intelligence** (FOVI) solution based on experiences they gained from two of their factories:

- A factory in Shimane where notebooks are manufactured
- A factory in Yamanashi where network appliances are manufactured

Fujitsu's goals for the FOVI project are as follows:

- Timely product manufacturing and shipment
- Quality improvements and reduced rejection rates
- Reduced time for equipment repair
- Overall higher throughput in factory

FOVI's backend is to be deployed to Fujitsu's public cloud. BLE Beacons are to be used to locate and track products in the repair area in the Shimane factory. Video archives of operations will be generated and correlated with data from sensors. Factory personnel are traced using passive RFID. The architecture is designed to support simulations.

The following diagram provides a functional view of Fujitsu's FOVI architecture (`http://www.iiconsortium.org/images/test-beds/Figure-en.jpg`):

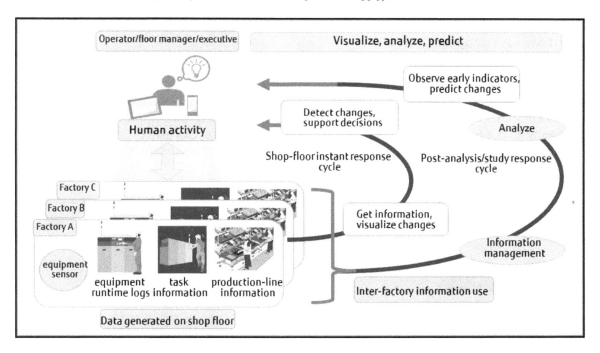

Hershey's, a manufacturer of candies, has already deployed a similar architecture. Temperature data is gathered from sensors in extruders on the plant floor and transmitted to the Microsoft Azure cloud where machine learning algorithms are applied. Adjustments to temperature are made in near real time to optimize the production process, improving quality and yield.

Omnichannel initiatives

Omnichannel initiatives are usually associated with retailers. Omnichannel strategies generally refer to multiple touch points with buyers through multiple channels, including retail stores, outlet stores, and websites. However, many CPG companies and other manufacturers fear disintermediation from their ultimate customers, the consumers. Until the recent past, they have had limited information about the consumers as their products were sold through distributors. So, CPG companies and manufacturers are pursuing strategies that now sometimes include direct sales to the consumers and/or deployment of smart displays into retail stores.

The ability to track the proximity of a consumer to a specific aisle or product, coupled with loyalty history, can help determine whether to make targeted offers and provide other useful information. A key to this solution is an **Indoor Positioning System** (**IPS**), which uses a combination of a light point (such as an LED and smartphone application) to locate a person within a few inches of their position. Such information can also be used to provide way finding in the store and help the customer locate the desired product.

The following diagram illustrates a digital retail store:

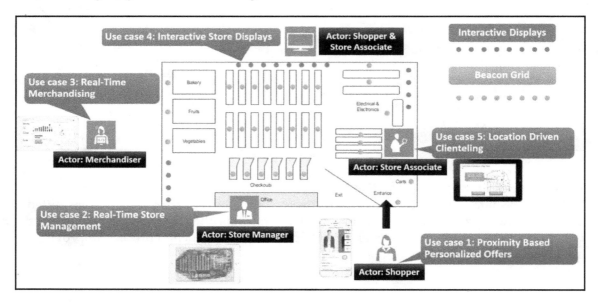

Indoor positioning is enabled by **Visible Light Communication** (**VLC**) along with the smartphone app (`http://www.gelighting.com/LightingWeb/na/solutions/control-systems/indoor-positioning-system.jsp`). The modulation of the LED light in the retail store ceiling is detected by the camera on the smartphone to pin-point the location of the customer relative to the aisles and shelves of the products. Data can be gathered about the dwell time of the shopper near an aisle or product.

This data, combined with PoS data and historical loyalty data, facilitates the following use cases:

- Proximity-based real-time personalized offers
- Real-time store management
- Real-time merchandising
- Interactive store displays
- Location-driven clienteling

The industry-oriented reference architectures we've introduced here help speed deployment of solutions. Next, we'll explore some of the IIoT solutions and architectures that can be repurposed in many industries.

Predictive maintenance

Performing maintenance prior to the failure of parts and equipment can lead to better service levels in the transportation of people and goods, more consistent production in manufacturing, and improved quality of care in healthcare. Predicting where such failures might occur soon and taking corrective action can positively impact revenue, result in cost savings, and potentially save lives. It should come as no surprise that many IIoT projects are focused on such initiatives today.

In this section, we'll focus on the aviation industry, but the use case has applicability in the other industries we have just mentioned. We'll also refer to this industry in some of the other examples of use cases in this chapter.

Airline industry background

The global airline industry transports between 3.5 to 4 billion people annually. Its economic impact is over $2.7 trillion annually. To understand how an Industrial Internet project can be used to improve maintenance planning and scheduling and for future reference in other sections, we will begin with a simple description of the major parts of the aircraft:

- **Fuselage**: The fuselage or the body of the airplane provides a connection point for all major assemblies. The front of the fuselage is the cockpit where the pilot controls the aircraft while passengers and cargo are carried in the rear. The aircraft fuel in carried in some cases in the fuselage, while others carry fuel in the wings.

- **Wings**: The wings help to balance and improve the aircraft's stability when flying. The wings generate thrust to allow the aircraft to take off and climb to the cruise altitude. There are two wings that are joined by a fuselage. The shape of the wings is designed and optimized for thrust and fuel efficiency.

- **Engines**: The engines are critical parts of the aircraft that enable its movement on the runway and generate the thrust for the flight. The diverse types of aircraft require engines that are made in accordance to the aircraft size and weight. There are different types of jet engines, but the two types that are widely used are turbofan and turbojet. Generally, commercial aircraft have two or four engines.

- **Landing gear**: Landing gear is the undercarriage of the aircraft that is used for either takeoff or landing. The landing gear supports the aircraft when it is not flying, allowing it to take off, land, and taxi on the runway, safely.

- **Avionics**: Avionics are the electronic systems of the aircraft. It consists of the navigation system, the display and management of multiple systems, and the communications systems. It may include some early warning and control systems as well.

The following diagram illustrates the structure of a simple aircraft:

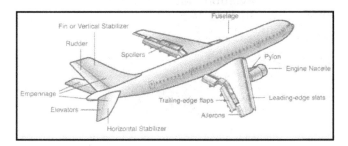

The components and their suppliers for present day commercial aircraft are very complex, consisting of many parts and subsystems. This complexity is apparent during commercial operations and aircraft maintenance on the part of airlines. The following diagram illustrates the structure and major suppliers for the Boeing 787 (`https://www.researchgate.net/figure/268209377_fig4_Figure-4-Vehicle-Level-Health-Reasoner-Overview-Diagram-with-information-exchange-data`):

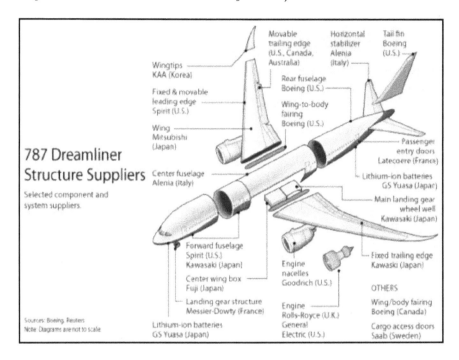

Airlines are in the core business of flying passengers and their baggage or cargo from one place to another. They continuously make complex decisions on how to maintain the fleet of aircraft in a good condition. Airlines such as Delta and Lufthansa are known to have their own MRO operations, while many other airlines rely on manufacturers and other parties.

What is MRO?

MRO stands for **Maintenance, Repair and Overhaul**, a phrase very commonly used to describe aircraft maintenance activity. Commercial aircraft are maintained in predetermined conditions of airworthiness to safely transport passengers and cargo.

The airlines that operate commercial services are overall responsible for MRO activities, including the inspection or modification of an aircraft or aircraft subsystems and components. These maintenance activities can include such tasks as ensuring compliance with Airworthiness Directives or Service Bulletins.

Airline proactive and preventive maintenance

Maintaining aircraft in good condition is a prerequisite for improved aviation safety and maintaining service levels. Aircraft maintenance is divided into four checks that are carried out at predetermined intervals based on the number of flight cycles (landings and take-offs) or flight time. These checks originated from Boeing's Maintenance Steering Group (MSG) in 1968 and were designed to ensure the safety of the Boeing B747-100 aircraft.

The checks are defined as follows:

- **A Check**: This is a *light* check usually carried out overnight at an airport gate. This check is carried out every month or every 500 flight hours (depending on the type of aircraft).
- **B Check**: This *light* check is also carried out overnight at an airport gate, normally every 3 months.
- **C Check**: A *heavy* maintenance check is usually carried out every year or 1.5 years. Since this check includes the disassembly of critical parts, it is performed in an aircraft hangar.
- **D Check**: This check is also known as an overhaul check or heavy maintenance check; it is performed every 4-5 years and inspection of the entire aircraft is carried out.

With this MSG-3 approach, the aviation industry moved away from the tradition of MRO activities at fixed time intervals to one that considered the operations and intervals needed to keep the aircraft safe. This approach was successful due to time and money savings, and due to unnecessary interference with components. Boeing started to recommend the same approach to all their aircraft models.

When an airline is scheduled to fly, the crew performs several checks apart from those just mentioned to assure the plane is safe to fly. Some potential problems are difficult to detect using traditional checks. Landing gear falls into that category.

Often, landing gear problems are not detected until the plane pushes back from the gate. Uncovering problems with the landing gear during this taxi out stage could result in an unscheduled flight delay. Each delay costs the airline between $25,000 and $40,000 and impacts customer satisfaction. If the delay occurs in the morning, it can have a cascading effect that impacts the entire day's flights. Problems with landing gear have traditionally had unclear causes that could not be determined until repair crews began working.

The following diagram illustrates the complexity of the components present in the landing gear (`https://www.faa.gov/regulations_policies/handbooks_manuals/aircraft/amt_airframe_handbook/media/ama_Ch13.pdf`):

The mechanical motion of the landing gear initially limited the use of sensors due to the amount of wiring required and the potential for problems. In older aircraft, sensors were limited to capturing the following:

- Position (extension or retraction)
- Wheel speed
- Weight on wheel
- Skid (and antiskid)

Today, additional sensors can improve the analysis of the state of landing gear and provide the intelligence needed for predictive maintenance. The sensors use wireless communications to the **Quick Access Recorder** (**QAR**), and data is downloaded when the plane reaches the gate. Additional information is collected in this manner, including the following failures and conditions:

- Failing to retract/extend
- Failing to get up-locked after retraction / down-locked after extension
- Exceeding retraction/extension time limits
- Failing to give indications in cockpit of down-locking, transit, and up-locking
- Loss in nitrogen pressure and oil in oleos due to leak
- Loss in pressure in tires due to leak
- Binding of wheel bearings and brakes
- Fully worn out friction pads
- Brake unit-related issues, such as overheating of brake unit
- Leakage of brake fluid and sponginess in brake pedals
- Failure of antiskid
- Leakage of nitrogen pressure in emergency extension cylinder
- Low brake pressure in emergency accumulator
- Low line pressure in emergency system
- Low brake line pressure
- Low battery voltage in emergency system

The following diagram indicates typical placement of these sensors:

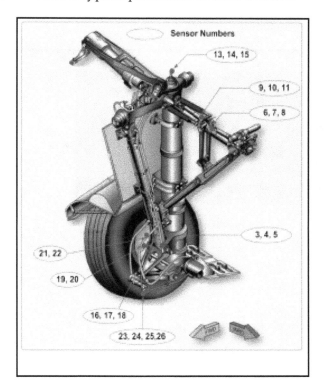

Source: https://www.faa.gov/regulations_policies/handbooks_manuals/aircraft/amt_airframe_handbook/media/ama_Ch13.pdf

To solve problems related to potential brake pad heating and hydraulic oil pressure problems in the landing gear, we can use sensors in the landing gear subsystems to gather data on the wearing of the brake pads and the hydraulic pressure profile. The data gathered from such sensors can be used to test a digital twin of the landing gear.

In this case, a solution team identified 34 sensors that can be applied to provide data for the early detection of wear or malfunction related to the brake pads and hydraulic oil pressure. Using the data from these 34 sensors, a digital twin of each aircraft's physical landing gear is tested and analytics is applied. The digital twin is updated as new data comes in, typically after each flight. This enables the MRO crew to diagnose the current issues. The remaining useful life can be predicted based on the accumulated historical data and the manufacturers' specifications.

The MRO crew would use a dashboard like the following one to understand potential hydraulic pressure issues and when it might make sense to replace a pump based on when failure thresholds will be reached:

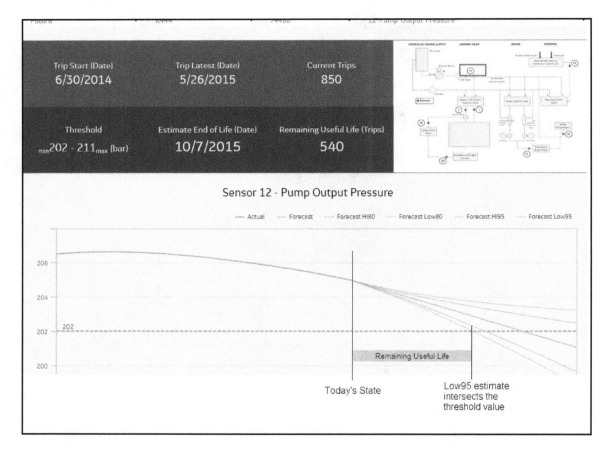

The MRO team might view a dashboard like the following one to understand brake pad temperatures and the optimal time to replace brake pads:

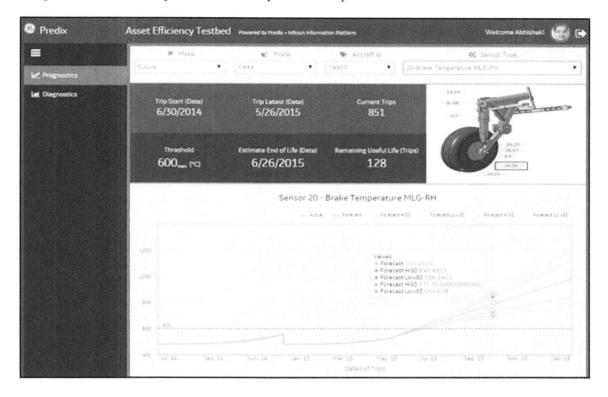

The data pictured in these illustrations was collected from the sensors and transmitted to the GE Predix Platform. Data services were used to persist the time series data and an asset service was used to model the sensors and subsystems in the landing gear. Analytic services, including custom algorithms, were applied against the asset model to determine anomalies and the remaining useful life of the subsystems.

The GE's Predix architecture for this solution is shown in the following diagram:

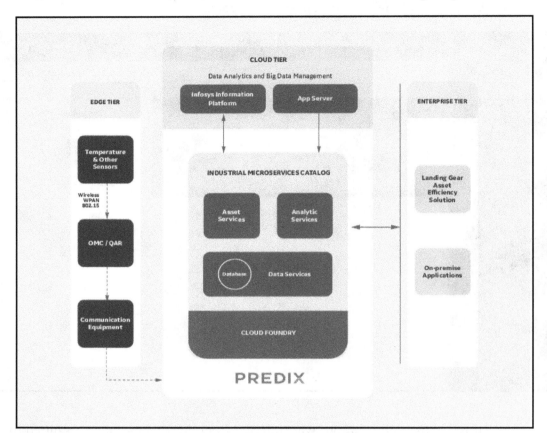

We'll describe the importance of this framework and some of the other emerging frameworks in the next chapter of this book.

Automated Service Requests

Airlines, aircraft manufacturers, and other transportation companies are experimenting with applying algorithms to use predictive failure information such as that presented here to optimally schedule service-based parts availability, the availability of skilled technicians able to perform the work, and the likelihood of parts failure, impacting schedules.

Preventive maintenance as a business

Manufacturers are building advanced predictive maintenance solutions that they package with their products and are widening their business focus into providing broader maintenance activities. For example, large manufacturers of elevators and people movers commonly found in public places maintain anything from tens to hundreds of thousands of these machines annually. A primary goal they have is minimizing the downtime of their products, since that can disrupt the ability to move people through buildings and impact their reputation.

Today, many of these products are equipped with sensors that measure operating characteristics of the equipment. By measuring speed, temperature of key assemblies, and other aspects, and then transmitting the data to cloud-based machine learning and analytics engines, they can predict when failures are likely to occur. Service can be dispatched to repair worn parts before failure.

Some manufacturers are further widening their efforts to also monitor equipment that they did not manufacture and provide service capabilities. This gives them important insight and a leg up when it's time to replace the equipment.

Asset tracking and handling

Another popular area for Industrial Internet applications is the broad area of asset tracking and optimized handling of tools and resources. Throughout this book, we describe various aspects of supply chain optimization and IIoT. Here, we'll look at simply tracking the assets first. We'll describe typical use cases in baggage and cargo handling and in tracking tools used in manufacturing.

In addition to relevancy in transportation and manufacturing, these applications have relevancy in other industries such as healthcare and agriculture. The impact of deploying these solutions can include improved productivity, customer satisfaction, quality of products, and safety, all with significant impact on the business.

Baggage and cargo handling

Travelers can readily relate to problems caused by missing baggage or baggage that arrives late at a destination. According to The Baggage Report by SITA (2017), about 22 million bags were mishandled in 2016 globally. This translates to about six mishandled bags per 1,000 bags checked in. Mishandled bags generally fall into one of three categories:

- Delayed (77 percent)
- Damaged (16 percent)
- Lost (7 percent)

The **International Air Transport Association (IATA)**, a trade association of the major airlines, announced IATA Resolution 753 that will come into effect in June 2018. It promises to deliver major improvements in airline baggage services over and above the incremental improvement seen in recent years, with the goal of improving customer satisfaction. IATA Resolution 753 is an example of GRC at an industry vertical level. An IIC Testbed called **Smart Airline Baggage Management Testbed** (`http://www.iiconsortium.org/baggage-management.htm`) is creating an Industrial Internet solution to help airlines achieve compliance with this resolution.

The following airline baggage flow visual shows the typical flow of airline baggage from the arrival at the airport to the destination:

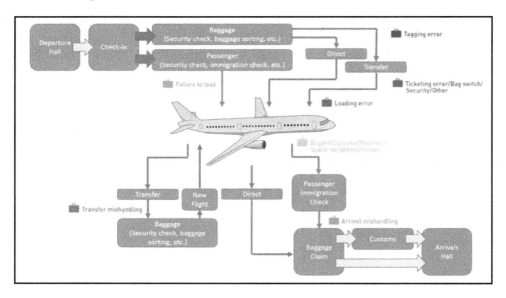

The passenger drops the bag at the drop-off location. The bag tag is printed either at the self-service kiosk or by the airline staff. The following figure is a typical baggage tag with a bar code indicating the flight details and the airline passenger (PAX) information as well as a readable portion:

The bags are transported via baggage belts and carts to the aircraft. The following baggage transfer should look familiar to anyone who has flown an airline:

The passenger journey may consist of a direct flight or connections. Accordingly, the bags are routed to the next aircraft at the transfer point. Today, the bags are constrained to travel no faster and no slower than the airline passenger, as most countries do not allow accompanied bags to fly in-flight. In other words, since bags must fly in the same flight as the passenger, bags cannot move faster than the passenger and make a tight connection, so the passenger misses it. Likewise, baggage cannot move too slowly or else the flight must wait for the bag to be loaded. As a net result of this, over 10 million bags were mishandled at the transfer point in 2016.

The typical points for mishandling baggage are as follows:

- **Tagging errors**: The airline bag tag is placed incorrectly, swapped between the bags of different passengers, or not pasted properly and falls off (a more common occurrence at self-service bag drop kiosks)
- **Security checks**: When a checked-in bag is flagged for additional security screening, it might get delayed and not make it in time for its designated flight
- **Failure to load**: The bag might not make it to the correct aircraft in time, go to the wrong aircraft, or fall off the baggage belt or cart and not be detected in time
- **Transfer issues**: Failure to route baggage to the right handlers and carts in time
- **Weather issues**: Inclement weather conditions may cause a reduction in cargo weight and lead to bags not being loaded on designated flights
- **Arrival issues**: At the arrival airport, the bag may not get unloaded from a flight that has a stopover at the passenger's final destination or the bag might get routed to the wrong bag carousel
- **Theft**: On rare occasions, there could be theft of the bag or other security breaches

Today, the use of printed bag tags with the bar code is prone to reading errors due to line-of-sight scanning. We refer to it as 2D scanning, and multiple scanners are used on the baggage belt. The currently used airline baggage tag has printed bar codes. These bar codes can be scanned in the line-of-sight only. Mainly two types of scanners are used:

- **Hand-held scanner**: This is often used by the airline staff or ground handling crew while transferring the bag from the cart to the aircraft and vice versa.
- **In-line arrays**: These are built into the baggage conveyor system and use a 360-degree array of lasers to read the bar code tags from multiple angles. It tries to account for any shift in the baggage and the orientation as the bag travels through the conveyor belt system.

The airlines paste a few bar code stickers on different sides of the bag to increase the scan changes. These are printed at points where the bags change hands or at kiosks in the airport.

Though the previously mentioned baggage-mishandling issues might seem unique, most (if not all) of the conditions could impact cargo handling by air carriers and other transportation carriers such as trucks and trains. To solve these sorts of issues, **Radio-Frequency Identification (RFID)** tags have been used for many years on cargo shipping containers. As RFID tags became cheaper over the years, they have appeared on much smaller shipping containers and pallets.

The use of RFID tag can improve the read efficiency as it becomes 3D scanning. The RFID readers are not limited by line of sight. The use of active or passive RFID as a bag tag essentially makes it an IoT end point.

The Smart Airline Baggage Management solution uses connected bags using RFID tags, connected readers, and other connected fixed and mobile assets for ground handling at the airports. This near real-time tracking of bags will help save the air transport industry about $3 billion. Once the airlines implement this solution, they will be able to do the following:

- Demonstrate delivery of baggage when custody changes
- Demonstrate acquisition of baggage when custody changes
- Provide an inventory of bags upon departure of a flight
- Exchange information about these events with other airlines as needed (data sharing by use of Baggage **eXtensible Mark-up Language (XML)**).

What is a Baggage XML?

It is a new messaging standard that is being developed by IATA using XML, based on established best practices. It will allow future developments at a reasonable cost using technology that is almost universally adopted in other industries. The Baggage XML project is striving for a sustainable standard for messaging related to airline baggage.

The high-level architecture of the solution is illustrated in the following diagram:

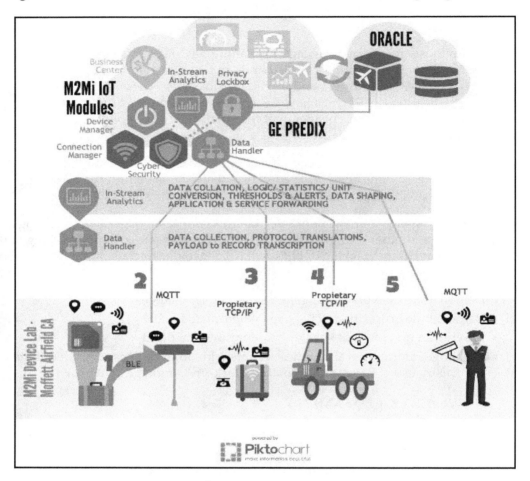

In this solution, the RFID tags contain information that is traditionally stored in the printed barcode tag. RFID tags can be active or passive, which will determine the range and storage capability. The data from RFID tags is read via the connected reading devices. It is then sent to the IoT Cloud Platform via a secured connection. The sensor data is stored in a time series data store. The enterprise data elements from the different airline systems are stored in an airline data model (the Oracle Cloud component pictured). The integrations between the two systems provide the necessary data for real-time scenarios and batch mode analytics scenarios.

The real-time scenarios help track the bag in near real time and react to exceptions, such as the bag falling of the conveyor belt and not getting scanned at the next point in the expected range of time. The batch mode can be used to help figure out which kinds of bag exception are occurring at a site and then come up with mitigation strategies.

Expanded baggage-handling services

As is common in many IIoT initiatives, new business capabilities enabled by these architectures lead to consideration of new business offerings. For example, when connected bags can be tracked end to end using GPS-like capabilities, services can be expanded to customers in areas such as door-to-door pickup or delivery. Airline passengers are often willing to pay an additional fee for bag pick-up or drop-off at their home, hotel, office, or other convenient location. This can also save travelers time in that they avoid waiting in bag drop-off lines and pickups. This creates an additional revenue source for airlines.

The following diagram illustrates this vision:

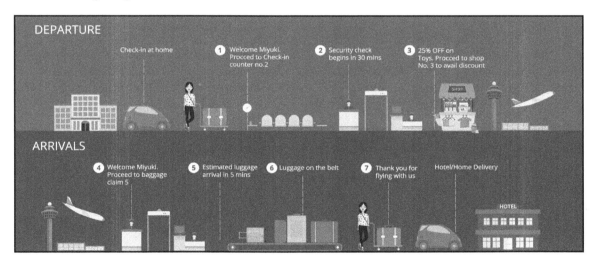

Tracking tools in manufacturing and construction

Manufacturing and construction workers often use specialized and extremely expensive tools during the assembly of products and building facilities. Improving the tracking and traceability of these tools can improve the productivity of the manufacturing assembly line process, help enforce critical processes and regulatory compliance safely by allowing stricter audit trails, and minimize unauthorized usage of the equipment. Such a system can also enable the business model of *Tools-as-a-Service*.

Track & Trace (T&T) is an IIC testbed, developed by Bosch, Cisco, and Tech Mahindra. It aims to deliver tangible benefits to the aerospace industry by *connecting* a variety of engineering tools. T&T allows the user to track every connected tool on the shop floor. The tools may have built-in connectivity, that is, they are *smart* or can be retro-fitted with sensors. Tools become the IoT end point and send information about their location as well as status. An example of the status would be the amount of torque applied for a specific assembly process. Then, the same aircraft comes back for repair, and the same amount of torque can be used to disassemble it.

The location service allows tracking the tool relative to the aircraft. This enables automation. For instance, if the tool is near the rear door, the system can download the amount of pressure to apply to the *smart tool*. Thus, the tool can perform the programmed action with almost zero human intervention in certain scenarios. Sensors in the tool are designed to record key parameters such as rpm or torque. The data is stored in a central database. This data is invaluable to ensure quality and conformance to stringent aviation industry regulations.

The solution consists of different modules such as the following ones:

- **Local Tool Control (LTC)** to manage power tool integration into individual work cells
- **Central Tool Control (CTC)** for complete remote tool control for the assembly line and for managing multiple, distributed LTCs
- Business rules and configuration management that automatically flows from the CTC to LTCs
- Geo-fencing to automatically disable tools outside the allowed or configured work area
- Data analytics for insight into operational metrics of the tool usage
- Comprehensive data security for identity management for safeguards against accidental or deliberate misuse

A variety of other tools and other manufacturers also have produced and enabled *smart* products as we noted earlier in this chapter in the section on use cases in construction and manufacturing.

Chemical industry automated tracking and replenishment

Next, we'll look at applying IIoT to the tracking and replenishment of industrial gas containers.

Replenishment of industrial gas containers or cylinders requires many manual steps. Often, cylinders are moved using manually operated transporters. People sort and clean the cylinders, attach them to the appropriate hoses, ,and fill the cylinders with the right amount of gas. These manual steps result in operational inefficiencies and are prone to human error.

The chemical industry uses an **air separation unit** (ASU) to separate atmospheric air into its primary components, typically nitrogen and oxygen, and sometimes also helium, argon, and other rare inert gases. After the gases are separated, they are supplied either by gas pipelines or cylinders. The composition of air is shown in the following diagram:

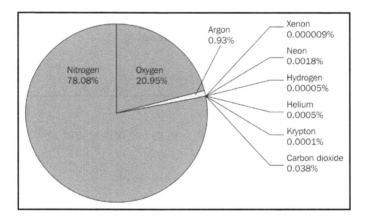

A unique characteristic of this industry is that the raw material is air, obtained freely from the atmosphere. Most of the complexity is in the plant equipment and the replenishment and distribution of the cylinders. Air Separation by Cryogenic Distillation is illustrated in the following diagram (`http://www.chemicalprocessing.com/articles/2011/digital-positioner-aids-air-separation/`):

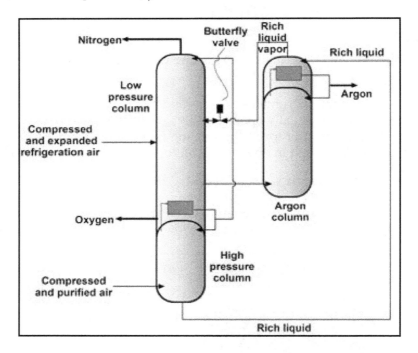

At a simplistic level, the manual steps in the process of filling and refilling the cylinders are as follows:

- Cylinders are transported to the plant by truck
- Sorting and cleaning of the cylinders occurs
- Cylinders are moved to the filling station
- The cylinder is connected to the right hose for filling
- The hose is disconnected
- Measurement, testing, and labeling of the cylinder occur
- The cylinder is dispatched based on an order

In our future state, optimizing operations leverages IIoT with the help of RFID-based asset tracking and use of robots. The following simplified steps take place:

- Cylinders are transported to the plant by truck, and cylinders are identified by RFID-based asset tracking
- Automated fork-lifts move the cylinders to the cleaning station during the sorting and cleaning operation
- Automated fork-lifts move cylinders to the filling station
- Data from the PLC drives the robotic actions to connect the cylinder to the right hose for filling
- Data from the PLC drives the robotic actions to disconnect the hose
- Digital gauges record a reading during the measurement, testing, and labeling phases
- An automated fork-lift moves the cylinder when an order is received for its dispatch

The high-level architecture of the robotic solution is shown here:

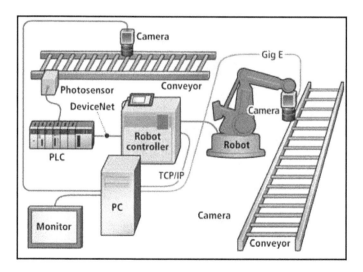

As you can readily tell, we've eliminated much of the potential human error that can occur during the sorting, cleaning, refilling, and transport of the cylinders using this approach (https://www.researchgate.net/figure/268209377_fig4_Figure-4-Vehicle-Level-Health-Reasoner-Overview-Diagram-with-information-exchange-data).

Environmental impact and abatement

Many companies pursuing Industrial Internet applications face environmental impact and abatement challenges. These can include companies involved in agribusiness, alternative energy and environmental control, construction, logistics and transportation, manufacturing and GPGs, oil and gas, pharmaceuticals, medical equipment and healthcare, and utility companies. In fact, an IIoT project is often considered is specifically to address these challenges.

In this section, we will describe IIoT for noise detection and abatement. Though we return to an aviation example, the architecture has wide applicability in all the industries just mentioned.

The three airports in the San Francisco Bay Area handle a large amount of air traffic. Airplanes arriving, taxiing, departing, and circling generate a lot of noise that can adversely impact residents near airports and under flight patterns. The following diagram captures the typical flight patterns in a 24-hour period in the Bay Area (https://speier.house.gov/sites/speier.house.gov/files/documents/NoCal-Initiative-Phase-One-Report.pdf):

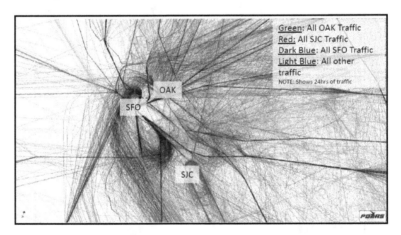

The Federal Aviation Authority (FAA) has an initiative to address noise concerns in Santa Cruz, Santa Clara, San Mateo, and San Francisco counties. This is a multi-phase approach, including review and response to community proposals, and explores such areas as flight procedure criteria and the overall fly ability of proposed **Performance Based Navigation (PBN)** procedures. Procedural modifications such as speed and altitude adjustments, airspace changes, rerouting over water, altered braking patterns on the runway, and increased night time operations are considered.

Airport authorities must ensure that they meet or exceed all Federal and State aircraft noise regulations and that flights operate as quietly as possible. If residents complain about noise, the airport must pay for noise reduction in those buildings.

The main source of noise pollution is the landing approach of the aircraft to the runway and the engines. Often the engine keeps running after the aircraft is already at the gate. This leads to unnecessary noise pollution. The **San Francisco airport** (**SFO**) is addressing this noise problem by implementing an IIoT solution involving noise sensors that gather data, and reporting and analytics solutions for analysis of the data. The goal is to create a safer and quieter airport environment that operates with a cleaner emissions footprint to benefit both the airline passengers and other nearby community stakeholders.

Noise sensors help pinpoint which aircraft have engines and **Auxiliary Power Units** (**APUs**) still running when they are not required to. SFO will monitor APU usage by aircraft at each of its gates. The data collected from noise sensors is monitored in real-time events and is also used in historical analysis.

Technical requirements of the solution include the following ones:

- Monitoring APU noise-detection levels per aircraft in alignment with SFO noise policies
- Visualization of noise levels per aircraft in real time
- The ability to sense, detect, store, and transfer noise data digitally and with low latency
- Accurate detection of acoustic data for individual aircraft within a specified area (apron, gate, parking location) without distortion and negative effects from other sound sources such as adjacent aircraft, runways, and airfield vehicles
- Seamless integration of the solution with SFO's technology systems, both physically and logically

The simplified solution architecture will consist of these three tiers:

- **Edge tier**: This tier includes IIoT sensors for capturing the noise level at various locations
- **Platform tier**: Noise data will be stored in the data store in the platform tier and analytics will help locate the precise location of the aircraft (the main challenge being the isolation of the source of noise when there may be several aircraft in the line of sight)
- **Enterprise tier**: This tier will combine IIoT data with enterprise systems from the airport and provide the end user with decision support reports

A potential sample of the reporting solution might be as follows:

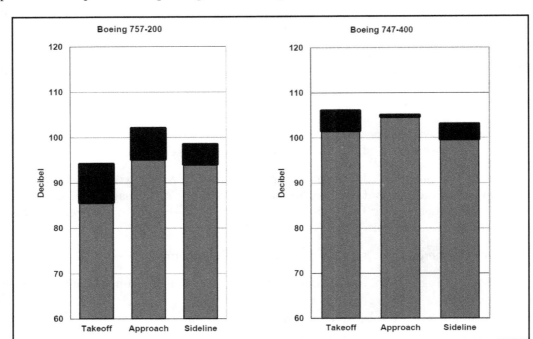

Summary

You should now understand some of the common use cases in agribusiness, alternative energy and environmental controls, construction, logistics and transportation, oil and gas, pharmaceuticals, medical equipment and healthcare, and utility companies, and have an even greater depth of understanding of architectures and use cases in manufacturing and CPGs, including the manufacturing test bed, factory operations, visibility and intelligence, and omnichannel initiatives. You should also understand some of the use cases that cross many industries, including predictive maintenance, asset tracking and handling, and environmental impact and abatement IIoT initiatives.

While each scenario is unique, the building blocks of IIoT solutions, such as the sensors, gateway devices, connectivity, and backend platforms, apply in these use cases. Hence, it is crucial to architect the solution using sound principles that will enable future extensibility into new use cases.

Many of the architecture diagrams and solutions presented in this chapter were based on the familiarity the authors have with certain of these solutions. However, you'll find a wide variety of emerging platforms as we'll describe in the next chapter. Though the focus of much of the material here was on use cases, rapid IIoT adoption and deployment ensures that there will be many more case studies also appearing in the future documenting the business gains companies are achieving (once they are less concerned about sharing details of the competitive advantages they are gaining).

It should also be increasingly clear to you from some of these descriptions that building Industrial Internet solutions is a team sport. Testbeds are reference solutions developed collaboratively by groups of companies highlighting the power of the ecosystem. Beyond the formal process promoted by various consortia, tactical building of solutions is occurring, driven by businesses with vision partnering with technology vendors, solutions providers, and systems integrators.

These efforts are helping to achieve the following goals:

- Improve the overall experience level, both technical and domain knowledge
- Reduce risk by distributing it among various parties whose increased skills improve the ability to mitigate concerns and challenges
- Accelerate adoption through increased evangelism, global awareness, and proven success

In the next chapter, we'll present a vision of the future. We'll pick up where we leave off here, discussing the importance of these emerging frameworks and applications. However, we'll also describe the edge device and network evolution, the evolution in human machine interfaces that is occurring, the impact all of this will have on robotics, and more distant technologies that will be incorporated, such as blockchain and quantum computing.

11
A Vision of the Future

In Chapter 1, *The Industrial Internet Revolution*, we described the evolution of today's Industrial Internet. Over the past decade, the pace of introduction of smarter edge devices and the ability to analyze massive amounts of data have greatly increased. New IIoT backend infrastructure deployments more frequently take place in flexible and highly scalable public clouds.

However, today's architecture remains complex and requires a broad mix of skills to properly design and implement a solution. Security holes exposed in incompletely planned architectures or poorly implemented solutions can be and have been exploited. The task of creating a viable and sustainable IIoT architecture is challenging.

In this closing chapter, we will describe some of the technological changes and advancements that we believe could impact IIoT architecture in the future and will provide answers to some of these challenges. Many of these recent advancements were substantial, so you might consider their adoption depending on their maturity when you read this book. As an architect of Industrial Internet solutions, you will be expected to understand the potential impact of upcoming technologies as you evaluate design choices and decide which components to use and the architecture to deploy.

Historically, emerging technology platforms have shared a common pattern of transitioning through multiple stages of maturity. Initially, there is a period of rapid innovation and development driven by competing research efforts, each having a goal of establishing an early market presence. Initial iterations of new platforms are usually more focused on meeting the needs of developers. As platforms begin to become established, competing platform companies seek to drive standards adoption, usually around the platforms they have developed.

Standardization improves the flexibility platform providers have in mixing components from various vendors and this, in turn, can drive further platform adoption. Mass adoption occurs when applications become available for the platforms and can be deployed by a much wider audience beyond developers. Applications can not only greatly simplify initial deployment, but also simplify support and upgrades.

The following diagram illustrates the timeline of this pattern and represents the relative degrees of customization, complexity, and skills required at each stage of maturity over time:

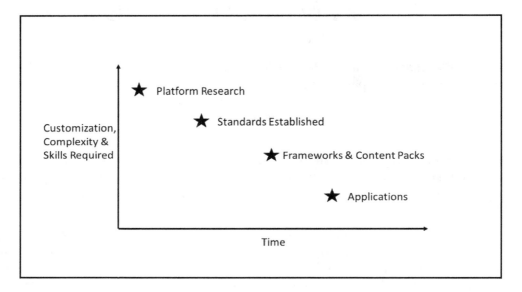

Today, the Industrial Internet is in a period in which many IIoT standards are still being proposed, debated, and then accepted and adopted. However, some vendors are simultaneously establishing themselves as leaders in building starter solutions with pre-integrated components (including devices), even as some of the standards are still developing and maturing.

In prior chapters, we focused on defining architectures to deploy Industrial Internet solutions based on the maturity of today's offerings. In this chapter, we'll describe the emergence of IIoT frameworks and applications development workspaces, as well as the growth in more complete applications. We'll also describe the evolution that is occurring in devices and networks, efforts to improve **human machine interfaces** (**HMIs**), how industrial robotics will evolve, how blockchain technology will enable a more secure infrastructure, and the possible impacts of quantum computing and nanotechnology.

There is also much speculation about the impact that these sorts of projects will have. While you might not initially see this debate as being relevant to your role, we believe that it will be important for architects to understand possible objections and more positive views when defending proposed projects in the future.

With that in mind, the major sections in this chapter are as follows:

- Maturing IIoT frameworks and applications
- Evolving edge devices
- The evolution of networking
- Cognitive and mixed reality HMIs and deep learning
- The impact on robotics and mobile devices
- Improved security through blockchain technology
- Quantum computing
- The Industrial Internet's impact on society

Let's now look at near-term and more distant anticipated changes and advancements. We will begin by discussing the rapid maturation of IIoT applications and application frameworks that is occurring.

Maturing IIoT frameworks and applications

In Chapter 5, *Assessing Industrial Internet Applications*, we described some considerations regarding applications and emerging frameworks. As this book was being published, industrial providers of applications and public **Cloud Services Providers** (**CSPs**) were continuing to develop frameworks of components useful in developing these applications, along with new IIoT applications. While some of the industrial providers initially focused on deploying their applications and frameworks to their own clouds, there appears to be movement by many of these companies to redeploy their offerings upon public clouds, leveraging the significant investments in infrastructure and aggressive pricing provided by leading CSPs.

The major CSPs (such as AWS, Google, IBM, Microsoft Azure, Oracle, and others) continue to extend functionality of components in their IIoT frameworks. Some have created applications development workspaces focused on broad areas with preconfigured components to speed applications development. A sample of the areas being addressed by packaged development environments includes the connected factory, remote monitoring, predictive maintenance, and connected field services. Systems integrators frequently team with the CSPs to offer services needed to build out these IIoT solutions.

Many industrial manufacturers have adopted one or more of these frameworks and offer IIoT applications that manage and monitor the equipment that they sell. For example, Rockwell Automation offers solutions for providing intelligence and manages manufacturing and production and energy utilization on the plant floor. Johnson Controls offers IIoT applications to control and manage building HVAC systems and enable enhanced troubleshooting.

As some of the extremely large and diversified industrial companies created IIoT applications for their **line of business** (**LOB**) and the devices that they manufacture, they saw an opportunity to promote their underlying frameworks for usage in further development. This appears to be a growing trend. GE's Predix platform is probably the most well-known example.

GE focused initially on building applications used in deploying and managing GE assets in industries that included transportation, aviation, healthcare, industrial manufacturing, mining, oil and gas, power distribution and generation (including wind), transportation, and water resources. GE Digital is creating a new architecture for applications – combining systems of record with systems of innovation – to power digital industrial companies. The Predix platform enables the building of solutions that include scheduling and logistics, connected products, intelligent environments, field force management, and predictive and prescriptive asset optimization and repair. The pre-built applications powered by Predix platform include **Asset Performance Management (APM)**, **Operations Performance Management (OPM)** and **Brilliant Manufacturing Suite (BMS)**. The APM suite gives industrial businesses a complete, integrated view of their assets and equipment at all levels, allowing for more intelligent decision-making and improved operations. The OPM provides advisory analytics from the boardroom to the asset level, combining real-time and historical data to power decision-making with a single dashboard view. Brilliant Manufacturing is the digital technology behind Brilliant Factories. It enables manufacturers to make precise, real-time decisions through data-driven insights. With the acquisition of ServiceMax, a leader in cloud-based field service management (FSM) solutions, GE Digital is poised to reinvent the way assets are managed, maintained and serviced, reducing downtime and removing costs.

The Predix foundation utilizes microservices, an increasingly popular approach that speeds code reuse, development, and deployment. Microservices are self-contained software services with well-defined APIs, and they communicate with each other using a standard communications protocol. Predix has defined microservices that address assets, analytics, data, security, and operations.

Microservices for managing devices and assets

Microservices are sometimes deployed to manage single aspects of a physical asset. By breaking the management into microservices, upgrades for each management aspect become faster and simpler.

Predix applications are deployed in the multi-tier architecture that we described throughout this book and consist of edge devices, networks, and backend components. The Predix foundation can be looked at as a PaaS model and utilizes Pivotal's **Cloud Foundry**.

The Cloud Foundry is an industry standard open source cloud application platform for developing and deploying enterprise cloud applications. It helps automate, scale, and manage cloud-based applications throughout their life cycle. Microservices and applications can be written in multiple languages and are deployed in container images in many different cloud infrastructures.

Many other frameworks were being promoted by other industrial applications providers as this book was being published. Emerson, Honeywell Process Solutions, and Schneider Electric each promoted their own frameworks (known as **PlantWeb**, **Uniformance Suite**, and **Exostructure**, respectively). For example, Schneider Electric's Exostructure framework provides an energy-focused IIoT architecture and platform. It is used primarily for managing buildings, data centers, industrial facilities, and power grids. The architecture was created to solve problems in machine automation and process automation, especially in the oil and gas industry, food and beverage industry, mining and metal industry, minerals and cement industry, and at water and wastewater facilities.

These frameworks share much in common. They rely on popular communications protocols for networking, usually including support for emerging popular standards. They typically support certain devices and sensors that have been tested and that are certified to be part of the solution. Some examples of the devices offered in these frameworks include transmitters, flow meters, analyzers, actuators, and controllers.

The frameworks and applications are continuing to mature. Some industry analysts speculated a few years ago that every industrial company would need to become a software company in the future. However, we believe it is more likely that most industrial companies will simply purchase complete integrated suites that include specific devices, networking, and backend cloud-based infrastructure from a few of the major vendors and industrial companies making large investments in developing these solutions.

Multi-cloud deployment

A growing trend in many industrial companies is the deployment of multi-cloud solutions. One reason for doing this is the belief that deploying on multiple CSPs will assure highly competitive pricing among the CSPs in the future. Another driver of multi-cloud strategies are the frequent mergers and acquisitions common for many industrial companies. For example, a company managing plants that have a mixture of Emerson, Honeywell, and Schneider Electric controls from a headquarters location might want to gather data that resides in multiple CSPs and multiple regions. Network exchange vendors are typically engaged to provide a network bridge among these sites to facilitate data exchange. It is important for the architect to consider the need for and cost of highly available network architectures that connect the devices to clouds or are used to transmit data among multiple clouds.

Evolving edge devices

In earlier chapters, we described the growing trend of computing activities taking place in smart edge devices, thus enabling immediate actions to take place prior to the transmission of data to the backend infrastructure. Some are now referring to this paradigm as fog computing. As this book was being published, consortia were in the initial stages of defining fog computing reference architectures and establishing standards through standards bodies.

Edge devices themselves are becoming smaller and consolidating. Previously, the controllers, HMIs, cameras, motion controls, and SCADA devices were physically separated and then networked together in field locations. Increasingly, these components reside in single units that also contain ever more powerful processors and **field-programmable gate arrays (FPGAs)** for customization.

The edge devices are sometimes deployed to locations where it is difficult to replace worn batteries that supply power. One source of the power drain is the voltage that is applied to microprocessors that normally operate at about 1.8V. Recently, several start-ups have begun manufacturing processors with greater precision that can operate at voltages less than 0.5V, thus greatly extending the life of batteries. In 2017, success in the commercialization of such microprocessors was still to be determined.

A manufacturing device that has drawn interest for many years is the 3D printer. These *printers* produce three-dimensional objects from data that is held in digital files. The promise of 3D printing includes rapid production of customized products and parts, reduced logistics costs, and faster time to market. The research and development of such printers is continuing, with the goal of enabling a wider variety of parts and assemblies to be produced using a wider variety of materials and at greater speed. This is often referred to as additive manufacturing
(https://www.technologyreview.com/s/513716/additive-manufacturing/). Many of the deployment strategies and security concerns we have discussed throughout the book are relevant, since the 3D printers are deployed as IIoT devices.

The evolution of networking

Qualcomm
(https://www.qualcomm.com/news/onq/2017/05/16/private-lte-networks-industrial-iot-how-spectrum-sharing-will-expand-lte) has been one of the pioneers in highlighting the emergence of private **Long-Term Evolution** (**LTE**) networks for Industrial Internet infrastructure and applications. The fifth-generation mobile networks or fifth-generation wireless systems, abbreviated as 5G, are the next proposed telecommunications standards beyond the current 4G standard. Carriers in the United States are targeting 2020 for widespread deployment of 5G technology. Marc Tracey, a Verizon spokesman, said, *"Basically, 5G will provide a wider pipeline and faster lanes"* for data-rich applications as such as IoT. However, until 5G becomes mainstream technology over the next few years, private LTE networks can help speed up the realization of benefits for Industrial Internet applications.

The following illustration shows some of the industries that can benefit from private LTE networks, according to *Harbor Research* (February 2017):

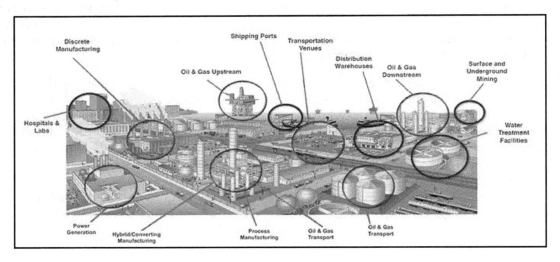

The concept of private LTE networks implies that the enterprise customers run their own local network with dedicated equipment and settings, rather than relying on the carrier. The key characteristics of the private LTE networks are as follows:

- **Rapid deployment**: Due to the availability of shared and unlicensed spectrum, deployment of private LTE network can be done easily today
- **Local control**: This refers to the use of local deployment equipment at the enterprise customer's site; it is relatively immune to traffic surges and provides better and reliable performance
- **Optimization**: It can be optimized for the specific IoT applications by controlling the **Quality of Service (QoS)** and other network settings

As this book was being published, **Low Power wireless Wide Area Networks (LPWANs)** were being explored as an alternative in many organizations. LPWAN is designed for long-range communications at low bit rates and is ideal for sensors operating on battery power. Battery life can be extended to provide power for over 10 years or more. A variety of LPWAN protocols were undergoing development and beginning to establish themselves in 2017, including **LTE advanced for Machine Type Communications (LTE-MTC)**, Haystack Technologies, LoRaWAN, Symphony Link, and **Ultra Narrow Band (UNB)**. Given these technologies were in early adoption and many were initially considered proprietary, it was expected that it would require a few years to determine which would gain widespread adoption and become broad standards.

Recently, the **Open Platform Communications Unified Architecture (OPC UA)** has gained increased adoption for IEEE 802.1 based networks. OPC UA replaces an early OPC protocol that was Windows-based and relied on COM/DCOM as a communications model. The OPC UA architecture is built on **Time Sensitive Networking (TSN)**, an extension of the IEEE 802.1 standard that enables network devices such as **programmable automation controllers (PACs)** to operate according to synchronized clocks. The following diagram illustrates this stack:

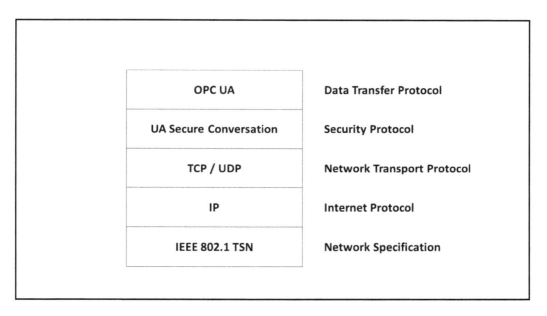

Authentication over OPC UA is via X.509 certificates and provides better security than the original OPC stack. APIs are available for multiple programming languages.

An indication of the growing popularity of OPC UA is its adoption by multiple device manufacturers. For example, GE Energy utilizes OPC UA for transmitting weather data to real-time controls in some of its devices. Given the frequent changes in what is popular, most device manufacturers usually provide adapters for previous commonly used protocols as well.

Networking layers are sometimes simply represented in just three layers consisting of an applications layer, a controls layer, and an infrastructure or hardware layer. We'll use the following diagram to introduce two abstraction levels, SDN and NFV, that are growing in popularity and are pictured between the three layers as shown here:

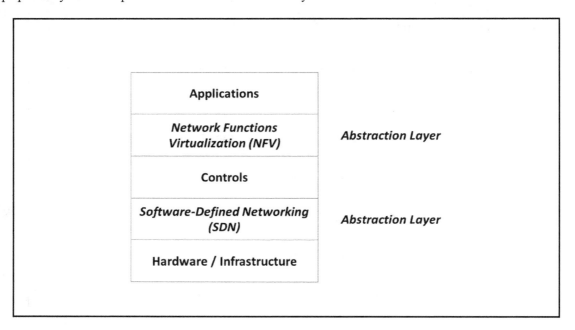

Software-Defined Networking (SDN) gained widespread data center adoption, especially among CSPs, in the past decade. It enables network management and control that is not tightly bound to underlying hardware and networks with centrally defined control policies for physical and virtual networks. SDN was expected to continue to move beyond data centers into wired and wireless networks, enabling programmability and automation across all networks in an IIoT architecture. Indeed, SD-WANs were growing in acceptance as a deployment strategy in IIoT architecture footprints as this book was being written.

Network Functions Virtualization (**NFV**) provides a layer of abstraction between the network applications and controls layer. Network functions (applications) are decoupled from hardware devices and under the control of a hypervisor. Network services previously provided by dedicated hardware devices such as routers, firewalls, and load balancers can instead be deployed using commodity servers. Many of the providers of dedicated hardware solutions have transitioned their software to supporting generic servers. Given that most public clouds are also built on massive numbers of generic servers, these configurations are particularly popular among CSPs.

Either of these abstraction layers can be deployed independently of each other. Since they reside between different layers of the stack, they can also be deployed in combination with each other.

Cognitive and mixed reality HMIs and deep learning

Over the past decade, HMIs evolved for many edge devices, from simple digital displays to dashboards rendered by business intelligence tools. The data gathered can be presented at the device on mobile devices that are connected via networks or transmitted to a central location. In some implementations, automated actions are initiated based on certain thresholds being reached.

The interfaces are becoming more varied as cognitive APIs are deployed as part of the HMI. Cognitive APIs deliver interfaces that can be used to speed searching, critical for use in many industrial-oriented applications where technicians must deal with mountains of engineering plans, circuit diagrams, and maintenance instructions. Cognitive APIs can also enable vision and speech recognition and language translation. The APIs are used in the construction of new knowledge-based applications (such as those making recommendations based on responses to questions, using the answers that are provided). Behind the APIs, one often finds machine learning algorithms and artificial intelligence making the recommendations and delivering insight.

Advances in artificial intelligence were drawing tremendous interest as this book was being written. Neural network algorithms, available in machine learning and data mining tools for many years, evolved in sophistication for use in deep learning projects. Recurrent neural networks are being deployed to **Long Short-Term Memory (LSTM)** networks and are used to predict future metrics values based on previous readings and for natural language processing. The following diagram is a typical representation of a recurrent neural network, illustrating multiple inputs to a hidden layer feeding multiple outputs and feedback provided to the hidden layer:

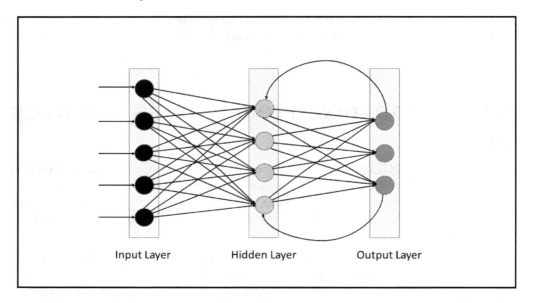

Input Layer   Hidden Layer   Output Layer

Deep neural network (DNN) models consist of multiple hidden layers. As each layer accurately performs analysis, the results are passed on to the next layer for further learning and refinement. Today's huge cloud-based analysis engines consisting of many nodes are beginning to make such analyses possible. These workloads are driving a need for next generation computing engines featuring nodes containing more powerful **Graphics Programming Units (GPUs)** and FPGAs, as well as quantum computers.

Google released TensorFlow as an open source software library in 2015. The overall goal is to make it easier for developers to design, build, and train deep learning models. TensorFlow has a Python library to allow users to express computation as a graph of data flows. Google developed a **tensor processing unit (TPU)** to speed up the required computing for machine learning. This TPU is an **application-specific integrated circuit (ASIC)**.

To understand the computing ability of TPU, consider the example of Google Photos. An individual TPU can process over 100 million photos a day. We expect that IIoT platforms and applications will use the power of such machine learning paradigms to solve complex problems that often involve image and video analysis. TPUs are available through the **Google Compute Platform** (**GCP**) only. Each GCP Cloud TPU will offer up to 180 teraflops of computing performance, as well as 64 GBs of ultra-high-bandwidth memory. However, when architects are developing platforms and applications for a multi-cloud, they have to be aware of the propriety nature of these hardware acceleration devices.

Augmented reality (**AR**) and **mixed reality** (**MR**) eyewear devices provide a means of viewing data superimposed on real-world industrial machines and devices. Augmented reality provides heads-up displays of data around real physical objects as the objects are being looked at through the eyewear. Mixed reality has 3D spatial awareness of real objects, such that virtual objects can be anchored in real space. Unlike the totally immersive **virtual reality** (**VR**) that many of us are familiar with in gaming systems, these devices feature small, embedded computers and sensors in the eyewear and can be mobile as the human wearing them moves about in the real world. Interactions are typically through gaze, gesture, and voice input.

The following Venn diagram represents the interactions that MR, AR, and VR have with the real world:

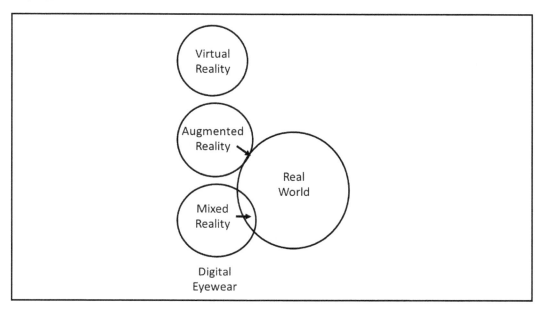

In Industrial Internet applications, eyewear devices might be worn by technicians in the field and by others monitoring devices and equipment. Industrial machines that might pose a hazard in the real world can be safely explored in this virtual world during skills development and training exercises. The eyewear can deliver hands-free instructions, speeding tasks and enhancing safety. Management and field inspectors can see a duplication of what their technicians are seeing in the field by wearing networked eyewear and can provide real-time supervision and guidance. As the power of these embedded computers in the eyewear grows, so will their sophistication and capabilities.

The impact on robotics and mobile devices

While 3D printers show promise today in the manufacturing of parts and small assemblies, many products that industrial companies produce require the assembly of a massive number of diverse parts and subassemblies. Mass production has undergone a noticeable change in many industries over the past generation, most notably through the introduction of robotics in factories. Few would take issue with the argument that robotics have greatly improved quality and reduced costs in the manufacturing of automobiles, for example.

Robotics research and development has primarily focused on greatly improving dexterity of the devices and better programming interfaces. An IIoT infrastructure offers the promise of helping to define a new generation of industrial robotics.

Next-generation robotic devices will use 3D-embedded vision and multi-spectral imaging in this connected IIoT world. As we noted in our discussion of other edge devices, more processing power will enable greater use of analytics and artificial intelligence in robotics devices. Deep learning could enable the robotics to learn on the job through trial and error and deductive reasoning. A process called evolutionary robotics is sometimes utilized in which algorithms operate on a population of controllers, fitness is determined, and those controllers and software in the most successful group are chosen to move forward with.

In the future, robotic devices no longer need be single purpose. Instead, they will be repurposed as needed and, given their increased mobility, be redeployed to other factory locations as needed.

Many recent advances are already making it possible for robotics to execute repetitive tasks that humans were formerly required to perform. Robotic devices are now able to pick parts, compare them, and inspect them for quality, for example. There are also use cases outside of the factory, including managing supplies in distribution centers and performing maintenance activities in situations where human safety is a concern.

Recently, many of these capabilities have been incorporated into flying mobile devices known as drones. In industrial applications, drones are being utilized to help deliver parts in supply chains and provide visual inspections of physical infrastructure in hard-to-reach locations.

Improved security through blockchain technology

Blockchain technology provides a means of building a secure, shared, and distributed database that can't be modified, often referred to as a distributed ledger, ensuring that data remains in its original, unaltered state. Data is replicated across many nodes. New transactions are digitally signed for security, with private keys used to create signatures and public keys used to verify the signatures. When participating nodes agree the data is valid, it is written to the database. The unique digital signatures ensure no individual blockchain node can modify the transaction message.

Transactions contain information about the sender, receiver, time of creation, data to be transferred, and reference transactions. Transactions are grouped together in blocks and a chain is created that maintains a history of ownership of digital assets from previous transactions. Blocks are added to the blockchain when validity of transactions is assured through *consensus*. Each block includes a hash of the prior block.

Blockchains are implemented across geographically separated distributed systems and storage and attain better parallelism, reliability, and availability in such configurations. Consensus is achieved through weak consistency models, a practical approach when many nodes are used to determine validity.

Blockchains first came into being as the underlying architecture for Bitcoin. In November 2008, a paper was published by an author using the name of Satoshi Nakamoto (never validated as a real person) and entitled *Bitcoin: A Peer-to-Peer Electronic Cash System*. The first bitcoins were issued in January 2009. By 2014, **blockchain 2.0** had emerged, describing new applications that could be built on the distributed blockchain database.

Blockchains were being investigated for usefulness in several IIoT applications at the time this book was published in 2017. Possible use cases being explored included the application of blockchains to improve security in the IIoT infrastructure by doing the following:

- Maintaining tamper-proof logs of transactions
- Securing device directories and broadcasts of updates

- Ensuring that items in transit are genuine and unaltered when managing supply chains
- Ensuring secure control of electrical grids and the delivery of power only to validated endpoints

Blockchains and other, less sophisticated security mechanisms are believed to be under threat in the future from powerful quantum computers. However, there are already efforts underway to create quantum key distributions for use with blockchains to secure them when quantum computers become practical for use in attacking today's cryptographic solutions.

Quantum computing

Many leading cloud and technology vendors are researching and developing quantum computers that operate by manipulating subatomic particles. These vendors are driven by a vision that quantum computing devices could be millions of times faster than today's computers. Some of the first versions of quantum computers with more limited power were being advertised as this book was published.

Quantum computers are fundamentally different from mainstream binary computers that have existed from the beginning of the electronic computer age. In binary computations, bits can be in one of two states, off or on (represented as 0s or 1s). This basic concept drove the inner workings of the first electronic computers that relied on vacuum tubes, later computers that relied on transistors and, still later, computers relying on integrated circuits.

The quantum computation theory was defined in the 1980s in works published by Richard Feynman, David Albert, and David Deutsch. The additional computational power stems from the premise that quantum bits (qubits) can exist in additional states simultaneously through what is called **superposition**. Early efforts in creating superposition focused on manipulating photons or electrons using technologies such as ion traps, optical traps, quantum dots (a single electron trapped by multiple atoms), semiconductor impurities, and superconducting circuits.

Dealing with qubits in superposition is extremely tricky. If you try to look at a qubit in superposition, its value will appear to be 0 or 1 (so, it will appear to be binary). A technique called entanglement is used to detect the spin of the first atom by placing a second atom next to it. The second atom will assume the opposite spin of the first. Through superposition, two qubits can perform four calculations.

Much of the work over the past few years has been focused on increasing the number of qubits that can be manipulated, minimizing errors in detection, maintaining superposition, and moving qubits over small distances. Two early types of quantum computers emerged: adiabatic and quantum gate array computers.

Adiabatic quantum computers use a concept called annealing, usually associated with heating and then cooling metals in metalworking. Qubits can be stressed and then relaxed into patterns, making these computers useful in pattern matching types of problems. A company named D-Wave produced early quantum computers that relied on QPUs (quantum processing units) built using Niobium metal and superconductors that operated at 9.2 degrees Kelvin (-263.95 degrees Celsius).

Quantum gate array computers contain registers that hold numbers and support common mathematical functions. They are different from traditional computers, in that registers represent all numbers and, when multiplying, qubits register together. Every possible product is held in the register.

In 2016 and 2017, apparent breakthroughs in the creation of photonic chips and quantum computing were publicized. In a photonic chip, a laser fires light pulses into a micro-ring resonator etched in silica. The resonator emits tangled pairs of photons called qudits. Two qudits, each having a dimension of 10 different states, were entangled and performed 100 different calculations. The qudits were then sent through optical fiber to prove that entanglement could be preserved over distances. So, not only was this development potentially able to produce computers much more powerful than previous quantum-computing efforts, but it also showed promise to be more commercially viable.

It is currently not believed that quantum computers will solve all problems faster than conventional computers, given their unique way of operating. However, quantum algorithms do exist for factorizing large numbers (Shor's algorithm) and searching unsorted databases (Grover's algorithm). It is believed that quantum computers will eventually solve today's public key / private key combinations used in cryptography in minutes or seconds. However, they will also be useful in generating next-generation quantum keys that can't be copied without destroying them. They will provide much greater performance in machine learning, anomaly detection, and data-sampling problems.

DNA logic for faster processing and dense storage

A branch of nanoscale research with the goals of providing faster computing and increased storage capacity involves the manipulation of synthetic DNA molecules. Nanoscale computational circuits can be created using synthetic DNA and organized using a technique called **DNA origami**. Synthetic DNA is also being tested for usage in the encoding and decoding of stored data. A single gram of DNA can store almost a zettabyte (one trillion gigabytes) of data, and it is believed that storage of data in this format can exist for thousands of years. Wide availability of DNA-based computing and storage devices is thought to be many years in the future.

The Industrial Internet's impact on society

The popular press tends to focus on many of the potentially negative outcomes from next-generation technologies in general and Industrial Internet projects specifically. Privacy and security challenges and the danger of cyberwars targeting industrial production are raised as concerns. Such forums also call attention to potential job loss for workers possessing skills that are no longer in demand and accountability and liability challenges in IIoT implementations. While some of these concerns can be mitigated through proper architecture planning, other challenges being raised go well beyond the technology considerations.

Such challenges can cause a company to hesitate in pursuing IIoT projects. As an architect interested in moving such projects forward, you should be aware of potential concerns and objections and prepare responses and steps to mitigate them where possible.

While some think tanks and organizations call attention only to the potentially negative impacts of Industrial Internet, others (such as the World Economic Forum) provide a more balanced view. In addition to the challenges, they describe many positive outcomes that might be expected from these projects. Some of the potentially positive outcomes include the following:

- Increased efficiencies in using resources
- Improved productivity
- Lower cost in delivering products and services
- Better quality of life

- Environmental improvement
- Greater resource transparency
- Improved safety
- Better business management through data-driven decisions

In fact, improvement in the quality of products being produced and better management of resources has resulted from many IIoT projects. The introduction of digital twins as part of these projects has enabled better and more frequent testing of prototypes in safer environments. These projects can deliver tremendous economic benefits, and we described a methodology for identifying and documenting these benefits earlier in this book.

Industrial Internet solutions are leading to the creation of new kinds of businesses and the revising of old business models. Innovative companies are creating new jobs even as old ones disappear, albeit with a shift in the skills that are required. Workers are needed who possess skills in managing and maintaining the new footprints that are being deployed. Trainers possessing expertise in change management are required to develop the skills of people interacting with these devices. Demands for device and robotics designers continue to grow, as does demand for IIoT architects, programmers, data analysts and data scientists, managed services providers, and networking and security specialists.

A forthcoming role you might evangelize is that of Citizen Developers for Industrial Internet applications. Gartner (http://www.gartner.com/it-glossary/citizen-developer/) describes the *Citizen Developer* as a business person who creates new business applications for consumption by other business users. They will utilize rapid development and runtime environments approved by the architects and the software development team.

To empower *Citizen Developers*, the applications development environment must be relatively code free and feature enhanced drag-and-drop capabilities. Often, such environments are referred to as *studios*, providing both mashup and integrated workflow capabilities, thus enabling the rapid application development of day-to-day scenarios. We believe the involvement of the Citizen Developers will accelerate the rapid realization of value from Industrial Internet applications. The industry has seen tremendous success in business intelligence applications by involving similar Citizen Developers with strong domain knowledge.

Your organization will likely face many tradeoffs when it considers the societal implications of these projects. The following illustration summarizes many of the tradeoffs that your organization will likely balance:

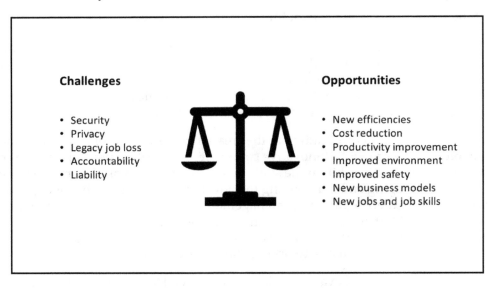

As with any technology, advances in IIoT can be used to create projects that test moral and ethical standards. Such projects might be envisioned to benefit just a few individuals and organizations to the detriment of others. Advancements in technology far outpace government bureaucracies and standards organizations and their ability to legislate and limit practices that might be viewed as unfair. Ultimately, architects and planners of these projects must take responsibility in considering the implications of their designs and their impact on privacy, safety, and other facets.

Summary

In this chapter, we provided guidance on some of the emerging trends and future technologies that could impact Industrial Internet projects that you are considering today. You should have gained a better understanding of the potential impact of maturing IIoT frameworks and applications, how devices and networks are evolving, new HMIs that will be used in monitoring and controlling devices, the roles of artificial intelligence and deep learning, how blockchain technology might be used to improve security, and the potential power and usefulness of quantum computing. We also hope that our brief discussion about the impacts on society leaves you with some food for thought.

Many of these advancements will help drive adoption of next-generation IIoT solutions. Integration will become seamless among devices running applications. The devices will become more intelligent in ever smaller footprints and become easier to manage through HMIs at the edge and in central locations. Securing these devices and backend footprints using advanced cryptography technologies will not be an afterthought. Backend infrastructure, including highly distributed database engines and other components, will continue to evolve at the nearly continuous rate of change that public cloud vendors already enable.

Prior to reading this book, you likely already thought of IIoT as a diverse infrastructure including devices in the field, networking, and data center components. You probably recognized some of the challenges in defining and implementing these solutions, but also saw the unique capabilities that these solutions could provide to help solve existing and emerging business problems.

This book was designed to provide you with a grounding in how to define an Industrial Internet architecture. As we traversed its chapters, we provided a perspective on the history of the Industrial Internet, architectural approaches, gathering business requirements and mapping those to a functional architecture, assessing applications, defining the data and analytics architecture, choosing a technology deployment architecture, securing the Industrial Internet, governance and assuring compliances, use cases, and a glimpse into the future.

Defining an architecture for these solutions requires a broad mix of skills and a diverse team. It will require continuous learning as the components and solutions continue to improve and advance. It is our hope that you now have a better understanding of the nature of these solutions. More importantly, we hope that you gained enough knowledge and confidence in your ability to define and move your own Industrial Internet project beyond its initial consideration and through its subsequent architecture design and deployment phases.

We conclude by offering you our best wishes as you design and deploy your Industrial Internet project, while hoping that we have started you on the road to success.

Sources

Chapter 1

- *Microsoft Azure IoT Reference Architecture, Microsoft*: `https://azure.microsoft.com/en-us/updates/microsoft-azure-iot-reference-architecture-available/`
- Stackowiak, Robert, A Licht, V Mantha, and L Nagode. *Big Data and The Internet of Things: Enterprise Architecture for a New Age.* New York, NY: Apress (Springer Media), 2015.
- The Open Group, TOGAF: `http://www.opengroup.org/subjectareas/enterprise/togaf`
- World Economic Forum: *Industrial Internet of Things: Unleashing the Potential of Connected Products and Services, January 2015*: `http://www3.weforum.org/docs/WEFUSA_IndustrialInternet_Report2015.pdf3`

Chapter 2

- Example of data for Aircraft from Aviation week: `http://aviationweek.com/connected-aerospace/internet-aircraft-things-industry-set-be-transformed`

Chapter 3

- *Business Architecture and Agile Methodologies,* Business Architecture Guild, February 2015: `http://c.ymcdn.com/sites/www.businessarchitectureguild.org/resource/resmgr/BA__AgileMethodologis.pdf`
- Business Architecture Institute: `http://www.bainstitute.org/`
- Deloitte, *Enterprise Value Map, 2004:* `http://public.deloitte.com/media/0268/enterprise_value_map_2_0.pdf`
- Ross, J., P Weill, and D Robertson, *Enterprise Architecture as a Strategy: Creating a Foundation for Business Execution.* Boston, MA: Harvard Business School Press, 2006.
- Westbrock, Tim. *True-IA? A True-EA Perspective for Information Architecture,* November 29, 2016: `http://www.eadirections.com/2016/11/true-ia-a-true-ea-perspective-for-information-architecture/`

Chapter 4

- Agile Alliance: `https://www.agilealliance.com`
- *Industrial Internet of Things Volume G1: Reference Architecture.* Industrial Internet Consortium, IIC:PUB:G1:V1.80:20170131, January 2017

Chapter 5

- Forbes article, related to custom software strategy: `https://www.forbes.com/sites/chuckcohn/2014/09/15/build-vs-buy-how-to-know-when-you-should-build-custom-software-over-canned-solutions/#34b55effc371`
- LNS Research, APM definition: `http://blog.lnsresearch.com/what-is-asset-performance-management`
- `http://www.reliasoft.com/newsletter/v11i1/asset_management.htm`
- Transportation Safety Board of Canada: `http://www.bst-tsb.gc.ca/eng/rapports-reports/aviation/2012/a12o0074/a12o0074.asp`
- Predictive analytics: `http://www.amadeus.com/blog/07/04/5-examples-predictive-analytics-travel-industry/`

- Optimization of Flight Path Descend: `http://your.heathrow.com/wp-content/uploads/2015/08/CDA-improvement.jpg`
- Augmented Reality for field service: `http://exelerate.com.au/wp-content/uploads/2017/02/Augmented-Reality-Field-Service.jpg`

Chapter 6

- *Azure Partner Community: Big Data, Advanced Analytics, and Lambda Architecture,* Microsoft Technet, January 27, 2016: `https://blogs.technet.microsoft.com/msuspartner/2016/01/27/azure-partner-community-big-data-advanced-analytics-and-lambda-architecture/`
- Chodorow, Kristina. *MongoDB: The Definitive Guide.* Sebastopol, CA: O'Reilly Media, 2013.
- *Graph Processing with SQL Server and Azure SQL Database,* Microsoft, July 18, 2017: `https://docs.microsoft.com/en-us/sql/relational-databases/graphs/sql-graph-overview`
- Greenwald, Rick, R Stackowiak, and J Stern. *Oracle Essentials: Oracle Database 12c.* Sebastopol, CA: O'Reilly Media, 2013.
- *Introduction to Azure HDInsight, the Hadoop Technology Stack, and Hadoop Clusters,* Microsoft, July 20, 2017: `https://docs.microsoft.com/en-us/azure/hdinsight/hdinsight-hadoop-introduction`
- *Introduction to Machine Learning in the Azure Cloud,* Microsoft, July 12, 2017: `https://docs.microsoft.com/en-us/azure/machine-learning/machine-learning-what-is-machine-learning`
- *Lambda Architecture for Batch and Real-time Processing on AWS with Spark Streaming and Spark SQL,* Amazon Web Services, May 2015: `https://d0.awsstatic.com/whitepapers/lambda-architecure-on-for-batch-aws.pdf`
- *Overview of the Azure IoT Hub Service,* Microsoft, June 16, 2017: `https://docs.microsoft.com/en-us/azure/iot-hub/iot-hub-what-is-iot-hub`
- Plunkett, Tom, B Macdonald, B Nelson, R Stackowiak, et al. *Oracle Big Data Handbook.* New York, NY: McGraw-Hill Oracle Press, 2013.
- *What is Stream Analytics?,* Microsoft, June 16, 2017: `https://docs.microsoft.com/en-us/azure/stream-analytics/stream-analytics-introduction`

Chapter 7

- *Architecture of Compromise* article: https://www.world-architects.com/en/architecture-news/reviews/architecture-of-compromise

Chapter 8

- Chavin, Ajit and M Nighot. *Secure CoAP Using Enhanced DTLS for Internet of Things*, Internation Journal of Innovative Research in Computer and Communication Engineering, December 2014: https://www.rroij.com/open-access/secure-coap-using-enhanced-dtls-forinternet-of-things.pdf
- *Industrial Internet of Things Volume G4: Security Framework. Industrial Internet Consortium*, IIC:PUB:G4:V1.0:PB:20160926, September 2016.
- *Internet of Things Security Architecture*, Microsoft, July 3, 2017: https://docs.microsoft.com/en-us/azure/iot-suite/iot-security-architecture
- NIST. *Cybersecurity Framework*, 2017: https://www.nist.gov/cyberframework
- Quinnell, Richard. *Low Power Wide-Area Networking Alternatives for the IoT*, EDN Network, September 15, 2015: http://www.edn.com/design/systems-design/4440343/Low-power-wide-area-networking-alternatives-for-the-IoT
- Rowe, Kim. *Making Sense of Internet of Things Protocols and Implementations*, ICC Media, 2013: http://files.iccmedia.com/pdf/rowebots140313.pdf
- *Securing your Internet of Things from the Ground Up*, Microsoft, July 3, 2017: https://docs.microsoft.com/en-us/azure/iot-suite/securing-iot-ground-up
- Yinbiao, Dr. Shu et al. *Internet of Things: Wireless Sensor Networks* (white paper). IEC, http://www.iec.ch/whitepaper/pdf/iecWP-internetofthings-LR-en.pdf, 2014.

Chapter 9

- Gilsinn, James and R Schierholz. Security Assurance Levels: A Vector Approach to Describing Security Requirements, October 20, 2010: http://ws680.nist.gov/publication/get_pdf.cfm?pub_id=906330
- IEC (International Electrotechnical Commission): http://www.iec.ch
- IEEE (Institute of Electrical and Electronics Engineers): http://www.ieee.org
- IETF (Internet Engineering Task Force): http://www.ietf.org

- ISA (International Society of Automation): `https://www.isa.org`
- ISAE (International Standard on Assurance Engagements): `http://isae.3402.com`
- ISO (International Organization for Standardization): `http://www.iso.org`
- Microsoft Azure compliance, 2017, `https://www.microsoft.com/en-us/trustcenter/compliance/complianceofferings`
- NIST Special Publication 800-53. *Security and Privacy Controls for Federal Information Systems and Organizations*, April 2013: `http://dx.doi.org/10.6028/NIST.SP.800-53r4`
- NIST Special Publication 800-82. Guide to Industrial Control Systems (ICS) Security, May 2015: `http://nvlpubs.nist.gov/nistpubs/SpecialPublications/NIST.SP.800-82r2.pdf`
- NIST Special Publication 800-171. *Protecting Controlled Unclassified Information in Nonfederal Information Systems and Organizations*, June 2015: `http://dx.doi.org/10.6028/NIST.SP.800-171`
- OASIS (Advancing Open Standards for the Information Society): `https://oasis-open.org`
- OMG (Object Management Group): `http://www.omg.org`
- W3C (Worldwide Web Consortium): `http://www.w3c.org`

Chapter 10

- *Enterprise Architecture Guides* (Planning for Big Data by Industry), Oracle, 2015-2016: `http://www.oracle.com/us/dm/seo100432412-na-us-wh-de1-ev-2578002.html`

Chapter 11

- Barbier, Francois. *5 Trends for the Future of Manufacturing*. World Economic Forum, June 22, 2017: `http://www.weforum.org`
- Bone, Simon and M Castro. *A Brief History of Quantum Computing*. Imperial College of London Department of Computing, June 9, 1997: `http://www.doc.ic.ac.uk`
- Buckup, Sebastian. *Fourth Key Questions for the Fourth Industrial Revolution*. World Economic Forum, June 26, 2017: `http://www.weforum.org`

- Casemore, Ben. *SD-WAN: Aligning the Network with Digital Transformation, Cloud, and Customer Engagement.* IDC, November 2016: http://www.idc.com
- Choi, Charles Q. *Qudits: The Real Future of Quantum Computing?* Institute of Electrical and Electronics Engineers, June 28, 2017: http://spectrum.ieee.org
- *Cognitive Services,* Microsoft, 2017: https://azure.microsoft.com/en-us/services/cognitive-services/
- Johnson, Dexter. *DNA Logic Gets Much Faster.* Institute of Electrical and Electronics Engineers, July 24, 2017, http://spectrum.ieee.org
- Johnson, Dexter. *Integrated Photonic Circuits Shrunk Down to the Smallest Dimensions Yet.* Institute of Electrical and Electronics Engineers, April 20, 2017: http://spectrum.ieee.org
- *Mixed Reality,* Microsoft, 2017: https://developer.microsoft.com/en-us/windows/mixed-reality/mixed_reality
- *Overview of IoT Suite,* Microsoft, 2017: https://docs.microsoft.com/en-us/azure/iot-suite/iot-suite-overview
- Savage, Neil. *Linking Chips with Light.* Institute of Electrical and Electronics Engineers, December 23, 2015: http://spectrum.ieee.org
- Schwab, Klaus. *The Fourth Industrial Revolution.* Geneva Switzerland: World Economic Forum, 2016.
- Stackpole, Beth. *Controller Evolution in the Age of IIoT.* Automation World, March 17, 2017: http://www.automationworld.com
- Wattenhofer, Roger. *The Science of the Blockchain.* Lexington, KY: Inverted Forest Publishing, 2016.
- Zhang, Mingchuan, H Zhao, R Zheng, Q Wu, and W Wei. *Cognitive Internet of Things: Concepts and Application Example.* International Journal of Computer Science Issues, November 2012: http://www.IJCSI.org

Index

A

Access Control Lists (ACLs) 219
additive manufacturing
  about 311
  reference link 311
advanced analytics
  about 58, 155
  creating, process 159
  descriptive analytics 58
  predictive analytics 58
  prescriptive analytics 58
Advanced Message Queuing Protocol (AMQP)
  105
Advanced Research Projects Agency Network
  (ARPANet) 11
agile approach 118, 119
agile movement
  DevOps 119
air separation unit (ASU) 297
aircraft maintenance
  checks 282
airline industry, use case
  about 280
  airline proactive 282
  maintenance 282
  preventive maintenance, as business 289
  reference link 283
Amazon Web Services (AWS) 8
analyst tool 158, 161
analytics applications
  assessing 132
  Brilliant Manufacturing 141
  descriptive analytics 133
  diagnostic analytics 133
  Field Service Management (FSM) application
    142
  fit gap analysis 137

predictive analytics 134
prescriptive analytics 136
analytics architecture design
  key constraints 199
analytics architecture
  mapping, to reference architecture 154
analytics tools 158
application adoption
  gaining 115
application domain
  about 45, 113, 154
  business analysts, assessing 113
  supply chain optimization application domain 115
  user skills, assessing 113
Application Performance Management 127
Application Service Providers (ASPs) 176
application-specific integrated circuit (ASIC) 316
architect's
  roles 19
  skill 19
architectural approach
  about 22
  Cloud computing 29
  connectivity framework, for Industrial Internet 26
  industrial data analytics framework 27
  multi-tier IIoT architecture 24
  reference architecture, for Industrial Internet 22
  security framework, for Industrial Internet 25
  user experience, consideration 29
architectural framework 34
architectural viewpoints
  about 35
  business viewpoint 36
  functional viewpoint 40
  usage viewpoint 38
architecture pattern
  for Industrial Internet 124

architecture type
  application architecture 19
  business architecture 19
  data architecture 20
  technology architecture 20
Argentina Personal Data Protection Act (APDA)
  251
artificial intelligence (AI) 17
Asset Performance Management (APM)
  about 125, 127
  reference link 128
asset tracking and handling
  about 289
  baggage and cargo handling 290
Augmented Reality (AR)
  about 142, 317
  reference link 142, 143
Auxiliary Power Units (APUs) 301

B

backend infrastructure cost models
  components 85
backend security
  about 229
  data lake security 231
  data warehouse security 233, 234
  ISO/IEC 27001 Security Standard 230
  NoSQL databases, security 232, 233
  strategies 230
baggage and cargo handling
  about 290
  chemical industry, automated tracking 297
  chemical industry, replenishment 297
  mishandling 292
  modules, used 296
  scanners , used 292
  services, expanding 295
  tools, tracking in manufacturing and construction
  296
basic edge device
  capabilities 104
batch layer
  about 167
  data lake 167
  data marts 169

data warehouses 169
Hadoop 167
relational databases 169
supply chain optimization 171
Binary Large Objects (BLOBs) 164
BitLocker 234
BlackEnergy malware 215
blockchain 2.0 319
blockchain technology
  about 319
  improved security 319
Bluetooth Low Energy (BLE) 16, 226
botnet 216
Brilliant Manufacturing 141
British Columbia Freedom of Information and
  Protection of Privacy Act (BC FIPPA) 251
build decisions
  versus buy decision 125
business analysts
  assessing 114
business case
  backend infrastructure cost models, components
  85
  building 84
  implementation costs, estimating 90
  networking cost 89
  smart device cost 89
  supply chain project, financial justification 91
Business Continuity Management System (BCMS)
  about 247
  goals, achieving 247
business discovery
  CSFs, gathering 76
  from data sources, to KPI delivery 80
  future benefits, documenting 90
  initializing 74
  KPI, gathering 78
  preparing, techniques 75
  solutions, building prioritization 82
  starting 75
business domain
  about 45, 116, 154
  computational deployment patterns 47
  cross-cutting function 46
  system characteristics 46

Business On-line Transaction Processing Systems
   116
business value
   creating 152
business viewpoint
   about 36
   security considerations 37

C

case study
   about 267
   versus use cases 266
Centers of Excellence (CoE) 259
Central Tool Control (CTC) 296
chemical industry
   cylinders, filling process 298
   reference link 299
Chief Executive Officer (CEO) 75
Chief Financial Officer (CFO) 75
Chief Information Officer (CIO) 21
Chief Security Officer (CSO) 20
cloud computing
   about 180
   advantages 180
   billing 182
   disadvantages 180
   Hybrid cloud 181
   private cloud 181
   public cloud 181
Cloud Controls Matrix (CCM) 247
Cloud Foundry 309
cloud gateway throttling limits 228
cloud service providers (CSPs) 248, 250, 307
cloud to device (C2D) 105, 165
cognitive APIs 315
commercial off-the-shelf (COTS) 125
composability 58
connectivity 59
connectivity transport layer
   about 206
   meshed network topology 207
   network layer consideration 206
   network topologies 207
Constrained Application Protocol (CoAP) 225
consumer packaged goods (CPGs) 265

containers
   used, for speeding DevOps 120
control domain
   about 41, 103, 154
   basic edge device, capabilities 104
   edge devices, selecting 106
   sensors, selecting 106
   smarter edge device, configurations 106
   supply chain optimization 107
Control Objectives for Information and Related
      Technologies (COBIT) 242
converged infrastructure
   about 194
   deployment considerations 195
critical success factors (CSFs)
   about 72
   gathering 76
cross-cutting function 46
Cross-Industry-Standard-Process for Data Mining
      (CRISP-DM) 159
Cryogenic Distillation
   reference link 298
Customer Relationship Management (CRM)
   about 45, 116, 185
   advantages 186
   disdvantages 186
Cyber-Physical System (CPS)
   about 26
   reference link 26
cybersecurity attacks examples 213
Cybersecurity Framework 220

D

data and analytics, IIoT
   about 55
   advanced analytics 58, 155
   advanced data processing 58
   analytics architecture, mapping to reference
      architecture 154
   automated interoperability 60
   business value, creating 152
   capabilities 146
   challenges 55
   composability 58
   connectivity 59

data analytics 148
data framework 151
data management 57
data reduction 148
description and presence 150
dynamic composition 60
functionality 152
integrability 58
integration 149
intelligent and resilient control 59
interoperability 58
publish 148
query 148
requisites 146
rights management 151
storage persistence 149
storage retrieval 149
subscribe 148
Data Distribution Service (DDS) 249
data framework 151
data governance 241
data lake
  about 167, 192
  advantages 193
  disadvantages 193
  management considerations 192
data marts 169
data mining
  versus machine learning 159
data warehouse
  about 169, 188
  advantages 189
  architecture 189
  big data 190
  big data analytics 193
  characteristics 188
  data lake 192
  data science 193
  decision support 188
  disadvantages 190
  functions 188
  Hadoop file systems 190
  management considerations 189
data wrangling tool 163
Datagram Transport Layer Security (DTLS) 225

Decision Support Systems (DSS) 188
deep learning 315
deep neural network (DNN) 316
Denial of Service (DoS) attacks 212
deployment architecture
  big data 187
  converged infrastructure 194
  current state, for IT systems 174
  data warehouse 187
  edge tier design 203
  engineered systems 194
  Enterprise Resource Planning (ERP) 183
  hosted systems 176
  IIoT constraints 195
  management and support infrastructure 210
  networking considerations 204
descriptive analytics 133
device to cloud (D2C) 105, 165
devices and edge security, to cloud gateway
  about 223, 224
  device considerations 224, 225, 226, 227
  device to gateway connections 227, 228
DevOps
  about 118
  agile movement 118
  speeding, containers used 120
  speeding, microservices used 120
diagnostic analytics 133
digital twins 109
Distributed Denial of Service (DDoS) attacks 212
DM-Crypt feature 234
DNA origami 321
Domain Name System (DNS) services 216
Dynamic Systems Development Method (DSDM)
  119

E

edge connectivity
  about 208
  Cellular 209
  LPWAN / LoRa / SIGFOX 209
  wired 208
  wireless 208
edge devices
  evolving 310

edge tier
  about 24, 50, 203
  design 203
Electronic Logging Devices (ELDs) 260
Electronic Medical Records (EMRs) 272
engineered systems
  about 194
  advantages 194
Enterprise Architect (EA) 20
enterprise asset management (EAM) 128
Enterprise Resource Management (ERM) 116
Enterprise Resource Planning (ERP)
  about 45, 183
  considerations, for SaaS cloud versus on-
    premises 183
    Customer Relationship Management (CRM) 185
    human resource management systems (HRMS)
    186
enterprise tier 24, 50
exabytes 15
Exostructure 309
eXtensible Mark-up Language (XML) 293
extraction, transformation, and loading (ETL) 111,
  149

F

Factory Operations Visibility and Intelligence (FOVI)
  about 276
  reference link 277
Feature-Driven Development (FDD) 119
field gateways 164
Field Service Management (FSM) application 142
field-programmable gate arrays (FPGAs) 310
fit gap analysis
  about 137
  cases study 138
Forms 175
functional viewpoint
  about 40
  application domain 45
  business domain 45
  control domain 41
  implementation viewpoint 48
  information domain 44
  operations domain 42

  security considerations 48

G

Gartner
  reference link 323
Google Compute Platform (GCP) 317
governance, risk, and compliance (GRC)
  about 221
  assessing 240
  data governance 241
  in supply chain optimization example 259
  trustworthiness, assessing 242
government and public institution compliance
  about 250
  non-U.S. government standards and
    certifications 251
  U.S. government standards 253
graph databases 169
graphical user interfaces (GUIs) 174

H

Hadoop file systems (HDFS) 190
Hadoop
  advantages 191
  disadvantages 191
Hardware Security Module (HSM) 227
heating, ventilation, and air conditioning (HVAC)
  13
hosted services
  about 177
  advantages 177
  disadvantages 178
  multi-tenancy 179
  single-tenant hosting 178
hosted systems
  about 176
  cloud computing 180
  hosted services 176
hubs 165
Human Capital Management (HCM) 125
human machine interfaces (HMIs) 213, 214, 306,
  315
Human Resource Management (HRM) 116
human resource management systems (HRMS)
  186

Hybrid cloud 181
HyperText Transfer Protocol (HTTP) 105

I

IIoT applications
  developing 307
IIoT architectures
  examples 274
  manufacturing 274
  test bed, manufacturing 274
IIoT constraints
  about 195
  analytics capacity considerations 198
  analytics considerations 199
  consumption models 197, 198
  incremental upgrades 195
  on-premises, versus cloud 196
IIoT frameworks
  developing 307
IIoT functional architecture
  application domain 154
  business domain 154
  control domain 154
  information domain 154
  operations domain 154
IIoT project
  benefits 270
IIoT security core building blocks 217, 219, 220
IIoT security guidelines 221, 222
implementation viewpoint
  about 48
  security considerations 54
Indoor Positioning System (IPS)
  about 278
  reference link 279
industrial data analytics framework
  about 27
  object related data 27
  relational data 27
  time series data 27
Industrial Digital Thread (IDT) 274
Industrial Internet applications
  abatement challenges 300
  asset, handling 289
  environmental impact 300

history 163
Industrial Internet Connectivity Framework (IICF)
  27
Industrial Internet Consortium (IIC) 23
Industrial Internet of Things (IIoT)
  about 7, 156
  challenges 18
Industrial Internet Reference Architecture (IIRA)
  23, 35
Industrial Internet Security Framework (IISF) 25
Industrial Internet security
  about 211
  backend security 229
  cybersecurity attacks examples 213, 215, 216,
    217
  devices and edge, securing to cloud gateway
    223
  IIoT security core building blocks 217
  IIoT security guidelines 221
  NIST cybersecurity frameworks 220
  risk assessments 234
  supply chain example security planning 236, 237
Industrial Internet
  architecture patterns 124
  business strategy framework 30
  connectivity framework 26
  evolution 9
  impact, on society 322
  need for 15
  reference architectures 22
  security framework 25
Industrial Revolution
  history 10
industry compliance certifications
  about 255
  guidelines, applying 257
information discovery tool 163
information domain
  about 44, 110, 111
  functional requisites, solving 111
  supply chain optimization information domain
    112
Information Systems Audit and Control Association
    (ISACA) 242
Information Technology (IT) 11
infrastructure as a service (IaaS) 65, 85

integrability 58
Interactive Flow Modeling Language (IFML) 249
international compliance certifications
  about 245, 246
  areas of control 246
international consortia 248
International Electrotechnical Commission (IEC) 242
International Organization for Standardization (ISO) 241, 242
International Society of Automation (ISA) 242
international standards
  about 248
  Business Strategy and Innovation Framework (BSIF) 249
  Industrial Internet Connectivity Framework (IICF) 249
  Industrial Internet Reference Architecture (IIRA) 249
  Industrial Internet Security Framework (IISF) 249
  Industrial Internet Vocabulary Technical Report (IIVTR) 249
Internet Engineering Taskforce (IETF) 225
Internet of People (IoP) 9
Internet of Things (IoT) 7
Internet of Things Reference Architecture (IoT RA) 250
interoperability 58

J

Java Management Extensions (JMX) 232

K

Kappa architecture 158
Kerberos 219
Key Distribution Center 231
key performance indicator (KPI)
  about 45
  gathering 78

L

Lambda architecture 16, 156
Layered Databus architecture pattern
  about 53
  benefits 54

Lightweight Directory Access Protocol (LDAP) 219
line of business (LOB) 249, 308
Local Tool Control (LTC) 296
Long Short-Term Memory (LSTM) 316
Long-Term Evolution (LTE) networks
  about 311
  characteristics 312
Low Power Wide Area Network (LPWAN) 90
Low Power wireless Wide Area Networks (LPWANs) 312
LTE advanced for Machine Type Communications (LTE-MTC) 312

M

machine learning tools 158, 160
machine-to-machine (m2m) 27
Machine-to-Machine Intelligence Corporation (M2Mi) 222
Maintenance, Repair and Overhaul (MRO) 281
management and support infrastructure 210
Manufacturing Execution System (MES) 116, 274
Manufacturing Resource Planning (MRP) 141
master data management (MDM) 241
meshed network topology
  advantages 207
Message Queue Telemetry Transport (MQTT) 105
message volume 165
microservices
  used, for speeding DevOps 120
Mirai malware 216
mixed reality (MR) 317
mobile devices
  impact 318
monitoring and diagnostic (M&D) 127
multi-cloud deployment 309
multi-tenancy
  about 179
  advantages 179
  disadvantages 179
multi-tier IIoT architecture
  about 24
  edge tier 24
  enterprise tier 24
  platform tier 24
Multiprotocol Label Switching (MPLS) 90

N

National Institute of Standards and Technology (NIST) 220, 242
National Science Foundation (NSF) 26
National Security (NSA) 223
Near Field Communications (NFC) protocols 226
Net Present Value (NPV) 96
Network Functions Virtualization (NFV) 315
networking considerations
  about 204
  connectivity transport layer 206
  edge connectivity 208
networking
  evolution 311
NIST cybersecurity frameworks
  about 220, 221
  Framework core 220
  Framework implementation tiers 220
  Framework profile 220
non-U.S. government standards and certifications
  about 251
  adoption, in various countries 251

O

OMA lightweight management standard for devices (OMA LW2M2M) 228
omnichannel initiatives 278
Online Transaction Processing (OLTP) 14, 103
Open Mobile Alliance (OMA) 225
Open Platform Communications Unified Architecture (OPC-UA) 27, 313
Operational Expenditures (OpEx) 88
operations domain
  about 42, 108, 154
  management 43
  Monitoring & Diagnostic 43
  optimization 43
  prognostics 43
  Provisioning & Deployment 43
Operations Technology (OT) 21

P

pattern
  about 23
structure 23
Performance Based Navigation (PBN) 300
personal computer (PC) 174
Personally Identifiable Information (PII) 247
Plant, Property, and Equipment (PP&E) 128
PlantWeb 309
Platform as a Service (PaaS) 8, 85
platform tier 24, 50
PoC
  building 65
  business case, considerations 62
  evaluating 68
  modifying 68
  production scale system 68
  prototype scale 67
  scope definition 61
  solution definition 62
  used, for evaluating design 61
Positive Train Control (PTC) 270
PowerBuilder 175
pre-shared keys (PSKs) 219
predictive analytics
  about 134
  reference link 136
predictive maintenance
  about 279
  airline industry, use case 280
prescriptive analytics 136
private cloud 181
Product Lifecycle Management (PLM) 116
production scale system
  about 68
  architecture 69
  components 69
  continuous engineering 69
programmable automation controllers (PACs) 313
project
  selling 97
proof of technology (PoT) 267
public cloud 181

Q

Quality Assurance (QA) 274
Quality of Service (QoS) 41, 312
quantum computing 320

Quick Access Recorder (QAR) 284

R

Radio-Frequency Identification (RFID) 293
  about 15
  using 299
reference architecture
  about 23
  analytics architecture, mapping to 154
relational databases 169
Remote Interface (RMI) request 232
Return on Investment (RoI) 61
rights management 151
risk assessments
  best security practices 234, 235, 236
Risk Management Framework (RMF) 220, 244
risk
  assessing 242
  overcoming, tasks 243
robotics
  impact 318
  using 299

S

San Diego project 270
scrum 120
security assurance levels (SALs)
  about 244
  foundational requirements 244
Sentient Hyper-Optimized Data Access Network
    (Shodan)
  URL 232
service level agreement (SLA) 127
Service Lifecycle Management (SLM) 116
Silicon Valley Innovation Program (SVIP) 222
single-tenant hosting
  advantages 178
  disadvantages 179
Smart Airline Baggage Management Testbed
  about 290
  reference link 290
smarter edge device
  configurations 106
Software as a Service (SaaS) 8, 85
software development kits (SDKs) 106

Software-Defined Networking (SDN) 314
solution definition 62
SPECK 222
speed layer 164
Standards Development Organizations (SDOs)
  about 240
  reference link 241
Statement on Standards for Attestation
    Engagements (SSAE 16) 248
Structured Assurance Case Metamodel (SACM)
    249
Stuxnet 215
subject matter experts (SMEs) 28
subscribers 148
superposition 320
Supervisory Control and Data Acquisition
    application (SCADA) 104
supply chain example security
  planning for 236
supply chain management (SCM) 183
supply chain optimization application domain 115
supply chain optimization control domain 107
supply chain optimization information domain 112
supply chain optimization
  example, in GRC 259
  in batch layer 171
Support Vector Machines (SVMs) 160
System and Organization Controls (SOC) 248
system characteristics 46
system integrator (SI) 22, 144

T

tensor processing unit (TPU) 316
test bed
  FOVI 276
  manufacturing 274
  omnichannel initiatives 278
The Open Group Architecture Framework
    (TOGAF) 19
Third Normal Form (3NF) 187
Ticket Granting Server (TGS) 231
Ticket-Granting Ticket (TGT) 231
Time Sensitive Networking (TSN) 313
Total Cost of Ownership (TCO) 61
Track & Trace (T&T) 296

transparent data encryption (TDE) 234
Transport Layer Security (TLS) 226
Treasury Architecture Development Guidance
    (TADG) 23
trusted platform module (TPM) 227

U

U.S. government standards
  Criminal Justice Information Services (CJIS) 253
  Department of Defense (DoD) 253
  Family Educational Rights and Privacy Act
    (FERPA) 254
  Federal Information Processing Standard (FIPS)
    254
  Federal Risk and Authorization Management
    Program (FedRAMP) 253
  Internal Revenue Service (IRS) 254
  International Traffic in Arms (ITAR) 254
  National Institute of Standards (NIST) 254
  Voluntary Product Accessibility Template (VPAT)
    254
Ultra Narrow Band (UNB) 312
Unified Component Model (UCM) 249
Uniformance Suite 309
United States Computer Emergency Readiness
    Team (US CERT) 216
Universal Plug and Play (UPnP) 217
usage viewpoint
  about 38
  security considerations 40
use case
  about 266
  benefits 271
  versus case study 266

use cases, IIoT
  environmental control 268
  in agribusiness 268
  in alternative energy 268
  in construction 269
  in energy generation 269
  in logistics 270
  in manufacturing and CPGs 271
  in manufacturing and CPGs, benefits 271
  in oil and gas, benefits 271
  in oil and gases 271
  in pharmaceuticals, medical equipment, and
    healthcare 272
  in pharmaceuticals, medical equipment, and
    healthcare, benefits 272
  in transportation 270
  in utility companies 273
  predictive maintenance 269
  with industry vertical 267
User Experience Design 29
user interfaces (UIs) 45
user skills
  assessing 114

V

virtual machines (VMs) 120
virtual private network (VPN) 228
virtual reality (VR) 317
Visible Light Communication (VLC) 279

W

Wireless Sensor Network (WSN) 225
work-in-process (WIP) 141
World Economic Forum (WEF) 126